Tennessee's
Forests, 2009

Christopher M. Oswalt, Sonja N. Oswalt,
Tony G. Johnson, Consuelo Brandeis,
KaDonna C. Randolph, and Christopher R. King

United States
Department of
Agriculture

Forest Service

Southern
Research Station

Resource Bulletin
SRS-189

Author Contributions

Christopher M. Oswalt contributed the outline of the report, initial analyses, and all text, tables, and figures not attributed to coauthors or acknowledged otherwise. Chris was also responsible for compiling coauthor contributions, the majority of the photographs, and completing two revisions of the report following peer review.

Sonja N. Oswalt contributed the text, tables, and figures for the Invasive Plants section.

Tony G. Johnson (retired) contributed text, tables, and figures for the Timber Removals and Utilization section.

Consuelo Brandeis contributed text, tables, and figures for the Forest Industry in Tennessee section.

KaDonna C. Randolph contributed text, tables, and figures for the Tree Crowns section.

Christopher R. King contributed text for the Highlights section and provided general editorial services and aided with both revisions.

Christopher M. Oswalt is a Research Forester with the Forest Inventory and Analysis Research Work Unit, Southern Research Station, U.S. Department of Agriculture Forest Service, Knoxville, TN 37919.

Sonja N. Oswalt is a Forester with the Forest Inventory and Analysis Research Work Unit, Southern Research Station, U.S. Department of Agriculture Forest Service, Knoxville, TN 37919.

Tony G. Johnson (retired) was a Supervisory Forester with the Forest Inventory and Analysis Research Work Unit, Southern Research Station, U.S. Department of Agriculture Forest Service, Knoxville, TN 37919.

Consuelo Brandeis is a Research Forester with the Forest Inventory and Analysis Research Work Unit, Southern Research Station, U.S. Department of Agriculture Forest Service, Knoxville, TN 37919.

KaDonna C. Randolph is a Research Statistician with the Forest Inventory and Analysis Research Work Unit, Southern Research Station, U.S. Department of Agriculture Forest Service, Knoxville, TN 37919.

Christopher R. King is a Forestry Technician with the Forest Inventory and Analysis Research Work Unit, Southern Research Station, U.S. Department of Agriculture Forest Service, Knoxville, TN 37919.

All photographs taken by Christopher M. Oswalt unless otherwise noted.

Front cover: top left, vibrant colored leaves such as these maples leaves provide a brilliant display each autumn; top right, Benton Mountain. (photo by Rob Howard); bottom, autumn lake. (photo by Ned Horton). Back cover: top left, aerial picture of Appalachian mountain ridges and valleys taken near Bristol, Tennessee. (photo by Bantosh, Wikimedia.org); top right, vibrant colored leaves such as these maples leaves provide a brilliant display each autumn; bottom, misty morning, Tennessee River. This shot was taken in the early morning as the sun was rising over an industrial area of Knoxville, Tennessee. The buildings were obscured by clouds, a gift. (photo by Rob Howard)

www.srs.fs.usda.gov

Cades Cove. (photo courtesy of Lost in Thought, Deviantart.com)

Tennessee's

Forests, 2009

Christopher M. Oswalt, Sonja N. Oswalt,
Tony G. Johnson, Consuelo Brandeis,
KaDonna C. Randolph, and Christopher R. King

Tennessee forest trail.
(photo by Jayne Shives,
Deviantart.com)

David Arnold

Robert L. Doudrick

The forests of Tennessee are as diverse as they are expansive. The unique shape of the State stretches across multiple regions of changing topography, geology, and ecology – each having significant influence on the type and breadth of the forest resource. From the Mississippi floodplain, across the Highland Rim, through the Nashville Basin, climbing the Cumberland Plateau and over to the Appalachian Mountains, Tennessee's forests cover half the State. Tracking forest resources changes and trends is important on many levels. As such it is vital to have the best available means for assessing the extent and condition of our State's forest resources.

Through the Forest Inventory and Analysis Program established by the U.S. Department of Agriculture (USDA) Forest Service in the 1930s, eight complete inventories, including this one, of our State's forest resources have been conducted on regular intervals. These inventories have provided valuable information to forest land managers and policymakers in making short- and long-term management and policy decisions working to strengthen the health and sustainability of our forests. The continued joint partnership between the Tennessee Department of Agriculture Division of Forestry and USDA Forest Service Southern Research Station provides a strong bond that ensures a timely and quality inventory. The quality of this report is a direct result of that sustained cooperation.

Tennessee's forests have historically faced multiple threats – insects, diseases, tornadoes, development – but over time have shown resiliency. As new threats emerge, our agencies' cooperative nature will work together through partnerships to manage them. Our forests are dynamic and ever-changing. Tracking these changes provides baseline information on the condition and health of the forest, and when compared to previous reports, provides a pulse on the health and sustainability of our forests over time.

This report contains information on the forest lands of Tennessee that is used by policymakers, agency and organization leaders, resource managers and owners, researchers, and students involved in forest resource management and forest-related issues. Because forests are much more than just tree volume and numbers of trees, this report includes information on forest age dynamics, forest health, ownership patterns, socioeconomic benefits, and emerging market opportunities such as forest biomass and carbon. It also contains a special section devoted to characteristics of the Cherokee National Forest, which holds the distinction as the largest tract of public land in Tennessee.

We are proud and pleased to introduce this valuable report on the extent and condition of Tennessee's forests as of the year 2009. It continues to be our goal that the partnership between our two agencies and the cooperative nature of this effort will continue to deliver the best information on the forests of Tennessee now and in the future.

David Arnold
Assistant State Forester

Robert L. Doudrick
Director, Southern Research Station,
U.S. Forest Service

Acknowledgments

It would be impossible to thank, by name, every individual who contributed to some aspect of this report. However, we would like to acknowledge the invaluable help provided by numerous organizations, individuals in the field, data processors, and scientists without which this report could not have been written.

First and foremost, the authors would like to thank the field crews from the Tennessee Division of Forestry and the U.S. Department of Agriculture Forest Service, Forest Inventory and Analysis (FIA) Program for collecting data across the State. The work done by the field crews can often be underappreciated. Without it, this report would contain empty pages.

The authors would like to thank the staff of the Tennessee Department of Agriculture Division of Forestry, especially Steven Scott and David Arnold, for their participation in the FIA inventory program in Tennessee.

The authors owe thanks to members of the Resource Analysis Section of Southern Research Station FIA for contributing portions of the Statistical Reliability section and Methods section in this report. Thanks are due to Dave Gartner for providing the analysis of measurement quality objectives in Tennessee and the South.

The authors would like to thank Dr. David Mercker, David Arnold, and Steven Scott for their frank and candid reviews of earlier versions of this report.

The authors owe a great deal of gratitude to Helen Beresford for programming the tools to generate many of the estimates used to populate the tables and figures in this report, and Jeff Turner and Jason Meade for tirelessly helping the entire Resource Analysis section make sure we are using the correct data. Special thanks is due Horace Brooks for providing critical mapping support.

The following people were responsible for collecting field data:

Tennessee Division of Forestry

John Mullins
Danny Osborne
Brian Rucker
Travis Trainer
Ellen Gray
John Ferris
Stephen Peairs
Michael Holder
Jason O'Shell
Steven Hacker
John Culclasure
Jeremy Norris
Shawn Hendrickson
Jamie Meyer
Brent Lecher
Steven Grindle
Douglas Godbee

FIA Staff

Sarah Combs
Lyndell Davidson
Angie Rowe
John Simpson
Jeffery Turner
Samuel Lambert
Andy Edwards
Jarrod Oglesby
Jason McHan
Ross Helm
Jason Meade
Mike Maki
Lucas Recore
Marcus Wood
Dan Stratton
Jason Hewitt
Jason Cooper
Lee McCord
Philip Fry
Trenton Girard

Warren Tucker
Christopher Oswalt
Horace Brooks
Danny Joe Johnson
Matthew Carr

The following people were responsible for editing and processing the collected data:

Helen Beresford
Jim Brown
Ali Conner
Jason McHan
Jason Meade
David Morgan
Ted Ridley
Jeffery Turner

The authors thank the following people for their tireless efforts with regards to editing, providing statistical support, and layout:

Anne Jenkins
Sharon Johnson
Janet Griffin
Charlene Walker

Crossvine (*Bignonia capreolata*) flower in Tennessee. (photo by William M. Ciesia, Bugwood.org)

Contents

Contents

A sunset on the Tennessee River.

Page

Text Figures

Page

Reelfoot lake, Tennessee. (photo by Ned Horton)

Page

Queen Anne's Lace. (photo courtesy of Lost in Thought, Deviantart.com)

Page

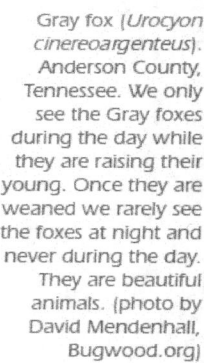

Gray fox (*Urocyon cinereoargenteus*). Anderson County, Tennessee. We only see the Gray foxes during the day while they are raising their young. Once they are weaned we rarely see the foxes at night and never during the day. They are beautiful animals. (photo by David Mendenhall, Bugwood.org)

Fern covered streambank in a hardwood dominated forest of east Tennessee.

Appendix Figures

The South Twin Arch at the Big South Fork National River and Recreation Area in Scott County, Tennessee. (photo by Brian Stansberry, Wikimedia.org)

List of Tables

List of Tables

Page

Appendix Tables

Appalachian mixed hardwoods stand in the Great Smoky Mountains National Park, Tennessee. (photo by Chris Evans, Bugwood.org)

Positive Developments

• Tennessee's forests occupied an area of 14 million acres (52 percent) across the State in 2009.

• From 1961 to 2009, forest land in Tennessee has comprised about one-half of the State's 26 million acres.

• Roughly 97 percent (13.5 million acres) of Tennessee's forest land was available for timber production (termed timberland) in 2009.

• A wide variety of species are found in Tennessee, including hardwoods such as yellow-poplar, several oak and hickory species, maple, beech, birch, and black locust. Softwood species occurring in the State include shortleaf pine, Virginia pine, loblolly pine, eastern redcedar, cypress, and others. Overall, 120 unique tree species were recorded from 2004 to 2009.

• Hardwood forest types have dominated the Tennessee landscape in every forest inventory and analysis inventory of the State conducted during the period 1948–2009.

• One-half of the 20 most dominant tree species in Tennessee are either oak or hickory species. Most of Tennessee's forests are therefore referred to as "oak-hickory" forest-type group, which comprised 73 percent (10.3 million acres) of the 14 million acres of Tennessee forest land in 2009.

• In 2009, red maple was the most common species in terms of number of individual stems recorded on forest land. In terms of volume, white oak is the most significant species, followed by chestnut oak and yellow-poplar.

Misty morning, Tennessee River. This shot was taken in the early morning as the sun was rising over an industrial area of Knoxville, Tennessee. The buildings were obscured by clouds, a gift. (photo by Rob Howard)

• In the 2009 inventory, an estimated 84 percent (11.8 million acres) of the forest land in Tennessee was in private ownership.

• Sixteen percent of the forest land in Tennessee was publicly administered by local, State, or Federal agencies in 2009. About one-third of the public forest land (5 percent of all forest land) is administered as national forest, one-third by other Federal agencies, and the remaining one-third (6 percent of all forest land) is owned and administered by various State and local governments.

• The effects of the southern pine beetle (SPB) in the eastern portion of the State were still evident in the 2009 inventory, but softwood live volumes are now recovering.

• Standing volume of all-live trees (≥5 inches diameter at breast height) on timberland exceeded 27 billion cubic feet in 2009. The overall standing inventory continues to increase at the rate of about 2 percent per year.

• In 2009, stands on Tennessee's timberland were predominantly of natural origin (i.e., not planted). Planted forests (which are mostly loblolly pine) still only makeup 5 percent of the State's forest land.

Interesting Trends

• Early successional or small diameter forest acres (forested stands with primarily small diameter trees) declined over the period 1961–2009, a result of aging forests.

• In 1999 forest industry accounted for ownership of an estimated 1.3 million acres (10 percent). Forest industry forest land has since steadily declined and now represents only 374,000 acres (3 percent) of all forest land in the State. This is largely due to the increasing trend of forest industry divesting their forest land holdings.

• The 1999 to 2002 SPB epidemic was the worst in Tennessee since the 1970s and caused significant financial losses. However, many of the impacted pine forests have either been replanted or have regenerated naturally to predominately hardwood types.

Fernleaf phacelia (*Phacelia bipinnatifida*). Cades Cove, Great Smoky Mountains National Park, Tennessee. (photo by William M. Ciesla, Bugwood.org)

• Tennessee forests are aging. The age class distribution during the period between 1999 and 2009 is, on average, shifting to older stands.

• While timber harvesting has continued on private forest land during the period of 1999 to 2009, timber harvesting on public lands has stagnated (and in some cases declined).

• The area of forests in the 0- to 10-year class has been increasing more recently, creating a bimodal age class structure. These young forests will be important as older forest begins to succumb to disturbances common to old stands.

• The small increase in forest land from 2004 to 2009 was also seen in timberland, which increased >290,000 acres in that time period.

Issues and Trends to Watch

• Slight gains in forest land for the period of 2004–09 continues what may be a "leveling-off" of the trend of increasing forest land in the State since 1971. This may be a precursor to anticipated declines due to fragmentation, parcelization, and associated land use changes as reversion from agriculture slows down.

• Emerald ash borer has been discovered in the State, and the movement of ash has been quarantined in some east Tennessee counties. Movement of black walnut has been quarantined in multiple Tennessee counties due to confirmed cases of thousand cankers disease. The presence of these two invaders may result in biological and economic damage in both ash and walnut species.

• In 2009, there was an estimated 46,000 acres of the "other exotic hardwoods" forest type (a 190-percent increase since 1999). This expanding population of exotic hardwood trees in just a 10-year period suggests that a future problem could exist.

• In 2009, an estimated 10 percent (8.0 billion board feet) of all sawtimber volume was classified as grade 1. Sawtimber volume within grade 1 trees has been steadily declining from a peak of 14.8 billion board feet in 1999 where grade 1 material represented about 21 percent of all sawtimber volume.

• From 1999 to 2009, several forest types experienced a large decrease, including Table Mountain, pitch, shortleaf, and Virginia pines due to SPB and hardwood replacement. Certain forest types such as cottonwood and several oak types decreased in area during this period as well. The most alarming forest-type change between 1999 and 2009 was the 190-percent increase in the other exotic hardwoods forest type.

• Invasive plants were detected on 1,932 plots across the State, or 71 percent of all forested plots measured from 2004 to 2009. This is a dramatic increase from the 52 percent of forested plots from 1999 to 2004 which contained invasive plants.

• Japanese honeysuckle (*Lonicera japonica*) was the most frequently detected nonnative species in Tennessee, followed by Nepalese browntop (*Microstegium vimineum*). Tree-of-heaven (*Ailanthus altissima*) was the most frequently detected invasive tree in the State.

Hikers enjoyng a path through hardwood forests.

Introduction

This resource bulletin consolidates data from the eighth complete survey of Tennessee's forest resources which was conducted during the period 2005–09 by the U.S. Department of Agriculture (USDA) Forest Service, Forest Inventory and Analysis (FIA) program in coordination with the Tennessee Department of Agriculture Division of Forestry (TDF). Data on the extent, condition, and classification of forest land and associated timber volumes, as well as growth, removals, and mortality rates are described and interpreted. Data on forest health and forest landowner characteristics are also evaluated. Estimates of forest resources are reported at multiple scales. The two most common scales discussed in this report are State and unit. The State of Tennessee is divided into five FIA units (fig. 1) that approximate broad physiographical sections of the State. The five FIA units are labeled: 1) West, 2) West Central, 3) Central, 4) Plateau, and 5) East.

In 1999, the Southern Research Station (SRS) FIA program and the TDF began implementing the new annual survey strategy in Tennessee. The strategy involves rotating measurements of five systematic samples (or panels), each of which represents about 20 percent of all plots in the State. A panel generally takes 1 year to complete and covers only one growing season. For Tennessee, data collection for all five panels was completed in 5 years. This analysis focuses primarily on changes and trends in recent years and their implications for Tennessee's forests, forest landowners, and citizens. (See the Data Sources and Techniques section for further information on data collection methodology.)

The inventory dates of 2009 and 2004 are repeated throughout this report. The inventory year of 2009 represents data that was collected from 2005 to 2009. The inventory year 2004 represents data that were collected from 2000 to 2004. Estimates of components of change (i.e., growth, removals, and mortality) are calculated based on plot measurements collected from 2000 to 2004 as compared to the same plots being remeasured from 2005 to 2009. The period of 1999 to 2009, often repeated in this report, represents the period of time where data in Tennessee was collected using the annual plot design (see Inventory Methods).

The 2009 inventory accounted for a total of 2,713 forested plots across the State. There were 707, 551, 551, 431, and 473 plots measured in the East, Plateau, Central, West Central, and West units, respectively. A total of 2,119 plots measured for the 2004 inventory were remeasured during the 2009 inventory. The remeasured plots were used to calculate estimates of growth, removals, and mortality, commonly referred to as GRM.

Note: This data was accessed and compiled from the FIA database (FIADB) in March, April, and May of 2011. Publicly available data from the FIADB is regularly updated when data collection and/or processing anomalies are found and corrected. Additionally, new data are added on a regular basis which may be reflected by small changes in the past or current estimates.

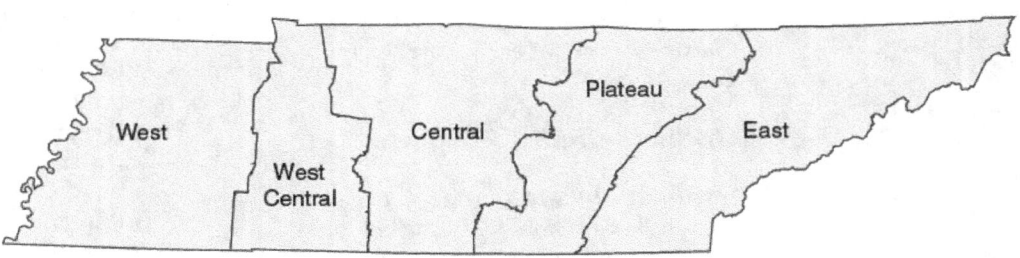

Figure 1—Survey unit boundaries, Tennessee.

View looking northwest across the northern Highland Rim from the Goodpasture Mountain fire tower at Standing Stone State Park in Overton County, Tennessee. (photo by Brian Stansberry, Wikimedia.org)

History of Tennessee's Forest Inventory

Seven previous inventories have been completed in Tennessee. The inventories of 1950, 1961, 1971, 1980, 1989, 1999, and 2004 provide statistics for measuring changes and trends over the past 60 years. Traditionally, FIA reporting of forest resource statistics has been oriented toward sustaining timber resources to meet the demand for forest products. Over time the idea of "sustainability" has evolved from a concept driven by commodity production to one that is defined by a diversity of values including timber resources, wildlife habitat, species richness, and cultural benefits among others. The USDA Forest Service FIA program has evolved alongside the broader concept of sustainability. The FIA program now reports on a diverse set of variables and attempts to help answer numerous questions surrounding the forest resources of each State, including Tennessee.

Updates of Past Estimates

In 2010 the SRS FIA program began the adoption of version 4.0 of the National Information Management System (NIMS) in order to meet national FIA program standards. The 2004 Tennessee forest resources report (Oswalt and others 2009)

was based on data processed through version 2.2 of the FIA NIMS. The FIA NIMS 4.0 processing system included programmatic changes that at times altered standard definitions and/or estimate derivation. For example, some forest types were retired, some forest types were consolidated, and others included changes to component tree species lists. In order to ensure the most valid comparisons possible across annual inventories, all data collected on the annual design (Bechtold and Patterson 2005) were reprocessed through version 4.0 of the FIA NIMS. The data and estimates available to the public and the estimates presented in this report reflect that reprocessing and therefore, some historical estimates may not match previously published reports. Estimates published in this report supersede estimates for the same period published in previous reports.

The SRS FIA program has made available some historic data in electronic form in the FIADB version 4.0. Historic data were converted to the current format of the FIADB. For Tennessee, electronic data are now available for all inventories from 1980 to present. Common comparisons in this report are made for the period between 1999 and 2009 for many forest land attributes and for the period between 1980 and 2009 for many timberland attributes.

Forest Extent

Tennessee Forest Land

Forests are an important characteristic of the Tennessee landscape. Forests play a vital role in Tennessee's economic, cultural, and biological landscape. The dependence of Tennesseans on the State's forests requires that attention be paid to their extent and condition. Today, portions of eastern Tennessee, along with the Plateau and West Central units, are the most heavily forested regions in the State (fig. 2).

In 2009, forests covered nearly 52 percent, or slightly >14 million acres (table 1), of the land base in Tennessee. Beginning with the 1961 inventory, forests have routinely remained about one-half of the land base in Tennessee. Recently, however, it appears small gains in forest land may have been realized. Between 2004 and 2009, there was an increase of about 183,000 acres

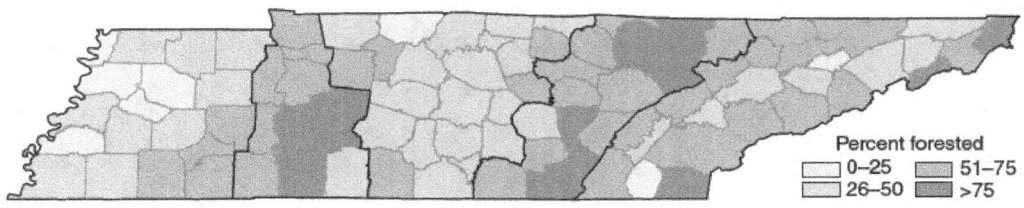

Figure 2—Percent forest for each county, Tennessee, 2009.

Table 1—Area by land class and survey completion date, Tennessee, 1961–2009

Land class	Survey completion date						
	1961	1971	1980	1989	1999	2004	2009
	thousand acres						
Timberland	13,432.4	12,819.8	12,879.0	13,265.2	13,305.2	13,254.5	13,547.2
Other reserved	263.5	316.5	429.5	337.3	406.9	566.1	456.1
Total forest land	13,695.9	13,136.3	13,308.5	13,602.5	13,712.2	13,820.6	14,003.3
Nonforest land	12,826.2	13,338.6	13,141.6	12,844.5	13,259.6	13,151.2	12,968.1
Total land area	26,522.1	26,474.9	26,450.1	26,447.0	26,971.8	26,971.8	26,971.4
Percent forested	51.6	49.6	50.3	51.4	50.8	51.2	51.9

Totals may not sum due to rounding.

Total land area estimates changed slightly over time due to improvements in measurement techniques and refinements in classification of small bodies of water and streams.

of forest land across the State. Slight gains in forest land for the period of 2005–09 continues what may be a "leveling-off" of the trend of increasing forest land in the State since 1971 (fig. 3). The small gains that have been realized have been concentrated in the West unit (fig. 4), as abandoned agricultural lands continue to revert to forests. The conversion of row crop management to forest due to conservation incentive programs may have also contributed to this change.

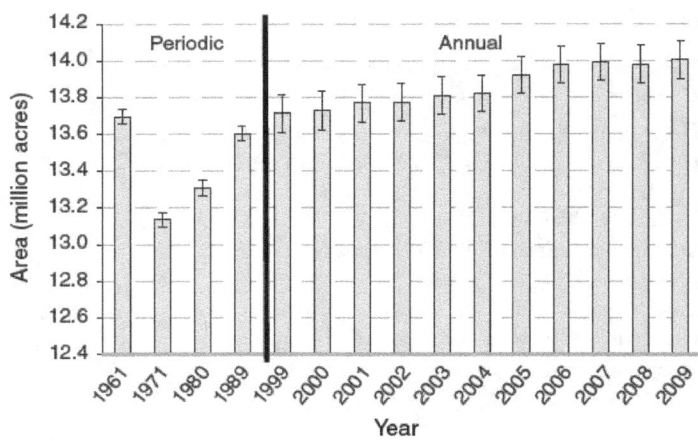

Figure 3—Area of forest land, Tennessee, 1961–2009. Error bars represent one standard error.

The Obed River.

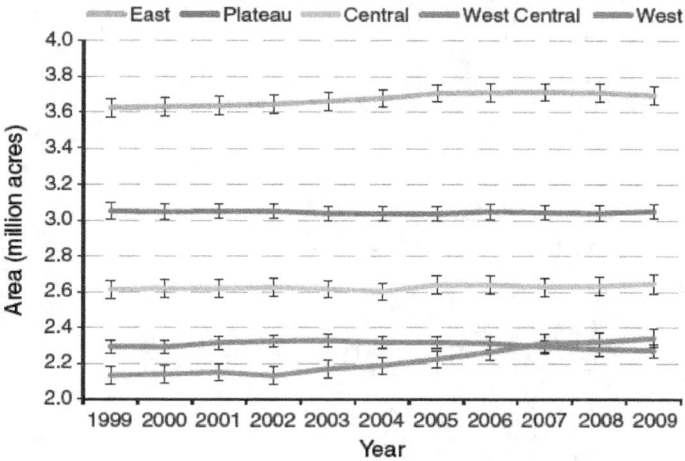

Figure 4—Area of forest land by survey unit, Tennessee, 1999–2009. Error bars represent one standard error.

Land Use and Land Use Change

According to the observed land use (forest, urban, agriculture, etc.) at the center of each plot, 53 percent of the plots (excluding water) were located in a forested condition (fig. 5). Agricultural land use accounted for 33 percent of plots, while developed uses accounted for 14 percent. While current land use estimates indicate the majority of land in Tennessee is forested, it is important to understand recent land use changes that have occurred. For example, each year forest land is converted to both agricultural land and to urban conditions, as well as abandoned agricultural lands reverting back to a forested condition.

Between the period of 2004–09, Tennessee lost an estimated 351,000 acres of forest land to nonforest land uses (table 2). However, during that same period, an estimated 555,000 acres reverted back to forest. Overall, Tennessee gained forest land between 2004 and 2009. (Note: the estimated net change in table 2 is not the same as the difference of the 2004 and 2009 estimates of forest land area, and is a result of a lack of complete overlap in plots used for each estimate. The estimates in table 2 utilize only plots measured during both inventories where the 2009 estimate presented earlier includes new forested plots. As a result, slight discrepancies exist among the different estimates.)

Forest losses occurred mostly as a result of forest conversion to agricultural and developed (urban) land uses. Statewide, 50 and 48 percent of losses were due to developed and agricultural land use, respectively (table 2). Change from a forested to a developed condition was greatest in the East unit (48,122 acres), and was similar across all units. Change from a forested to an agricultural condition was greatest in the

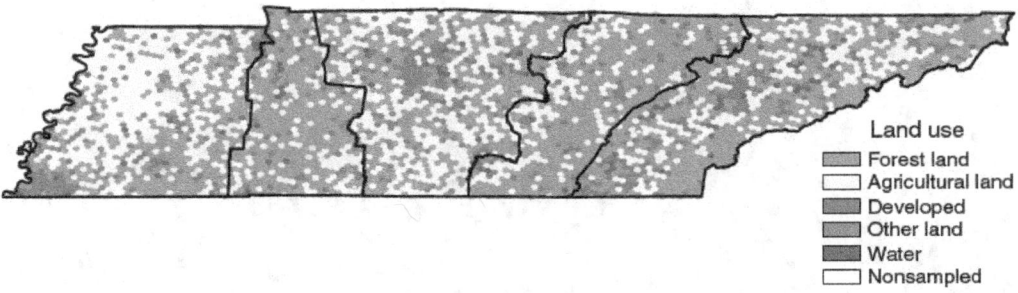

Figure 5—Assigned land use for each phase 2 hexagon of the 2009 annual inventory for Tennessee. Each phase 2 hexagon contains one plot. Land use at plot center was assigned to corresponding hexagon.

5

Central unit (45,890 acres) and lowest in the Plateau unit (15,887 acres). Forest gain from agriculture was greatest in the West (141,414 acres) and Central (114,749 acres) units and insignificant in the West Central unit (9,194 acres). Overall net change of forest land was positive in all units with the exception of the West Central unit which appears to have experienced a net loss of an estimated 35,000 acres. The West unit experienced an estimated net gain of about 140,000 acres of forest land.

Table 2—Change in land use by survey unit, Tennessee, 2004–09

Change/land use	West	West Central	Central	Plateau	East	Total
			acres			
Forest loss to						
Agricultural land	34,941	35,693	45,890	15,887	35,437	167,848
Developed	30,288	32,537	32,659	32,697	48,122	176,303
Other	0	0	0	0	0	0
Water	5,526	76	109	232	449	6,392
All	70,755	68,306	78,658	48,816	84,008	350,543
Forest gain from						
Agricultural land	141,414	9,194	114,749	47,401	68,749	381,507
Developed	54,738	23,452	16,881	20,295	41,376	156,742
Other	4,191	0	0	0	0	4,191
Water	10,705	706	207	1,122	0	12,740
All	211,048	33,352	131,837	68,818	110,125	555,180
Net forest change	140,293	-34,954	53,179	20,002	26,117	204,637

Totals may not sum due to rounding.

The brilliant blue sky is made even sweeter by the presence of the Appalachian mountains on a beautiful autumn day. (photo by Rachel Weeks)

Forest Composition

Tree Species Diversity and Distribution

The species composition of a forested stand defines its character, likely future development, ecosystem function, and dynamics, as well as providing insight into its historical evolution. For this reason, analyses of current and past species composition aid in understanding the existing forest character and potential developmental pathways of the future.

A wide variety of tree species are found in Tennessee including hardwoods such as yellow-poplar, oak, hickory, maple, beech, birch, and black locust. Softwood species occurring in the State include shortleaf pine, Virginia pine, loblolly pine, eastern redcedar, cypress, and others. Overall, 120 separate tree species (seedlings included) were recorded during the 2009 forest inventory (see appendix table D.1).

Tree species richness—Biological diversity can be quantified in a myriad of ways. Here, species diversity is primarily addressed

through quantifying the number of unique tree genera and/or species observed on Forest Inventory and Analysis (FIA) plots in Tennessee as species richness (Note: for a detailed discussion of using FIA data for assessing tree species diversity, see Rosson and Rose 2010). Statewide, 50 different genera were recorded on forested plots (see appendix table D.1). *Quercus* dominated with 22 different species recorded. *Carya* (eight species), *Acer* (six species), *Pinus* (six species), *Ulmus* (six species), and *Magnolia* (five species) were the other dominate genera found in forests across the State.

Statewide, there were 120 distinct species codes recorded. The East unit was the most diverse with 88 different species recorded followed by the Central, West, Plateau, and West Central units with 86, 85, 84, and 77 different species recorded, respectively. The counties with the most diverse species list were mostly in the East unit along the border with North Carolina and within the Appalachian Mountain region (fig. 6). The least diverse counties were in the agriculturally-dominated West unit. In general, there was a moderate relationship between the area of forest land within a given county and the number of distinct

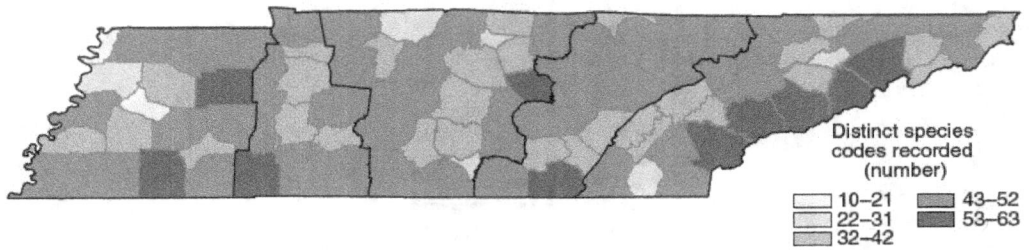

Figure 6—Number of distinct tree species codes recorded for each county, Tennessee, 2009.

tree species sampled within that county (fig. 7). As forest land area increased, the number of distinct tree species recorded also increased.

Red maple was the most abundant species in terms of number of individual stems recorded on forest land and was estimated to account for nearly 10 percent of the statewide population of all-live stems (fig. 8). It is important to note, however, that all oak species combined comprise a very substantial proportion of the total estimated number of stems. While 120 distinct species codes were sampled across the State, the top 20 species (fig. 8) account

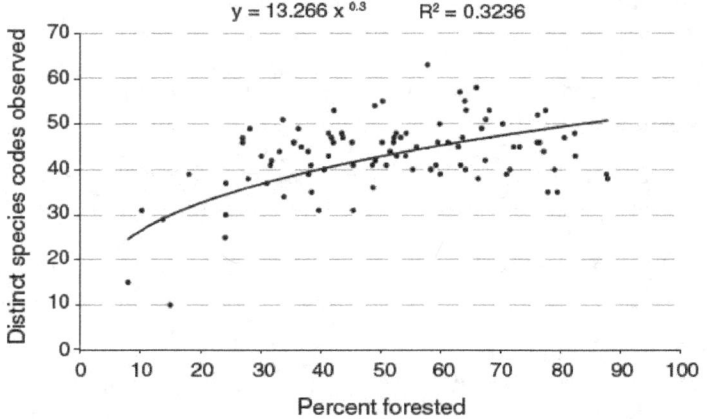

$$y = 13.266\ x^{0.3} \qquad R^2 = 0.3236$$

Figure 7—Relationship between the proportions of a county that is in forest and the number of distinct species codes recorded in the county, Tennessee, 2009.

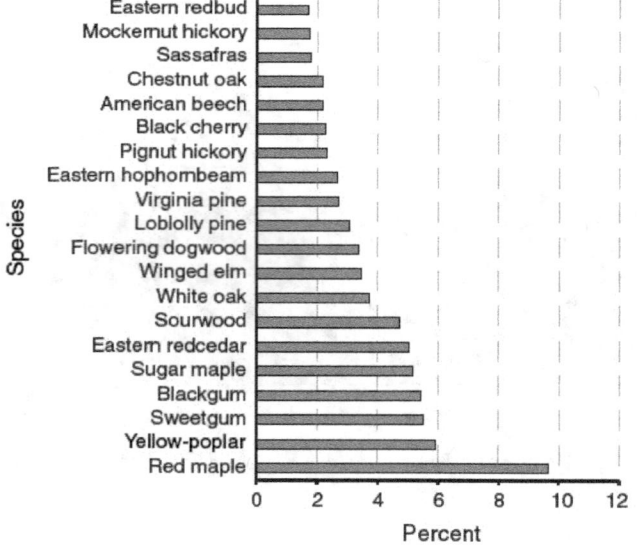

Figure 8—Proportion of all-live trees accounted for by individual species for the 20 most numerous tree species, Tennessee, 2009.

Dogwood blossoms provide a bright contrast against a bright blue Tennessee sky. (photo by Sonja N. Oswalt)

for about 75 percent of all-live trees (fig. 9). In addition to having large populations in Tennessee, red maple, sugar maple, and yellow-poplar are some of the most widely distributed tree species in the State (fig. 10).

While red maple accounted for the largest proportion of all-live trees statewide, this was not the case for every unit in the State. In the East and Plateau units, red maple accounted for slightly <20 percent of all-live trees (fig. 11). In the Central, West Central, and West units, however, eastern redcedar, yellow-poplar, and sweetgum were the most numerous tree species, respectively. With the exception of the Central unit, red maple was one of the top 10 most numerous tree species in each unit. Other numerous tree species common among units included yellow-poplar, flowering dogwood, white oak, and sugar maple.

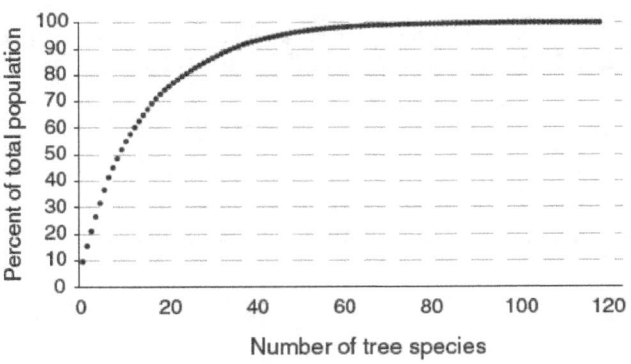

Figure 9—Cumulative percent of all-live trees accounted for by adding individual tree species in rank order from most numerous to least, Tennessee, 2009.

9

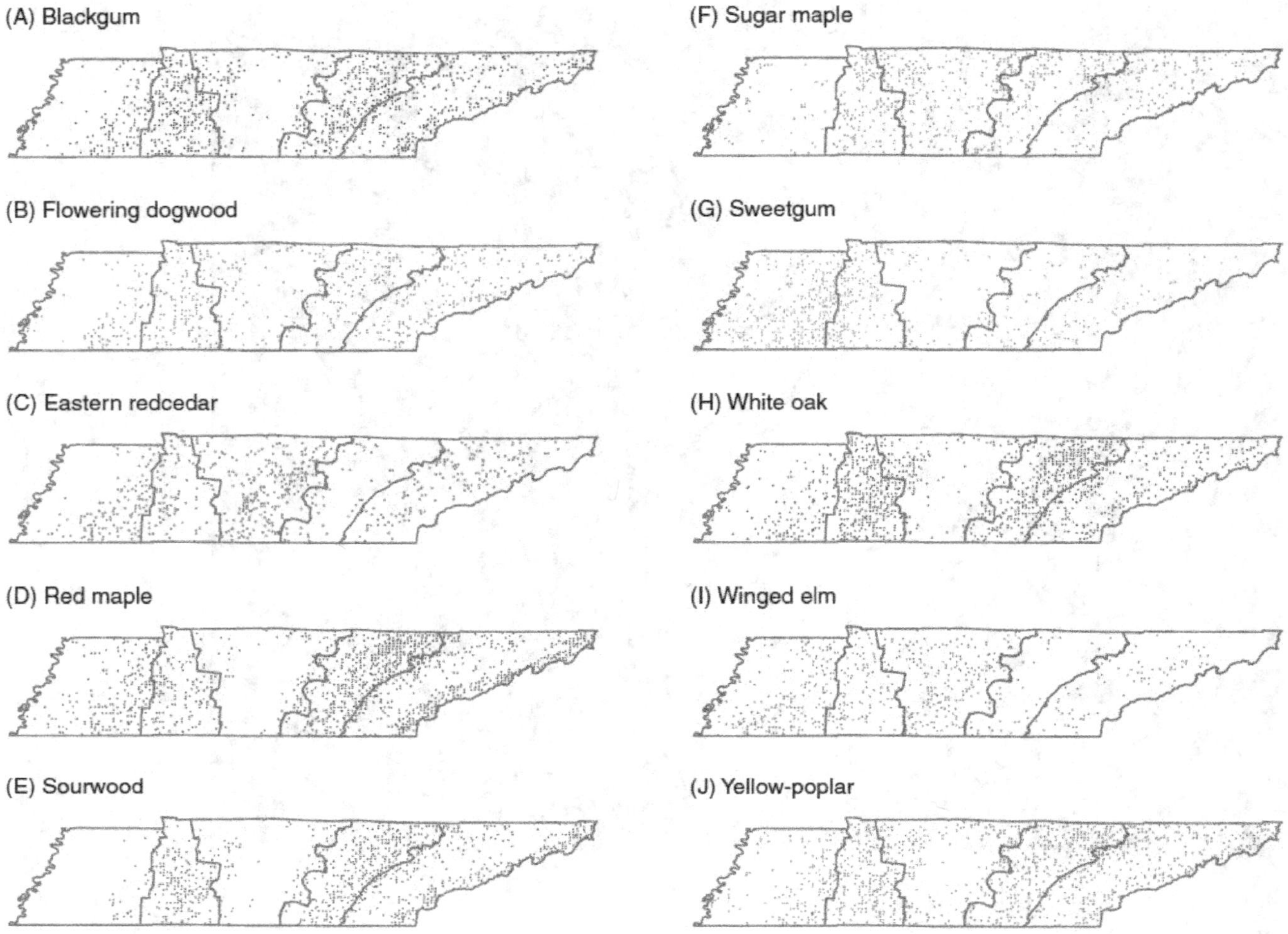

(A) Blackgum

(F) Sugar maple

(B) Flowering dogwood

(G) Sweetgum

(C) Eastern redcedar

(H) White oak

(D) Red maple

(I) Winged elm

(E) Sourwood

(J) Yellow-poplar

Figure 10—Sampled distribution of the 10 most numerous tree species, Tennessee, 2009 (A) Blackgum, (B) Flowering dogwood, (C) Eastern redcedar, (D) Red maple, (E) Sourwood, (F) Sugar maple, (G) Sweetgum, (H) White oak, (I) Winged elm, (J) Yellow-poplar.

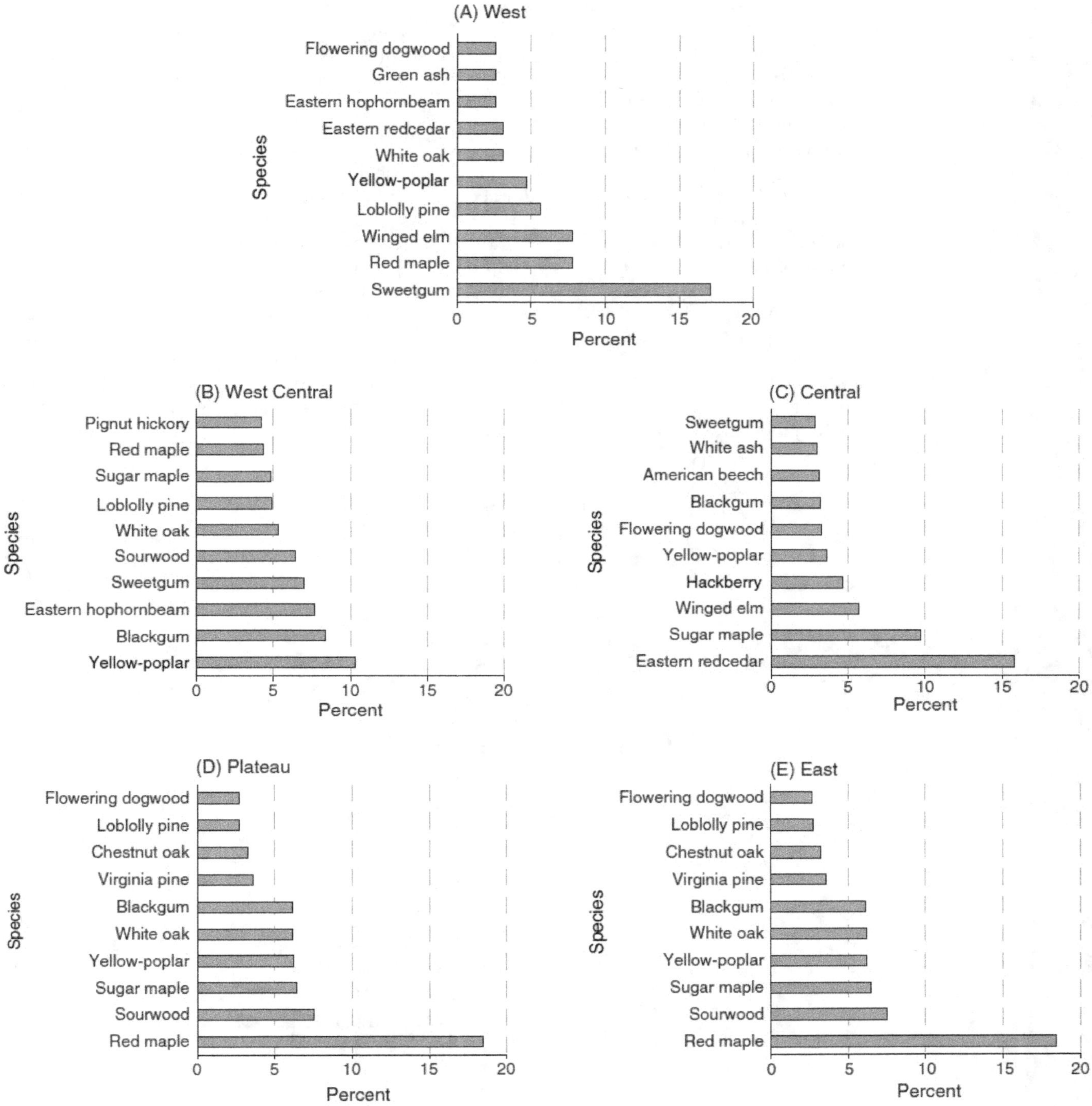

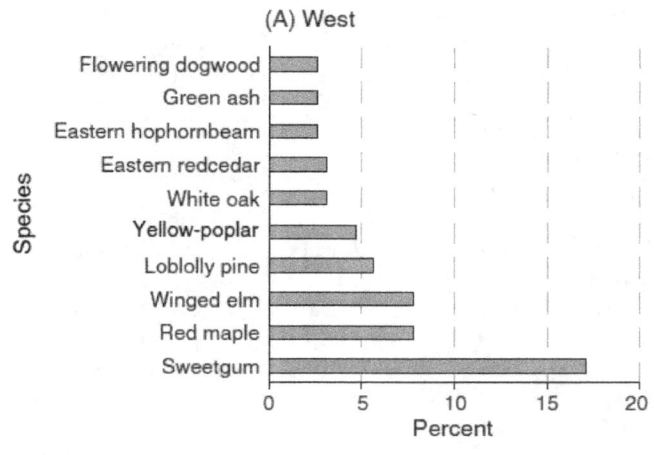

Figure 11—Proportion of all-live trees accounted for by unit and individual species for the 10 most numerous tree species, Tennessee, 2009 (A) West, (B) West Central, (C) Central, (D) Plateau, and (E) East.

Tree species dominance—Ecological dominance can be defined as the degree to which a species is more numerous than its competitors in an ecological community, or it makes up more of the biomass. Here, dominance is defined in terms of both total aboveground biomass and volume.

White oak is estimated to account for about 11 percent of all aboveground biomass found in trees on forest land across the State of Tennessee (fig. 12). Chestnut oak and yellow-poplar, the second and third most dominant trees species in Tennessee, represent an estimated 9 and 8 percent, respectively. Red maple, while the most numerous tree species across the State, is only the fourth most dominant tree species when measured by aboveground biomass.

Oak species account for 7 of the 20 most dominant tree species while hickory species account for 3. Thus, most forests in Tennessee are referred to as "oak-hickory" forests.

Not unlike with the total number of stems, the dominant tree species according to aboveground biomass differed among each FIA unit. In the East unit, chestnut oak was the most dominant tree species and accounted for an estimated 18 percent of all aboveground tree biomass (fig. 13). White oak is dominant in both the Plateau (15 percent) and West Central (24 percent) units, while yellow-poplar (8 percent) is dominant in the Central unit and sweetgum (12 percent) in the West unit.

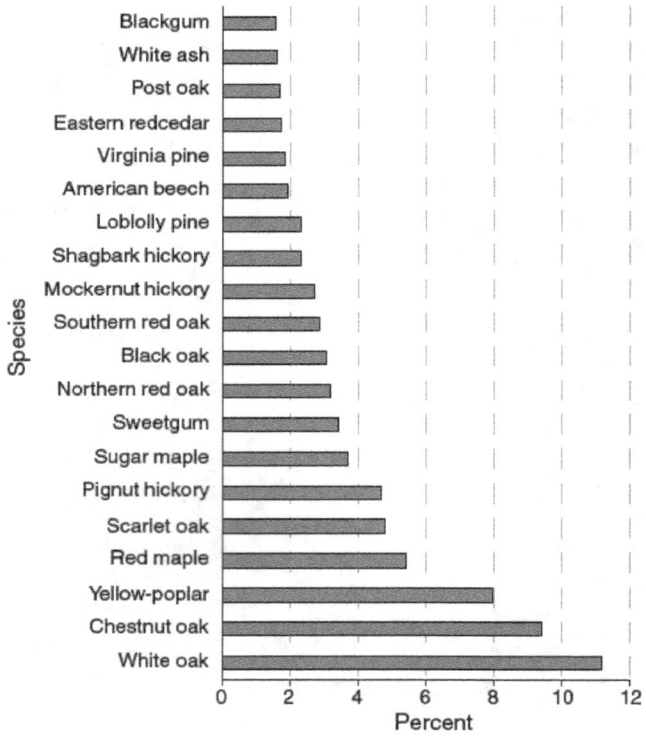

Figure 12—Proportion of all-live trees (≥1-inch d.b.h.) aboveground biomass accounted for by individual species for the 20 tree species representing the most aboveground biomass, Tennessee, 2009.

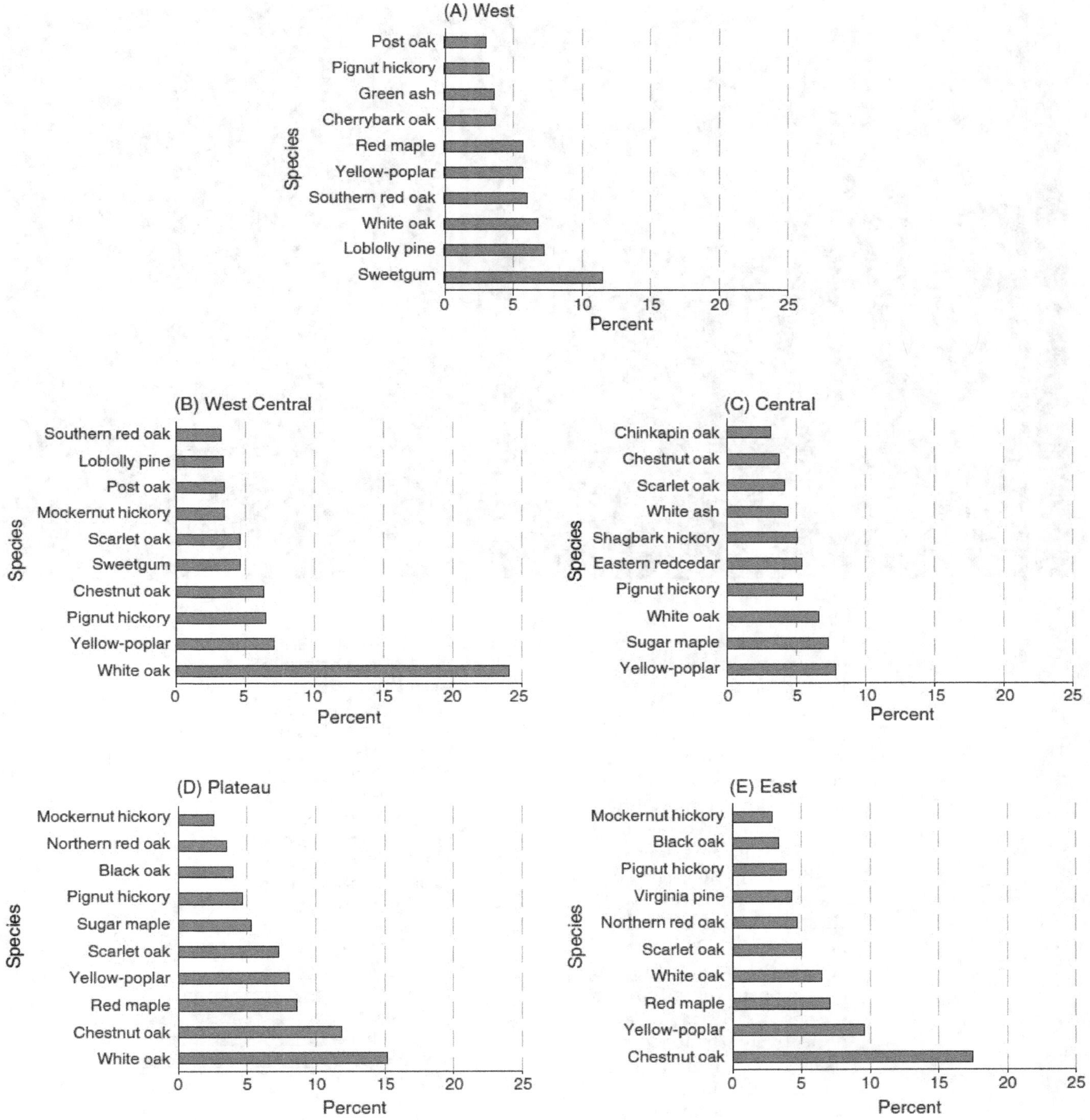

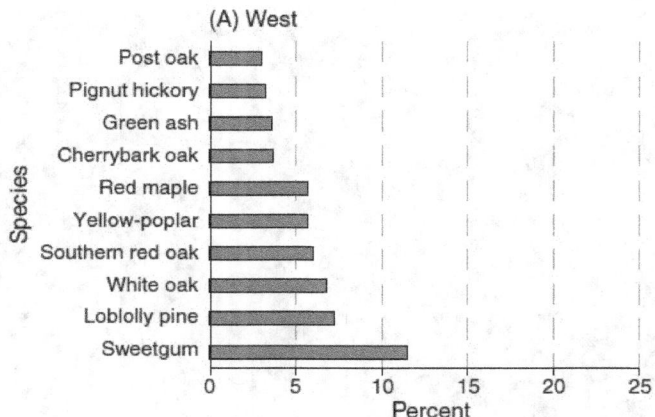

Figure 13—Proportion of all-live biomass accounted for by survey unit and individual species for the 10 most dominant tree species according to standing biomass, Tennessee, 2009 (A) West, (B) West Central, (C) Central, (D) Plateau, and (E) East.

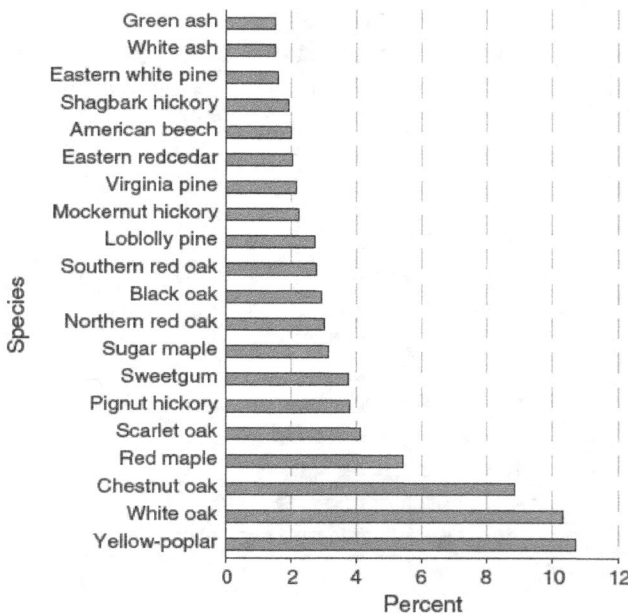

Large poplars await hikers near this hardwood forest trail. (photo by Sonja N. Oswalt)

When dominance is assessed on a volumetric (ft^3) basis (includes only stems ≥5 inches diameter at breast height [d.b.h.]), slight differences are realized among the most dominant tree species. State-wide, yellow-poplar (Tennessee's State tree) accounts for an estimated 11 percent of all-live volume (fig. 14). Six other oaks (white oak, chestnut oak, scarlet oak, northern red oak, black oak, and southern red oak) rank in the top 20 voluminous tree species at 2, 3, 5, 9, 10, and 11, respectively. The top 20 tree species accounted for about 80 percent of all-live volume across the State's forest land (fig. 15).

Figure 14—Proportion of all-live tree (≥5 inches d.b.h.) volume (cubic feet) accounted for by individual species for the 20 most tree species representing the most volume, Tennessee, 2009.

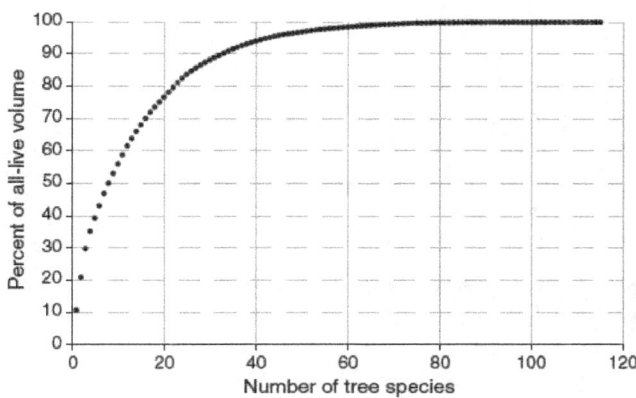

Figure 15—Cumulative percent of all-live tree (≥5 inches d.b.h.) volume accounted for by adding individual tree species in rank order from the species representing the most volume to least, Tennessee, 2009.

No one tree species dominates Tennessee's forest land in terms of both numbers of live trees and volume. The statistics reflect the ecological niches and silvical characteristics of the common species found in the State. Species such as yellow-poplar, white oaks, and many in the red oak group comprise the larger canopy species in much of the forest. Some of the more numerous species, such as red maple, flowering dogwood, and eastern redbud are smaller, but generally occupy the mid and understory in greater numbers.

Forest Types in Tennessee

Hardwood forest types have dominated the Tennessee landscape in every inventory of the State produced by FIA (Oswalt and others 2009) including the 2009 inventory (fig. 16). In fact, for the period between 2004 and 2009, softwood forest-type acreage was lower than any other period of FIA inventory of Tennessee forests (see Oswalt and others 2009 and fig. 16). Stands of softwood forest types have been mostly limited to mid- and high-elevation communities of the Appalachian Mountains, the Southern Cumberland Plateau in the east, and the Gulf Coastal Plain in the southwestern part of the State.

In 2009, the oak-hickory forest-type group accounted for 73 percent (10.3 million acres) of the 14.0 million acres of Tennessee forest land (fig. 16). The oak-hickory forest-type group was also the most widely distributed forest-type group in the State as the dominant forest-type group in each unit (table 3). The oak-pine, loblolly-shortleaf pine, elm-ash-cottonwood, and other eastern softwoods forest-type groups accounted for 991,000; 903,000; 727,000; and 245,000 acres, respectively. The other eastern softwoods forest-type group (primarily comprised of eastern redcedar), while found across the State, was mainly concentrated in central Tennessee (table 3) within the Inner and Outer Nashville Basins. Cedar glades and other cedar dominated communities are common in the Nashville Basin ecoregions (Baskin and Baskin 2003). In 2009, the least extensive forest-type group within the State (with the exception of the other hardwoods group) was exotic hardwoods (nonnative species such as tree-of-heaven, paulownia, and mimosa) with an estimated 52,000 acres across the State. However, acreage estimates for forest-type groups with such rarity are accompanied by significant error rates.

Since 1999 the area of forests classified as the oak-hickory forest-type group has significantly increased (fig. 16). Softwood forest-type groups have been stable or declining over the same time period. For the most part, the decline in softwood and the parallel increase in the oak-hickory forest-type group can be attributed to the southern pine beetle (SPB) epidemic that impacted Tennessee forests between 1999 and 2002 (Oswalt and others 2009).

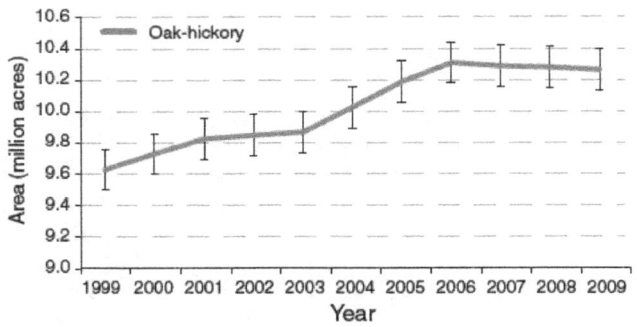

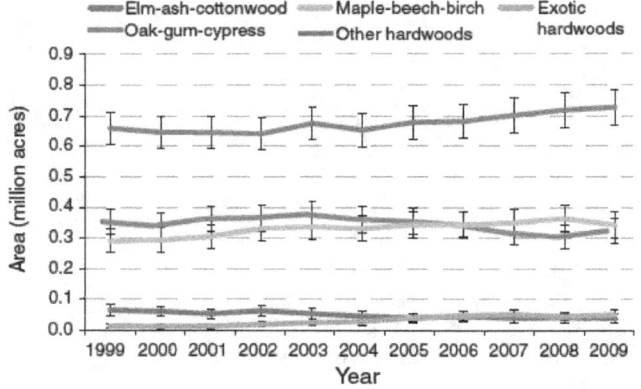

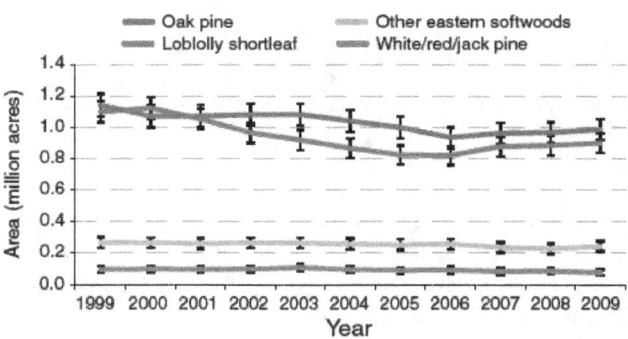

Figure 16—Area of forest land by forest-type group, Tennessee, 1999–2009.

Table 3—Area of forest land by forest-type group and survey unit, Tennessee, 2009

Forest-type group	Total	Survey unit				
		West	West Central	Central	Plateau	East
		acres				
White-red-jack pine	76,179	—	—	3,276	22,991	49,913
Loblolly-shortleaf pine	903,114	259,456	155,493	17,836	180,164	290,164
Other eastern softwoods	245,209	9,718	5,916	152,661	17,715	59,200
Oak-pine	990,862	159,019	102,823	214,486	157,949	356,585
Oak-hickory	10,261,072	1,224,063	1,916,997	1,955,779	2,517,578	2,646,655
Oak-gum-cypress	324,036	258,676	17,748	23,946	13,392	10,274
Elm-ash-cottonwood	727,065	406,680	61,446	186,384	15,207	57,348
Maple-beech-birch	343,104	10,775	2,958	57,106	94,443	177,821
Other hardwoods	40,675	—	8,289	6,504	5,329	20,552
Exotic hardwoods	52,466	1,536	—	24,393	11,238	15,299
Nonstocked	39,501	10,961	—	3,269	14,840	10,430
Total	14,003,283	2,340,883	2,271,670	2,645,641	3,050,848	3,694,242

— = negligible; totals may not sum due to rounding.

A cedar glade at Cedars of Lebanon State Park in Wilson County, Tennessee. This particular glade is located along the Cedar Glades Trail, near the visitor center. (photo by Brian Stansberry)

The oak-hickory forest-type group covers the largest overall area in the State. This group consists of 15 different forest types (forest-type groups represent a collection of similar forest types) in Tennessee. In 2009, the six most common forest types within the oak-hickory type group were: (1) white oak-red oak-hickory, (2) mixed upland hardwoods, (3) chestnut oak-black oak-scarlet oak, (4) yellow-poplar-white oak-red oak, (5) chestnut oak, and (6) white oak. The white oak-red oak-hickory forest type was the most extensive, occupying an estimated 3.6 million acres in the State (table 4). Since 1999, the white oak-red oak-hickory forest type has experienced slight gains in the Plateau and Central units, while declining in the West Central unit (fig. 17). Some of the hardwood forest types with the most limited coverage were northern red oak, black locust, black walnut, and

cottonwood. It is estimated that these types accounted for 51,000, 50,000, 21,000, and 11,000 acres, respectively.

The loblolly-shortleaf forest-type group consists of five forest types in Tennessee: (1) loblolly pine, (2) Virginia pine, (3) shortleaf pine (4) pitch pine, and (5) Table Mountain pine. In 2009, the loblolly pine type (576,000 acres) accounted for the majority of area occupied by the loblolly-shortleaf pine type group (903,000 acres). This was followed by Virginia pine, which occupied an estimated 242,000 acres (fig. 18). Between 1999 and 2009 all forest types, with the exception of the loblolly pine forest type (representing the loblolly-shortleaf pine forest-type group), declined. In 2009, the scarcest forest types within the loblolly-shortleaf pine type group were Table Mountain pine and pitch pine,

Table 4—Area of each forest type observed and 10-year change on forest land, Tennessee, 2009

Forest type	Area	Change	Forest type	Area	Change
	- acres -	percent		- acres -	percent
Table Mountain pine	0	-100	Swamp chestnut oak/cherrybark oak	53,994	-7
Red maple/upland	0	-100	White oak	581,635	-6
Pitch pine	5,650	-57	White oak/red oak/hickory	3,598,044	4
Shortleaf pine	79,843	-56	Sugar maple/beech/yellow birch	218,884	5
Shortleaf pine/oak	107,003	-50	Eastern redcedar/hardwood	324,322	8
Cottonwood	10,811	-46	Sycamore/pecan/American elm	126,201	8
Virginia pine	241,897	-45	Cottonwood/willow	12,290	11
Overcup oak/water hickory	10,973	-45	Mixed upland hardwoods	1,075,839	15
Other hardwoods	40,675	-39	Loblolly pine/hardwood	211,128	16
River birch/sycamore	77,322	-31	Yellow-poplar/white oak/northern red oak	743,340	17
Eastern hemlock	12,381	-30	Sugarberry/hackberry/elm/green ash	372,168	17
Eastern white pine/eastern hemlock	4,721	-29	Chestnut oak	727,714	17
Sweetbay/swamp tupelo/red maple	58,408	-27	Sweetgum/yellow-poplar	567,637	24
Virginia pine/southern red oak	255,910	-26	Loblolly pine	575,724	28
Sweetgum/nuttall oak/willow oak	112,766	-21	Cherry/white ash/yellow-poplar	382,339	33
Elm/ash/black locust	325,042	-21	Willow	59,045	35
Northern red oak	50,761	-20	Scarlet oak	131,168	42
Sassafras/persimmon	165,591	-19	Yellow-poplar	279,406	48
Silver maple/American elm	10,366	-19	Hard maple/basswood	116,829	58
Eastern white pine	59,077	-17	Black locust	49,867	61
Eastern white pine/northern red oak/white ash	74,090	-15	Baldcypress/water tupelo	87,894	65
Chestnut oak/black oak/scarlet oak	1,074,423	-9	Black cherry	7,391	100
Post oak/blackjack oak	320,320	-9	Paulownia	5,992	100
Eastern redcedar	245,209	-9	Red maple/lowland	58,862	138
Other pine/hardwood	18,410	-9	Red maple/oak	167,224	152
Black walnut	20,720	-8	Other exotic hardwoods	46,474	190

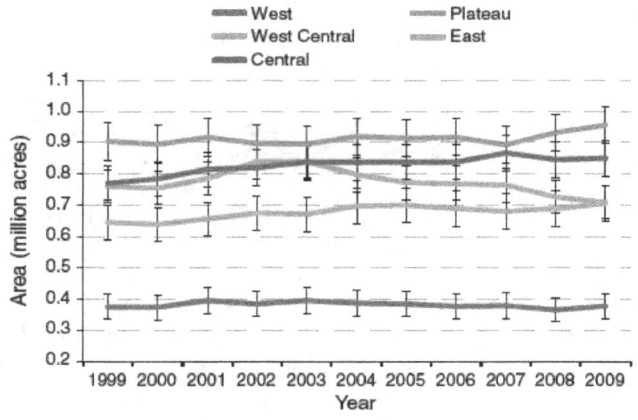

Figure 17—Area of forest land classified as white oak/red oak/hickory forest type by survey unit, Tennessee, 1999–2009. Error bars represent one standard error.

two forest types that are often found in mid-elevation communities in the Southern Appalachians and Cumberland Plateau. Following the outbreak of the SPB, these two forest types appear to be scarcer in the Tennessee landscape than before. In fact, the Table Mountain pine forest type, while accounting for an estimated 19,000 acres in 1999, has declined to the point that it is no longer detectable by the FIA inventory (fig. 18).

To gain a better understanding of changes in detailed forest types across the State, comparisons between 1999 and 2009 were made for each forest type sampled in Tennessee during that period (table 4). Table Mountain pine and the red maple-upland forest types have both declined below a point in which the FIA inventory can detect them on the landscape. This does not indicate that these forest types are no longer present within the borders of the State. However, it does indicate, particularly with Table Mountain pine, that the forest type has reached such low levels of areal extent, that conservation efforts may be necessary to increase the coverage of the type. In addition to the Table Mountain pine forest type, the largest declines in forest land area were realized by many softwood forest types, including pitch pine (57 percent decline), shortleaf pine (56 percent decline), shortleaf pine-oak (49 percent decline), and Virginia pine (45 percent decline), among others (table 4).

The white oak-red oak-hickory forest type was the dominant forest type in both 1999 and 2009 (table 5). Changes in the top 10 dominant forest types included declines (in rank) of the chestnut oak-black oak-scarlet oak, sweetgum-yellow-poplar, Virginia pine, and elm-ash-black locust types. Ten-year changes in forest types included gains in the mixed upland hardwoods, loblolly

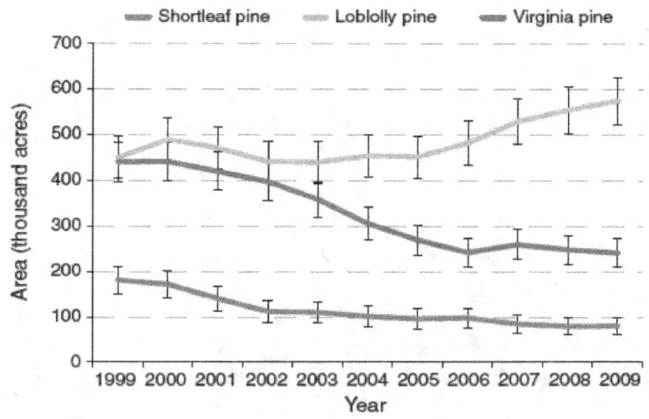

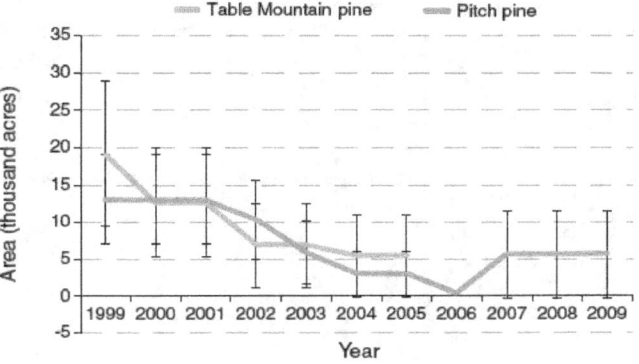

Figure 18—Area of forest land classified as belonging to the loblolly-shortleaf pine forest-type group by detailed forest type, Tennessee, 1999–2009. Errors bars represent one standard error.

pine, cherry-white ash-yellow-poplar, and sugarberry-hackberry-elm-green ash types. No one forest type, whether hardwood or softwood, young or old, can satisfy the needs of all forest-dependent organisms. A tapestry of different forest types, structures, ages, and forest conditions is needed to provide the many habitats required by the flora and fauna of Tennessee. Forest change and/or disturbance can give rise to a diversity of habitat types, and can therefore be positive.

Table 5—Top 10 forest types, according to forest land area for direction of rank change and estimate, Tennessee

1999		2009	
Forest type	Area	Forest type	Area
	acres		*acres*
White oak/red oak/hickory	3,456,062	White oak/red oak/hickory	3,598,044
Chestnut oak/black oak/scarlet oak	1,186,143	Mixed upland hardwoods	1,075,839
Mixed upland hardwoods	931,978	Chestnut oak/black oak/scarlet oak	1,074,423
Yellow-poplar/white oak/northern red oak	636,193	Yellow-poplar/white oak/northern red oak	743,340
Chestnut oak	621,828	Chestnut oak	727,714
White oak	620,792	White oak	581,635
Sweetgum/yellow-poplar	458,697	Loblolly pine	575,724
Loblolly pine	450,529	Sweetgum/yellow-poplar	567,637
Virginia pine	441,078	Cherry/white ash/yellow-poplar	382,339
Elm/ash/black locust	409,711	Sugarberry/hackberry/elm/green ash	372,168
Not a top 10 forest type		Dropped out of top 10 forest types	

Color blocks: Rust = a forest type that declined in rank between 1999 and 2009; Green = a forest type that increased between 1999 and 2009; Tan = no change.

The most significant forest-type change between 1999 and 2009 was the 190-percent increase in the other exotic hardwoods forest type (table 4). While in 2009 there was only an estimated 46,000 acres of exotic hardwoods across the State, a 190-percent increase signifies that a potential future problem could exist with an exploding population of exotic hardwood trees. While the increase is occurring in each unit, with the exception of the West Central unit, the largest 10-year increase occurred in the Central unit (fig. 19). The other exotic hardwoods forest type only recently appeared in the West unit in 2006.

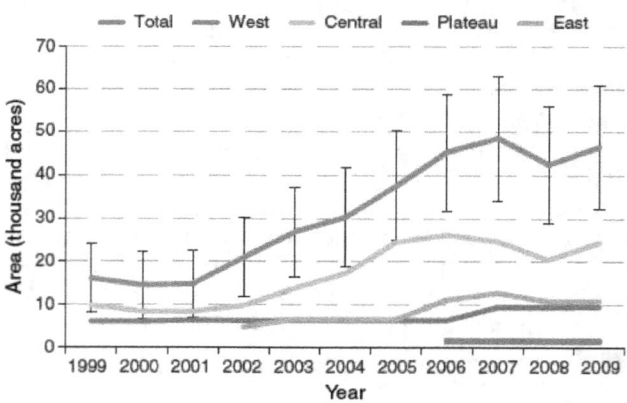

Figure 19—Area of forest land classified as other exotic hardwoods forest type by survey unit, Tennessee, 1999–2009. Error bars represent one standard error.

The Emory River, just downstream from Nemo Bridge, in Morgan County, Tennessee.
(photo by Brian Stansberry, Wikimedia.org)

Special Section—Forest-Type Conversions

A debate has surfaced in recent years in Tennessee regarding the conversion of hardwood forests to softwood forests through active forest management. To investigate the extent (if any) that hardwood forests are being converted through anthropogenic or natural means to softwood forests, we compared all forested plots measured in 2004 that were remeasured during the 2009 inventory. A comparison of broad forest types (softwood vs. hardwood) were made in order to estimate the acreage that shifted from hardwood to softwood forest types and from softwood to hardwood during the period of 2004–09. In addition, shifts to and from mixed oak-pine forests were estimated.

Very few acres (75,879) shifted from a hardwood forest type in 2004 to a softwood forest type in 2009 (table 6). Of the 342,000 acres that were estimated to have shifted from a hardwood to a mixed forest type, softwood forest type, or nonstocked condition, about 74 percent (255,000 acres)

Table 6—Broad forest-type group transitions between the 2004 and 2009 inventories, Tennessee

2004	2009			
	Hardwood	Softwood	Mix	Non-stocked
	acres			
Hardwood	10,828,334	75,879	255,102	11,493
Softwood	171,417	841,972	143,168	3,097
Mix	302,505	176,928	520,802	—
Nonstocked	36,461	11,214	7,267	18,422

— = negligible.

transitioned to a mixed oak-pine forest type (fig. 20). Shifts from softwood to a hardwood forest type were over two times greater than from hardwood to softwood types. Moreover, many mixed forests shifted to hardwood forests over the period. Over 300,000 acres of forests classified as mixed hardwood/softwood in 2004 were classified as hardwood in 2009. For the most part, hardwood forests largely remained hardwood forests and softwood forests remained softwood forests (fig. 21).

There is little evidence to support claims of widespread hardwood forest conversion in Tennessee. Data from this large-scale inventory illustrate that while conversions may be occurring, they are limited. Forest conversion from hardwood to softwood forests is scarcer than conversion from softwood to hardwood forests. Hardwood forest conversion does not appear to pose a threat to the forests of Tennessee at this time.

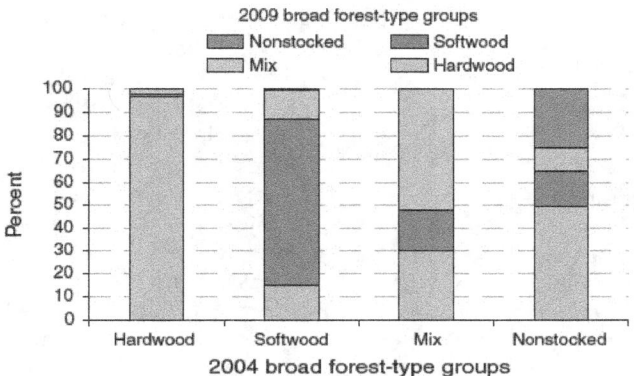

Figure 20—Broad forest-type group transitions (acres) between 2004 and 2009, Tennessee.

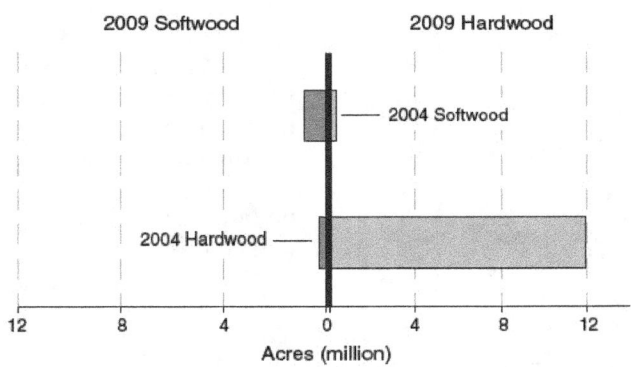

Figure 21—Broad forest-type group transitions between 2004 and 2009, Tennessee.

23

Stand Structure

Forests can be described by their composition, function, and structure (Franklin and others 1981). Most descriptions of forest stand structure are based on measures easily obtainable from the ground level (e.g., diameter at breast height). Oliver and Larson (1990) define forest stand structure as the physical and temporal distribution of trees in a stand and include within the description the distribution of species, vertical and horizontal spatial patterns, size of trees or tree parts, and tree or stand age. Here we use five common FIA metrics (stand age, stand size, stocking, basal area, and origin) to explore the structure of Tennessee's forests.

Stand Age

Stand age is the average age of the majority of live trees in the predominant stand-size class. Tennessee's forests are, for the most part, getting older. The age class distribution during the period between 1999 and 2009 is shifting to older stands on average (fig. 22). In 1980 the peak in the age class distribution for all forest land in Tennessee was the 31–40-year class. In 2000, the peak shifted to the 41–50-year class. By 2004 the age class distribution peak had shifted to the 51–60-year class and in 2009 the peak was shared by the

51–60- and 61–70-year class. Besides a shift in the peak of the distribution, there has been a broadening of the distribution as well, providing further evidence that Tennessee's forests are aging. The area of forests in the 0–10-year class has been increasing recently to provide for a bimodal-age class structure. This increase in the youngest age class suggests that some young forests are being established on the landscape. These young forests will be important as older forests begin to succumb to disturbances common to aging stands.

The temporal dynamics of the age class distribution of Tennessee forests is dependent upon broadscale ownership patterns. While both private and public forests are aging, forests of these different ownerships, in general, are not aging the same. Private forests largely mimic the overall forest land pattern in Tennessee because the vast majority of forest land in the State is privately owned. Since 1999 the age class structure on private forest land has slowly shifted from a peak in the 41–60-year age class to a peak in the 61–80-year class (fig. 23). Concurrently, the increase in young forests is apparent as well. On public forest land, overall, there are fewer young stands and the development of a bimodal-age class structure is not as apparent (fig. 24). In addition, older stands (100+-year class) have increased considerably on public lands during the period of 1999 to 2009, while remaining basically unchanged on private lands over the same period. The difference in the changes in age class distributions are likely in response to differing management objectives. While timber harvesting has continued on private forest land during the same period, timber harvesting on public lands has stagnated (Oswalt and others 2009).

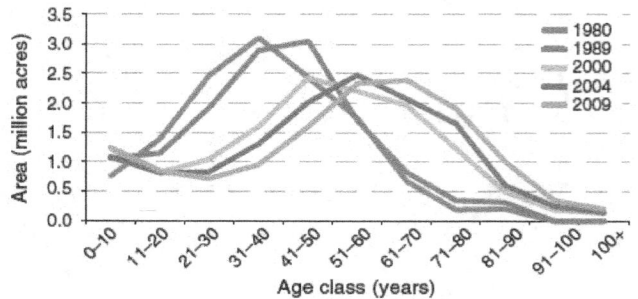

Figure 22—Age class structure for all forest land, Tennessee, 1999–2009.

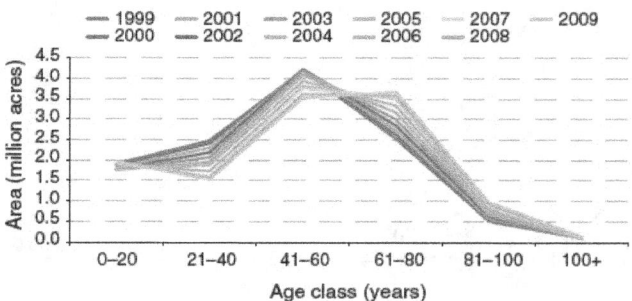

Figure 23—Age class structure for private forest land, Tennessee, 1999–2009.

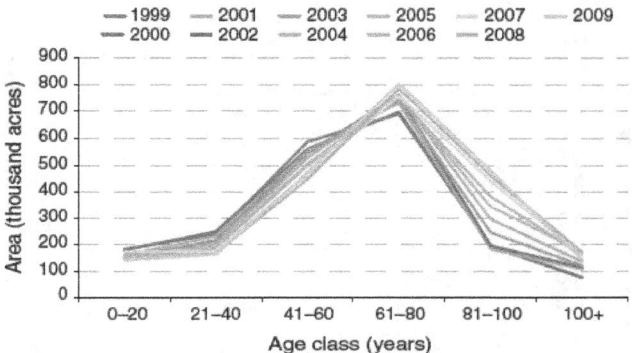

Figure 24—Age class structure for public forest land, Tennessee, 1999–2009.

The temporal dynamics of the age class distribution differed among each FIA unit as well (fig. 25). In the East and Plateau units a bimodal distribution has developed over time much like for all forest land in the State. The development of a bimodal structure is not occurring in the Central unit where the entire distribution is shifting to older age classes. In the West Central unit, a bimodal structure was apparent in 1999 and has been maintained to 2009. Maintenance of a larger population of young stands may be a response to active forest land management or widespread stand-replacing disturbances in the region. Overall, forests appear to be younger, on average, in the West unit where a significant increase in young stands has been realized over the period of 1999 to 2009. The recent reversions of agricultural lands to forest land played an important role in the increase of young stands in that region (see Land Use and Land Use Change discussion).

Considerable differences in age class structure exist among broad forest-type groups. In general, softwood forests in Tennessee are younger, hardwood forests are older, and mixed oak-pine forests are somewhere in between (fig. 26). Softwood forests are dominated by young stands with an estimated 39 percent of all softwood stands age 20 or below in 2009. This was an increase from 30 percent in 1999 and 33 percent in 2004. The majority of mixed oak-pine forests are within the 41–60-year age class and little change has occurred over the period between 1999 and 2009. Because Tennessee forests are largely hardwood forest types, the age class structure and change over time of hardwood forest types largely mimics the patterns of all forests in the State. It is promising that a younger cohort is developing that will help replace the hardwood forests of today (fig. 26).

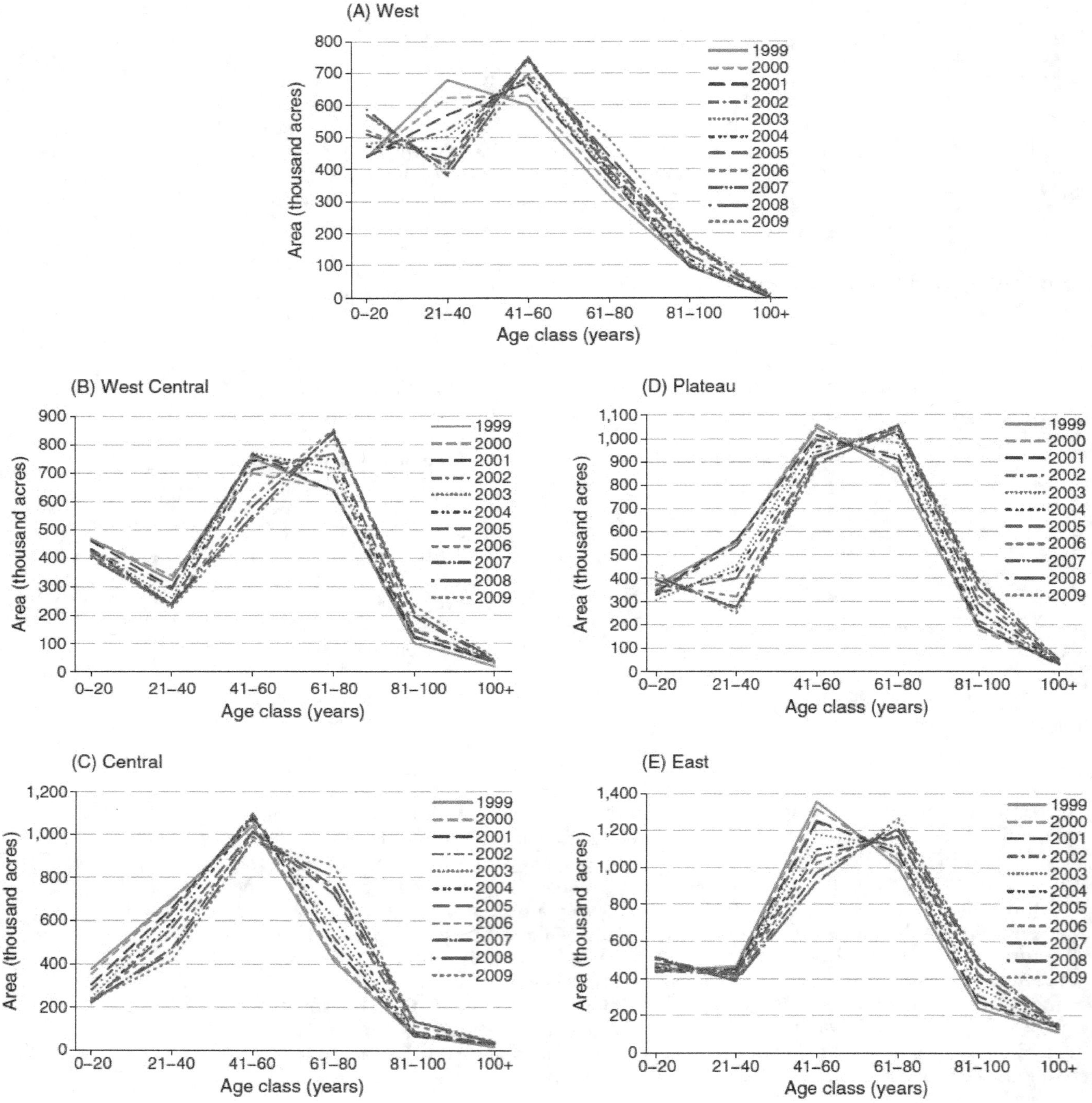

(A) West

(B) West Central

(D) Plateau

(C) Central

(E) East

Figure 25—Area of forest land by survey unit and age class, Tennessee, 1999–2009 (A) West, (B) West Central, (C) Central, (D) Plateau, (E) East.

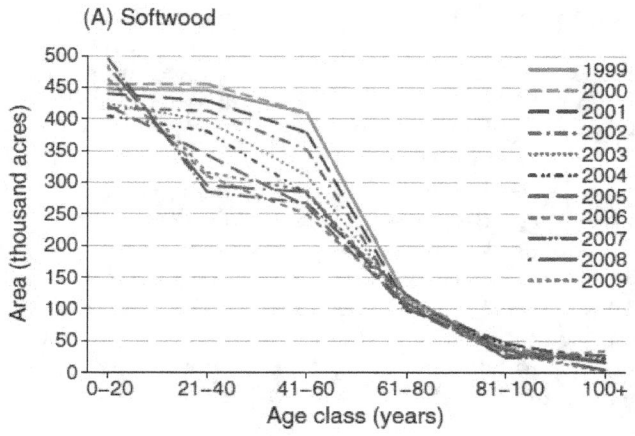

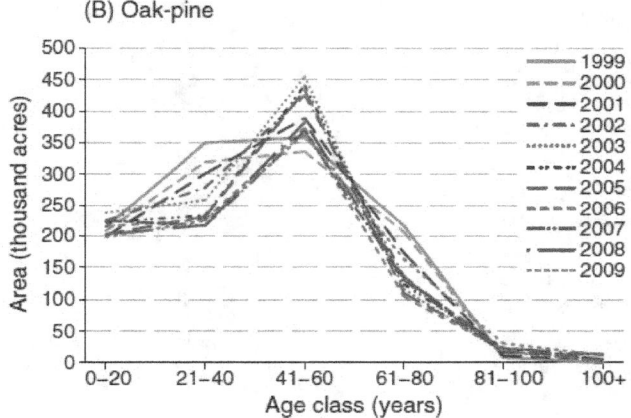

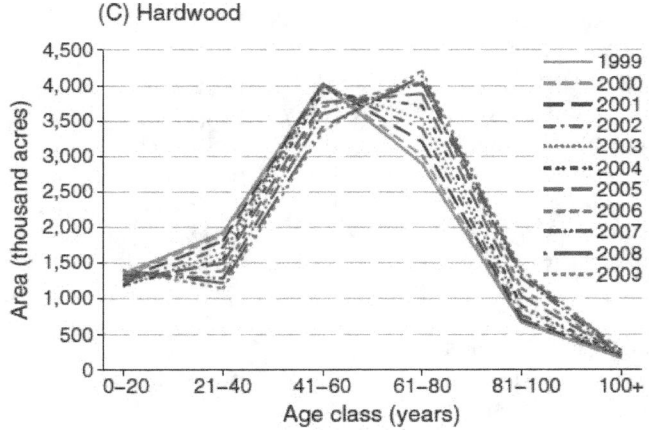

Figure 26—Age class structure for forest land by broad forest-type groups, Tennessee, 1999–2009 (A) Softwood, (B) Oak-pine, (C) Hardwood.

Stand-Size Class and Stocking

It is important to know the size of the trees that makeup the forests in Tennessee. Armed with this knowledge, resource managers are better able to understand the structure of the forested stands and the habitat that exists on the landscape. In addition, trend analysis of stand size (a classification based on stocking and the diameter of the majority of the live trees in a stand) facilitates understanding of the successional status and potential future development of the forest and the populations of its inhabitants.

The stand-size classes utilized by FIA are small, medium, and large diameter (formerly sapling-seedling, poletimber, and sawtimber, respectively), as well as nonstocked. Small diameter stands are forested areas where the majority of the trees are <5.0 inches d.b.h. Medium diameter stands are at least 5.0 inches d.b.h. but are not large enough to be considered large diameter. In order to be large diameter size, a softwood species must be ≥9.0 inches, while hardwood species must be ≥11.0 inches. Nonstocked means that although the land is considered forested, there are not enough trees on it to categorize it into a particular stand-size class. These are generally forested areas that have recently been harvested but new tree growth has not regenerated to an adequate level of stocking at the time of the field inventory.

In 2009, the majority of stands were in the large diameter size class (fig. 27). The area of forest land classified as large diameter has been increasing in recent years. In 1999, an estimated 60 percent of all forest land in Tennessee was in large diameter stands. In 2004, the percent of large diameter stands had increased to

63 percent and by 2009 had increased to 65 percent. Concurrently, stands classified as medium diameter declined from 27 percent in 1999 to 23 and 21 percent in 2004 and 2009, respectively. During the period of 1999 to 2009, the area of small diameter stands remained about 13 percent. However, the State has seen a declining trend in early-successional or small diameter forests over nearly 50 years (1961 to 2009) (Oswalt and others 2009). In 1971, early-successional forests accounted for about 35 percent of all forest land in the State.

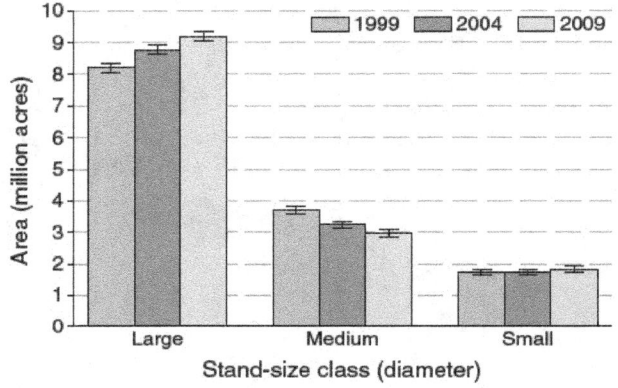

Figure 27—Area of forest land by stand-size class, Tennessee, 1999, 2004, and 2009. Error bars represent one standard error.

While relatively similar trends in stand-size class distribution exist among all FIA units in Tennessee, small but important distinctions do exist. For example, there appears to be a larger increase in small and medium diameter stands in the West unit (fig. 28). Additionally, change in any stand-size class appears to be minimal in the East unit while changes in the large and medium stand-size classes are more exaggerated in the West Central unit.

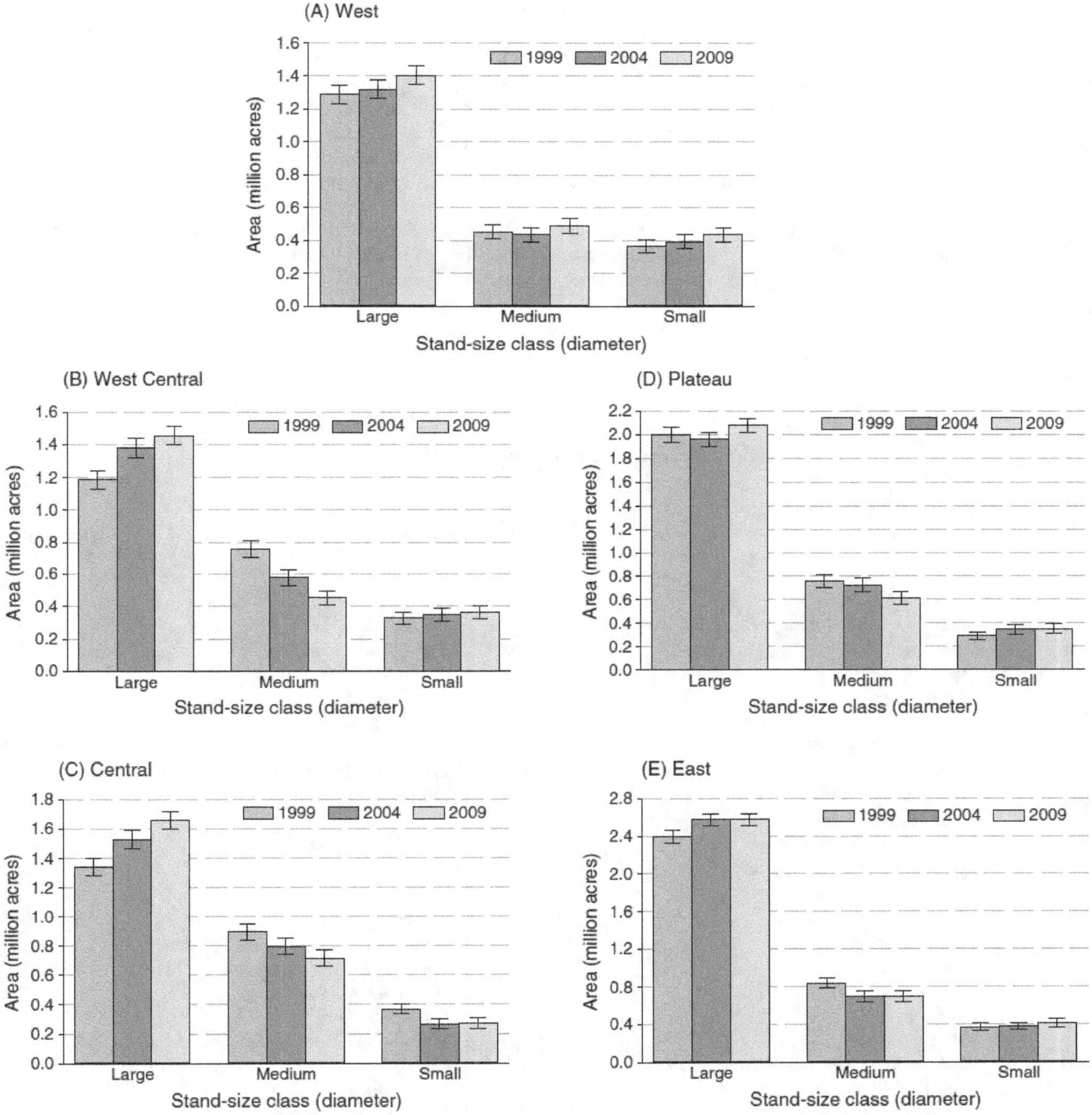

(A) West

(B) West Central

(D) Plateau

(C) Central

(E) East

Figure 28—Area of forest land by survey unit and stand-size class, Tennessee, 1999, 2004, and 2009 (A) West, (B) West Central, (C) Central, (D) Plateau, (E) East. Error bars represent one standard error.

Mean all-live stocking across all Tennessee forest land, with the exception of non-stocked stands, was 62.2 percent in 2009. Softwood forests types were maintained, on average, at higher all-live stocking levels (65.5 percent) than hardwood forest types (60.9 percent). Mixed oak-pine stands were maintained, on average, at an estimated 65.6 percent all-live stocking. The eastern white pine-eastern hemlock forest type, found in the East and Plateau units, had the highest average all-live stocking, estimated at 88.5 percent (table 7). Black cherry (27.1 percent) had the lowest average percent all-live stocking.

Public forest lands appear to have been maintained at higher all-live stocking levels than private forest lands. Forest land managed by the USDA Forest Service national forests had the highest mean stocking levels at 65.4 percent stocking (table 8). Other federally managed forest lands were similarly stocked at 64.9 percent all-live stocking. State, local, and private forest lands were maintained at lower mean stocking levels, 60.7 and 60.2 percent, respectively.

Table 7—Mean all-live stocking by forest type, Tennessee, 2009

Forest type	Mean all-live stocking	Forest type	Mean all-live stocking
	percent		*percent*
Eastern white pine	64.6	Chestnut oak/black oak/scarlet oak	63.7
Eastern white pine/eastern hemlock	88.5	Cherry/white ash/yellow-poplar	53.7
Eastern hemlock	62.0	Elm/ash/black locust	59.6
Loblolly pine	68.4	Red maple/oak	57.9
Shortleaf pine	55.8	Mixed upland hardwoods	57.9
Virginia pine	65.4	Swamp chestnut oak/cherrybark oak	65.9
Pitch pine	66.8	Sweetgum/nuttall oak/willow oak	72.4
Eastern red cedar	52.6	Overcup oak/water hickory	59.7
Eastern white pine/northern red oak/white ash	61.8	Baldcypress/water tupelo	59.9
Eastern redcedar/hardwood	50.5	Sweetbay/swamp tupelo/red maple	64.8
Shortleaf pine/oak	65.4	River birch/sycamore	58.6
Virginia pine/southern red oak	63.1	Cottonwood	53.9
Loblolly pine/hardwood	74.3	Willow	47.2
Other pine/hardwood	78.5	Sycamore/pecan/American elm	64.0
Post oak/blackjack oak	56.2	Sugarberry/hackberry/elm/green ash	62.3
Chestnut oak	68.4	Silver maple/American elm	69.4
White oak/red oak/hickory	59.6	Red maple/lowland	64.4
White oak	58.7	Cottonwood/willow	75.4
Northern red oak	62.3	Sugar maple/beech/yellow birch	60.8
Yellow-poplar/white oak/northern red oak	63.0	Black cherry	27.1
Sassafras/persimmon	69.4	Hard maple/basswood	59.1
Sweetgum/yellow-poplar	60.4	Other hardwoods	65.0
Scarlet oak	64.5	Paulownia	71.7
Yellow-poplar	56.4	Other exotic hardwoods	59.2
Black walnut	54.3	Nonstocked	4.0
Black locust	63.9		

Table 8—Mean all-live stocking by ownership group, Tennessee, 2009

Ownership group	Mean all-live stocking
	percent
Forest Service	65.4
Other Federal	64.9
State and local	60.7
Private	60.2

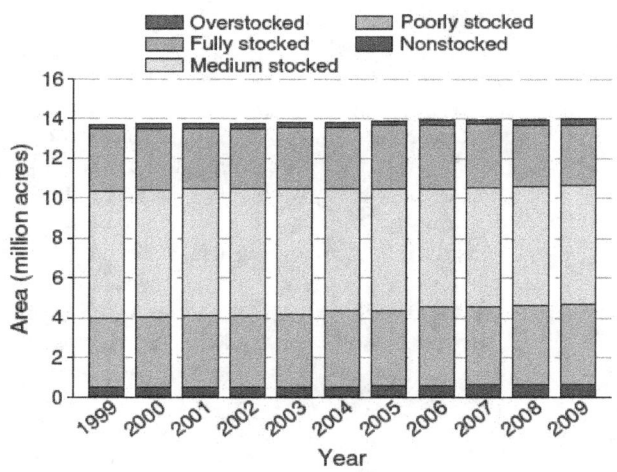

Figure 29—Area of growing stock on forest land by stand stocking class, Tennessee, 1999–2009.

The FIA inventory classifies all forested stands into one of five stocking classes (overstocked, fully stocked, medium stocked, poorly stocked, and nonstocked) based on both growing-stock seedlings and trees. Most of Tennessee's forest land was classified as medium stocked. In 2009, there were an estimated 6.0 million acres (43 percent of all forest land) in medium stocked stands (table 9) (fig. 29). There were

an estimated 4.0 and 3.0 million acres in poorly stocked and fully stocked stands, respectively. Somewhat concerning is the steady increase in stands poorly stocked with growing-stock trees. Poorly stocked stands increased from 25 percent of all forest land in 1999 to 28 percent in 2004 and 29 percent in 2009. The Central unit contains a larger than average percent of stands in the poorly stocked class (table 9).

Table 9—Area of forest land by survey unit and stocking class of growing-stock trees, Tennessee, 2009

Survey unit	Total	Stocking class				
		Over-stocked	Fully stocked	Medium stocked	Poorly stocked	Non-stocked
		acres				
West	2,340,883	71,002	485,966	908,827	737,658	137,431
West Central	2,271,670	35,771	534,895	1,077,642	565,826	57,535
Central	2,645,641	33,578	427,371	1,061,865	908,552	214,275
Plateau	3,050,848	82,687	686,374	1,310,442	878,632	92,712
East	3,694,242	59,911	893,605	1,606,241	988,749	145,736
Total	14,003,283	282,948	3,028,212	5,965,018	4,079,416	647,688

Totals may not sum due to rounding.

Stand Basal Area

Stand basal area, measured as the cross-sectional (at d.b.h.) area occupied by trees in a given stand, provides valuable information regarding stand density and dominance, and is significantly related to stand volume. In 2009, average stand basal area (basal area of all-live trees ≥1-inch d.b.h.) was 104 square feet per acre across all forest land in the State with the exception of non-stocked stands. Nonstocked stands averaged an estimated 14 square feet of basal area per acre.

The FIA program classifies each measured stand into one of four all-live basal area classes (typically 0–40, 41–80, 81–120, and ≥120 square feet per acre). The 81–120 square feet of live basal area class contained the greatest acreage across all Tennessee forest land (table 10), with an estimated 5.3 million acres. The second largest class across all forest land is the ≥120 square feet of basal area class.

Forest land in Tennessee managed by the USDA Forest Service national forest maintained the largest acreage, relative to overall forest land ownership, in the ≥120 square feet of basal area class (56 percent, table 10). Moreover, all public

forest land is skewed to the larger basal area classes. Private forest land is more evenly distributed among each of the basal are classes used by FIA (table 10). More than likely, this is an artifact of broad level differences in management strategies between private and public forest lands. Forest Service forest lands averaged about 125 square feet while private forest lands averaged 96 square feet of basal are per acre (table 11).

Table 11—Mean basal area by ownership group, Tennessee, 2009

Ownership group	Mean basal area
	square feet per acre
Forest Service	125
Other Federal	115
State and local	107
Private	96

Table 10—Area of forest land by ownership group and basal area class of all-live trees, Tennessee, 2009

Ownership group	Total	Basal area class (*square feet*)			
		0–40	41–80	81–120	120+
		acres			
National forest	705,668	17,546	104,928	186,315	396,878
Other Federal	664,985	27,447	118,709	199,100	319,729
State and local	836,132	67,163	123,366	348,510	297,092
Private	11,796,498	1,480,216	2,590,011	4,565,081	3,161,190
Total	14,003,283	1,592,373	2,937,015	5,299,006	4,174,889

Totals may not sum due to rounding.

Similar to all-live stocking, average stand basal area was highest for softwood followed by mixed oak-pine and hardwood forest types with an average of 146, 104, and 95 square feet of basal area per acre (table 12). In 2009, eastern white pine-eastern hemlock stands averaged >350 square feet per acre of basal area, the highest of any forest type in Tennessee. The black cherry forest type averaged a State low of 47 square feet per acre of basal area.

Table 12—Mean basal area by forest type, Tennessee, 2009

Forest type	Mean basal area	Rank	Forest type	Mean basal area	Rank
	square feet per acre	largest to smallest		square feet per acre	largest to smallest
Nonstocked	14	51	White oak/red oak/hickory	102	25
Black cherry	47	50	Red maple/lowland	105	24
Black locust	56	49	Overcup oak/water hickory	105	23
			Sweetbay/swamp tupelo/ red maple	105	22
Other exotic hardwoods	59	48	Hard maple/basswood	106	21
Paulownia	61	47	Virginia pine/southern red oak	106	20
Other hardwoods	61	46	Pitch pine	109	19
Black walnut	64	45	Scarlet oak	109	18
Red maple/oak	64	44	Yellow-poplar/white oak/ northern red oak	109	17
Willow	70	43	Yellow-poplar	110	16
Elm/ash/black locust	74	42	Sugar maple/beech/yellow birch	112	15
Sassafras/persimmon	74	41	Shortleaf pine/oak	117	14
Cherry/white ash/yellow-poplar	77	40	Northern red oak	119	13
Eastern redcedar/hardwood	79	39	Chestnut oak/black oak/ scarlet oak	121	12
Loblolly pine/hardwood	80	38	Shortleaf pine	122	11
Mixed upland hardwoods	83	37	Sycamore/pecan/American elm	123	10
Post oak/blackjack oak	84	36	Chestnut oak	124	9
Eastern redcedar	84	35	Swamp chestnut oak/cherrybark oak	127	8
Cottonwood/willow	86	34	Baldcypress/water tupelo	133	7
Cottonwood	87	33	Sweetgum/nuttall oak/willow oak	138	6
River birch/sycamore	91	32			
Sugarberry/hackberry/ elm/green ash	91	31	Eastern hemlock	140	5
Sweetgum/yellow-poplar	95	30	Silver maple/American elm	141	4
			Eastern white pine/northern red oak/white ash	146	3
Virginia pine	97	29	Eastern white pine	153	2
Other pine/hardwood	97	28	Eastern white pine/ eastern hemlock	358	1
Loblolly pine	101	27			
White oak	102	26			

Stand Origin

In 2009 there was a total of 683,000 acres of planted forest land in Tennessee, an increase from 604,000 acres in 1999 and 499,000 acres in 2004 (fig. 30). About 5 percent of all forest land in the State was classified as planted in 2009. For the period of 1999 to 2009, the proportion of forest land that was planted has

remained between 4 and 5 percent. All of the 683,000 acres of planted forests inventoried have been planted with one of three species (shortleaf pine, eastern white pine, or loblolly pine) (table 13). Ninety-seven percent has been planted with loblolly pine. Although there are known hardwood plantings throughout the State, the area of planted hardwood forests has not reached a level where the FIA inventory has detected it.

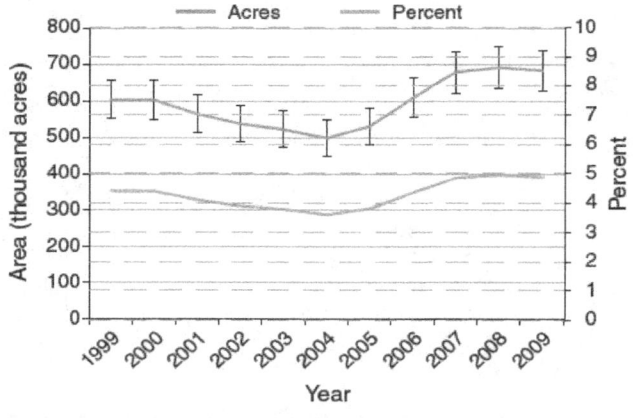

Figure 30—Area of planted forests and percent of forest land classified as planted, Tennessee, 1999–2009. Error bars represent one standard error.

Table 13—Area of planted forests by primary planted species, Tennessee, 2009

Primary planted species	Planted forests	
	- acres -	error percent
Shortleaf pine	14,065	56.48
Eastern white pine	3,276	94.02
Loblolly pine	665,900	8.39
Total	683,241	8.28

A young loblolly pine stand.

Planted forests are primarily located in the southern and eastern portions of the West unit, the West Central, and Plateau units and the southern portion of the East unit (fig. 31). The majority of the State, particularly in the East and Central units, has very little to no planted forests (fig. 32). The heaviest concentration of planted forests appears to be in the southern counties of the West and West central units.

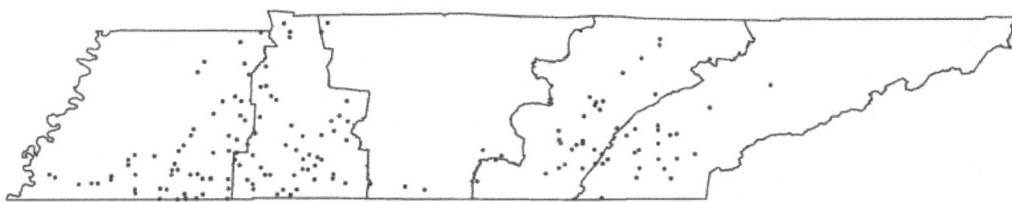

Figure 31—Location of planted stands, Tennessee, 2009. (Plot locations are approximate).

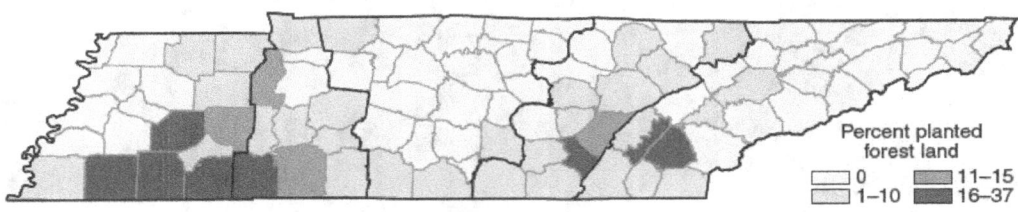

Figure 32—Percent of forest land with planted stand origin, Tennessee, 2009.

Shortleaf pine (*Pinus echinata*). (photo by Chris Evans, Bugwood.org)

Ownership Patterns in Tennessee

The FIA unit collects information about ownership of forested land in each State. Ownership at each forested phase 2 (see glossary) ground plot is determined from publicly available records at local county court houses. Area, density, and volume estimates are displayed by ownership classes such as nonindustrial private forest land (NIPF), public (including the U.S. Forest Service), and forest industry (defined as forest landowners who also own a wood processing facility).

According to the 2009 inventory, an estimated 84 percent (11.8 million acres) of the forest land in Tennessee is in private ownership (table 14). Sixteen percent of the forest land in Tennessee is publicly administered by local, State, or Federal agencies. About one-third of the public forest land (5 percent of all forest land) is administered as national forests and about one-third by other Federal agencies. The remaining public Tennessee forest land (6 percent of all forest land) is owned and administered by various State and local governments. The majority of the forest land owned and administered by the U.S. Forest Service is

Appalachian hardwoods in the Great Smoky Mountains National Park, Tennessee. (photo by Chris Evans, Bugwood.org)

Table 14—Area of forest land by ownership class and land status, Tennessee, 2009

Ownership class	All forest land	Unreserved			Reserved		
		Total	Timber-land	Un-productive	Total	Productive	Un-productive
				thousand acres			
U.S. Forest Service							
National forest	653.5	622.8	622.8	0.0	30.7	30.7	0.0
Other Forest Service	52.2	46.2	46.2	0.0	5.9	5.9	0.0
Total	705.7	669.0	669.0	0.0	36.6	36.6	0.0
Other Federal							
National Park Service	330.0	0.0	0.0	0.0	330.0	330.0	0.0
U.S. Fish and Wildlife Service	31.4	12.7	12.7	0.0	18.6	18.6	0.0
Dept. of Defense/Dept. of Energy	102.4	88.8	88.8	0.0	13.5	13.5	0.0
Other Federal	201.2	201.2	201.2	0.0	0.0	0.0	0.0
Total	665.0	302.8	302.8	0.0	362.2	362.2	0.0
State and local government							
State	724.8	680.8	680.8	0.0	44.0	44.0	0.0
Local	105.5	99.6	99.6	0.0	5.8	5.8	0.0
Other non-Federal public	5.8	0.0	0.0	0.0	5.8	5.8	0.0
Total	836.1	780.4	780.4	0.0	55.7	55.7	0.0
Forest industry							
Corporate	344.6	344.6	344.5	0.0	0.0	0.0	0.0
Unincorporated local partnership/association/club	5.2	5.2	5.2	0.0	0.0	0.0	0.0
Individual	24.0	24.0	24.0	0.0	0.0	0.0	0.0
Total	373.9	373.9	373.9	0.0	0.0	0.0	0.0
Nonindustrial private							
Corporate	1,899.6	1,899.6	1,899.6	0.0	0.0	0.0	0.0
Conservation/natural resources organization	32.0	32.0	32.0	0.0	0.0	0.0	0.0
Unincorporated local partnership/association/club	74.2	74.2	74.2	0.0	0.0	0.0	0.0
Native American	3.1	3.1	3.1	0.0	0.0	0.0	0.0
Individual	9,413.8	9,413.8	9,412.2	1.6	0.0	0.0	0.0
Total	11,422.6	11,422.6	11,421.0	1.6	0.0	0.0	0.0
All classes	14,003.3	13,548.8	13,547.2	1.6	454.5	454.5	0.0

Totals may not sum due to rounding.

0.0 = no sample for the cell or a value of >0.0 but <0.05.

within the Cherokee National Forest in the East unit and the Land Between the Lakes National Recreation Area in the West unit. The highest density of publicly administered forest land is in the East and Plateau units (fig. 33).

most likely in response to forest companies shifting to a different business model. In addition, there has been a slight increase in State and local forest land ownership (fig. 34).

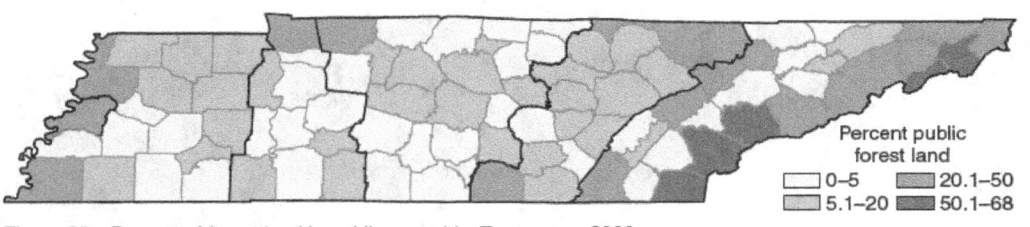

Figure 33—Percent of forest land in public owership, Tennessee, 2009.

Loss of Forest Industry Landholdings

Forest land ownership has been dramatically changing in Tennessee over the last decade. Forest industry forest land has been steadily declining since the late 1990s and now represents only 3 percent of all forest land in the State (fig. 34). In 1999 forest industry accounted for ownership of an estimated 1.3 million acres or 10 percent of Tennessee's total forest land. Today, forest industry accounts for about 374,000 acres. There have been concomitant gains in NIPF ownership as forest industry has divested the majority of its forest land base. This is

All regions in the State have been impacted by the loss of industry ownership, with exceptional losses of >75 percent in many counties in the East, Plateau, and West Central units (fig. 35). Over the last decade, spanning the period between 1999 and 2009, statewide forest industry ownership has declined about 72 percent (table 15). The largest change (absolute = -369,834 acres, relative = 82 percent) occurred within the West Central unit. While forest industry ownership declined only an estimated 13,000 acres in the Central unit, this represented about 41 percent of that ownership category in Central Tennessee. The significant loss of forest industry forest land ownership between 1999 and 2009 represents the largest shift in forest land ownership patterns across the State since FIA began tracking forest land ownership in Tennessee in the early 1960s.

Debris dam developing in an Appalachian mountain stream. (photo by Rachel Weeks)

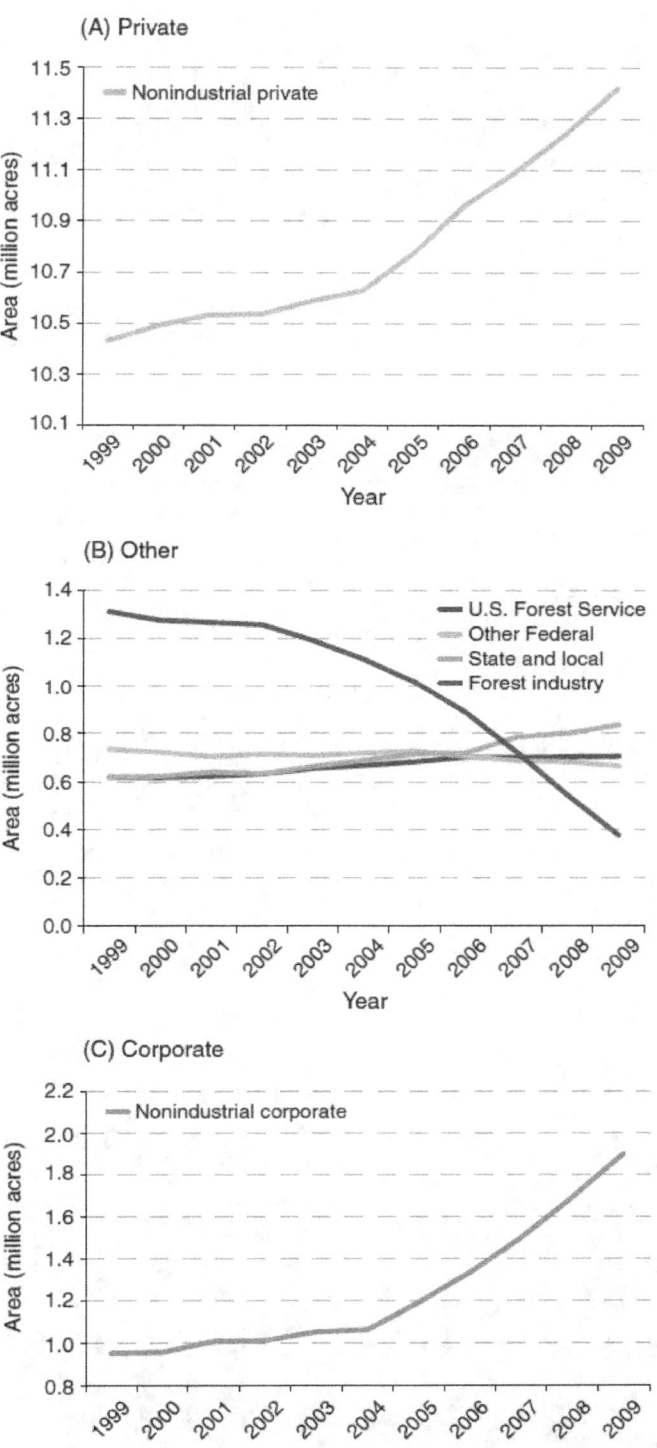

Figure 34—Area of forest land by ownership category, Tennessee, 1999–2009 (A) Private, (B) Other, (C) Corporate.

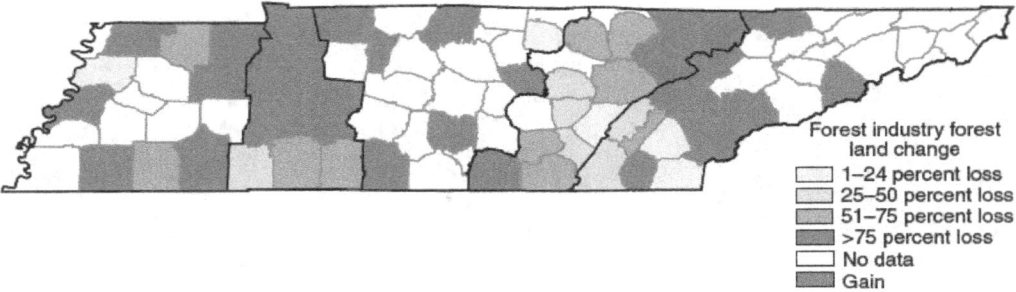

Figure 35—Percent change in forest land area with forest industry ownership, Tennessee, 1999–2009.

Table 15—Area of forest land in forest industry ownership and absolute and relative change by survey unit, Tennessee, 1999 and 2009

Survey unit	Year		Change	
	1999	2009	Absolute	Relative
	- - - - - - - - - - acres - - - - - - - - - -			percent
West	126,845	26,708	-100,137	-78.9
West Central	449,130	79,296	-369,834	-82.3
Central	30,883	18,362	-12,521	-40.5
Plateau	493,461	173,754	-319,707	-64.8
East	211,561	75,754	-135,807	-64.2
Total	1,311,880	373,873	-938,007	-71.5

View from Pinnacle Overlook in Cumberland Gap National Historic Park. (Wikimedia.org)

Special Section—The Cherokee National Forest

The Cherokee National Forest (CNF), located in the Southern Appalachian Mountains of east Tennessee, is the largest tract of public land in the State. The CNF is comprised of about 650,000 acres separated into a northern and southern section by the Great Smoky Mountains National Park. The CNF adjoins the George Washington/Jefferson National Forest in Virginia, the Pisgah and Nantahala National Forests in North Carolina, and the Chattahoochee National Forest in Georgia. As a result, the public land complex that the CNF is a part of is an extremely important expanse of forest land for a myriad of ecosystem services. Since the CNF represents a significant portion (about 5 percent in 2009) of Tennessee's forests, a very brief glimpse at the extent and condition of its forests has been included. The CNF forest is both biologically rich and socioeconomically important.

Visitors of the CNF can enjoy more than 600 miles of trails including 150 miles of the Appalachian National Scenic Trail, hundreds of miles of cold water streams, 7 whitewater rivers, 3 large lakes managed by the Tennessee Valley Authority, 11 congressionally designated Wilderness areas, 30 developed campgrounds, 45 developed day-use sites and abundant populations of wildlife. In addition, the CNF provides habitat for 43 species of mammals, 154 species of fish, 55 species of amphibians and 262 species of birds (see www.fs.usda.gov/cherokee).

Sample based estimates of forest land within the CNF have remained near 650,000 acres (fig. 36). The majority (73 percent or 475,000 acres) of the CNF forests are of the oak-hickory forest-type group (fig. 37). The CNF, during the period between 1999 and 2009, realized declines in area of the loblolly-shortleaf forest-type group while gaining maple-beech-birch forests.

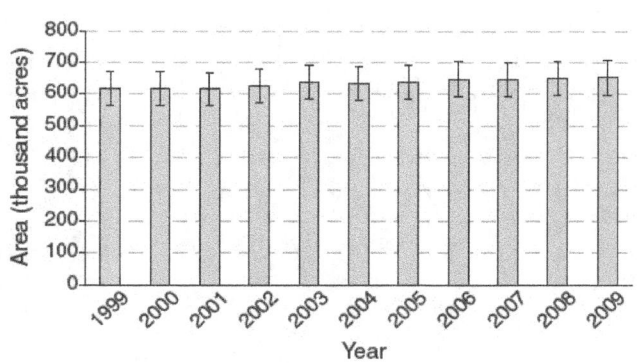

Figure 36—Area of forest land under the management of the U.S. Department of Agriculture Forest Service, Cherokee National Forest, Tennessee, 1999–2009. Error bars represent one standard error.

The FIA program classifies sampled plots into physiographic classes (see glossary) that help describe the local ecology of the sampled forests. Physiographic class accounts for the general effect of land form, topographical position, and soil moisture available to the trees. In 2009, the CNF was largely comprised of rolling uplands and moist slopes and coves with 42 and 39 percent of all CNF forest land area, respectively (fig. 38). An estimated 14 percent of CNF forest land area was classified as dry slopes and 4 percent classified as dry tops. Very little area was within the flatwoods physiographic class.

Charred ground after a recent fire in a small diameter stand of Table Mountain pine in east Tennessee.

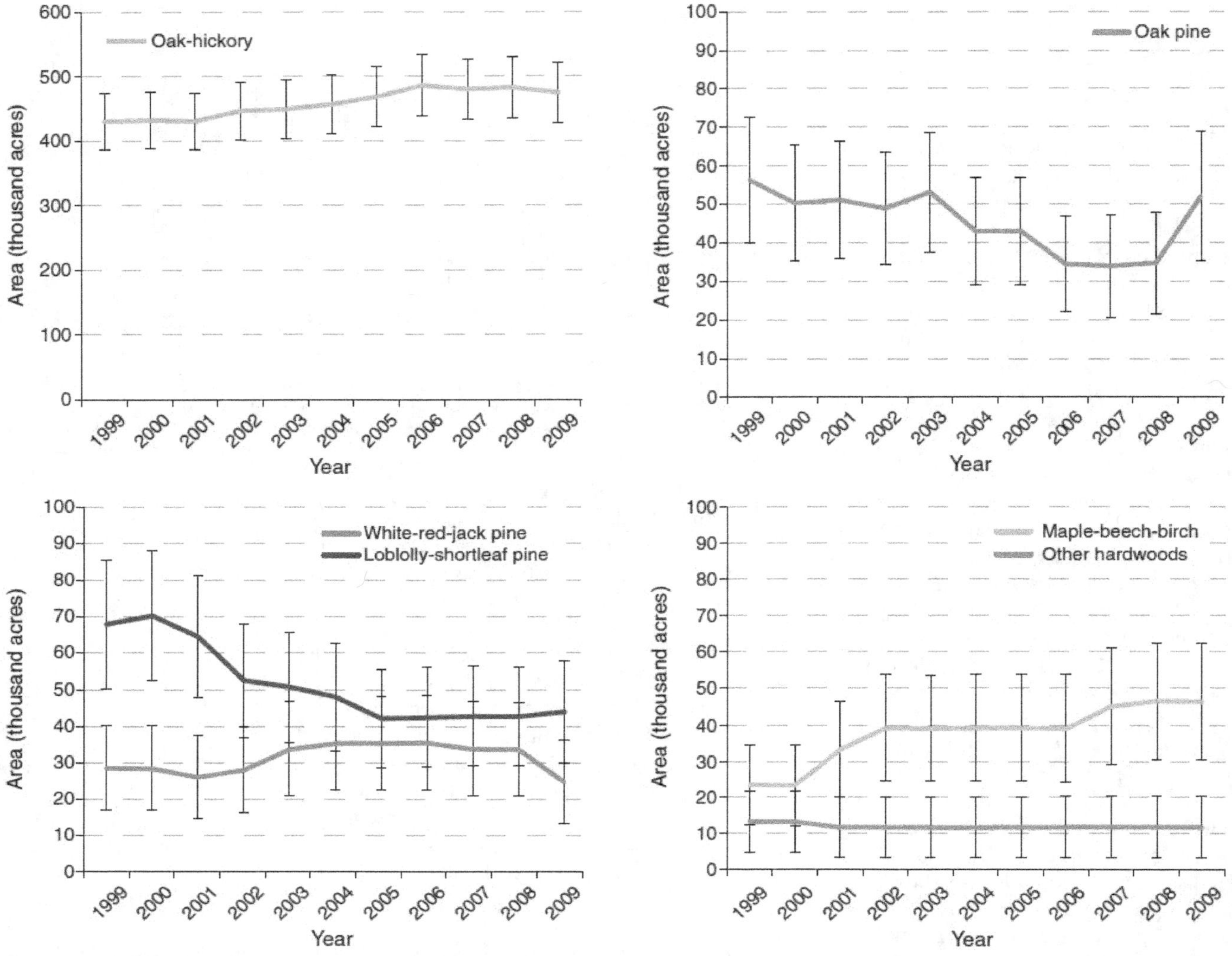

Figure 37—Area of forest land under the management of the U.S. Department of Agriculture Forest Service, Cherokee National Forest by forest-type group, Tennessee, 1999–2009. Error bars represent one standard error.

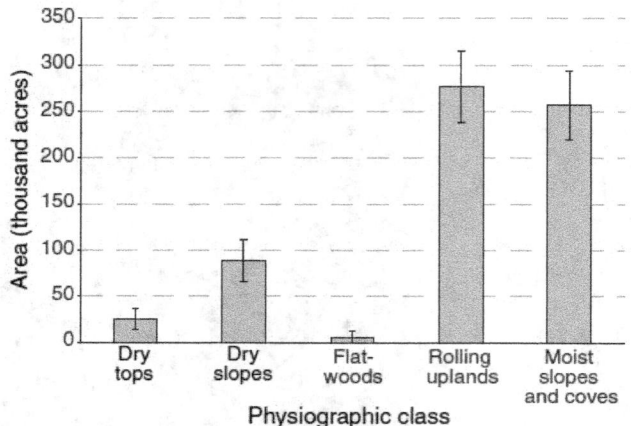

Figure 38—Area of forest land under the management of the U.S. Department of Agriculture Forest Service, Cherokee National Forest by physiographic class, Tennessee, 1999–2009. Error bars represent one standard error.

In 2009, an estimated 64,000 acres (10 percent) exhibited signs of a significant disturbance. Primary disturbance agents included insect, fire, and other unclassified disturbances. Fire and insects were recorded as the primary disturbance agent for 61 and 30 percent, respectively, of the forest land area where a disturbance was observed (fig. 39). In 2009, the disturbance agent responsible for the largest number of acres disturbed was fire, while in 1999 weather accounted for the greatest number of acres disturbed (75,000 acres). In 2004, weather related disturbed acreage had dropped to about 12,000 acres and insect-disturbed acreage had increased to 73,000 acres. Insect-disturbed acreage peaked in 2005 with an estimated 81,000 acres (fig. 40). The peak in SPB activity

in Tennessee occurred between 2000 and 2001 (Oswalt and others 2009). Therefore, it can be assumed that the estimated peak in insect-disturbed acreage in 2005 lags behind the peak in activity (fig. 40). More than likely the time-lag is an artifact of the manner in which FIA data is collected (e.g., 20 percent of plots measured each year over a 5-year period).

Between 1999 and 2009 the area of forest land in the CNF that exhibited signs of fire related disturbance increased nearly 450 percent. In 1999 and 2000, the area of forest land within the CNF with evidence of a fire disturbance was estimated to be slightly over 7,000 acres (fig. 41). By 2004 that estimate had increased to 16,000 acres and by 2009 was about 39,000 acres.

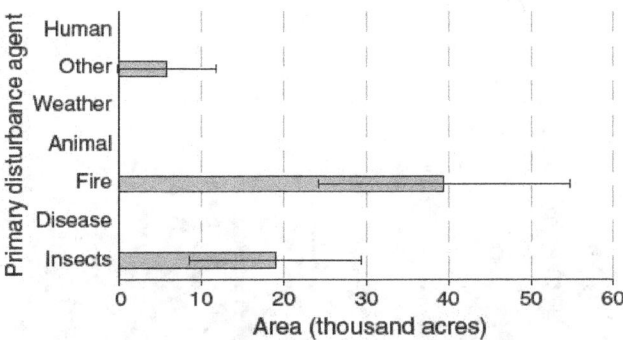

Figure 39—Area of forest land under the management of the U.S. Department of Agriculture Forest Service, Cherokee National Forest by primary disturbance agent, Tennessee, 1999–2009. Error bars represent one standard error.

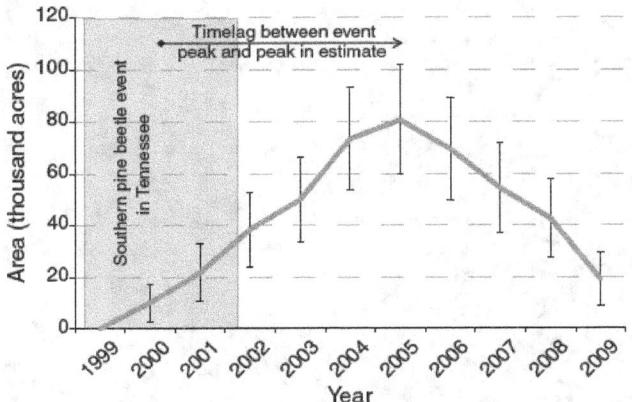

Figure 40—Area of forest land under the management of the U.S. Department of Agriculture Forest Service, Cherokee National Forest impacted by insect disturbance, Tennessee, 1999–2009. Error bars represent one standard error.

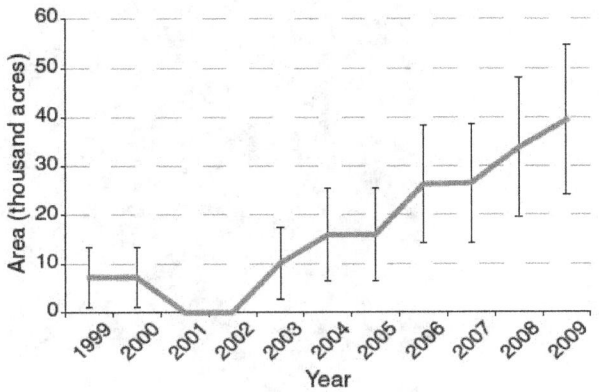

Figure 41—Area of forest land under the management of the U.S. Department of Agriculture Forest Service, Cherokee National Forest impacted by fire disturbance, Tennessee, 1999–2009. Error bars represent one standard error.

43

The changes in age class structure of CNF forest land over the past decade are much different than for forest land statewide. Over the past 10 years, younger stands have transitioned to older age classes (fig. 42). Unlike all forest land in the State, however, there is a lack of a younger cohort being developed. In fact, the area of CNF forest land within the 0–20-year age class has declined from an estimated 49,000 acres in 1999 to an estimated 38,000 acres in 2004 and 20,000 acres in 2009. Moreover, there have been declines in the 21–40- and 41–60-year age classes as well. All age classes >60 years

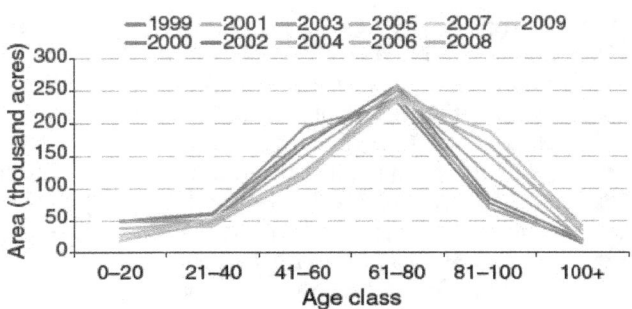

Figure 42—Age class structure for Cherokee National Forest forest land, Tennessee, 1999–2009.

have experienced gains in area. As a result, the forests of the CNF are aging much like those across the State, however, there is not a replacement cohort developing at this time.

New plant growth shortly following a prescribed fire in east Tennessee.

Productive Capacity of Tennessee Forests

Productive capacity refers to the ability of forests to produce goods and services for humans (U.S. Department of Agriculture 2004b). This definition incorporates aspects of both the environmental and economic sustainability of Tennessee's forest systems. Maintaining the productive capacity of the State's forests is essential because humans and wildlife rely on a productive, healthy forest to supply livelihoods, wood products, food, fuel, cover, water filtration, recreation, and many other goods and services year after year.

FIA defines timberland as any forested land that is available for timber production. That is, forested land not withdrawn from timber harvesting by law. A good example of forest land withdrawn from timber harvesting by law in Tennessee is the Great Smoky Mountains National Park. Thus, timberland is the land base from which Tennessee citizens can obtain multiple timber and nontimber products and services. The timberland base in Tennessee should remain productive.

Because few changes occur in the acreage of reserved forest land, the area of timberland in Tennessee tracks closely to that of forest land (see table 1 and fig. 3). In 2009, timberland covered an estimated 13.5 million acres across the State. This estimate was slightly higher than in 2004 (13.3 million acres), however should not be interpreted as a significant change. The interpretation of reserve status has been inconsistent in past surveys and has necessitated the correction of past data. Therefore, real change is confounded by inconsistently applied definitions. Timberland in Tennessee has consistently remained near 50 percent of all land and about 97 percent of all forest land in the State (see table 1 and fig. 3). The counties with large proportions of timberland relative to total land base are primarily in the West Central and Plateau FIA units (fig. 43). The counties with the largest timberland to forest land ratios in 2009 were in the West and East units (fig. 44).

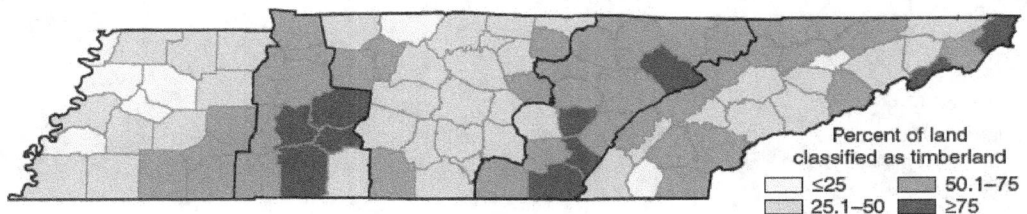

Figure 43—Percent of land classified as timberland, Tennessee, 2009.

Figure 44—Percent of forest land classified as timberland, Tennessee, 2009.

Composition of Timberlands

The oak-hickory forest-type group accounted for an estimated 73 percent (9.9 million acres) of the timberland in Tennessee in 2009 (table 16). The loblolly-shortleaf pine type group accounted for only 7 percent, the majority of which (541,000 acres) is located in the East and West units. Mixed stands of the oak-pine type group accounted for an estimated 7 percent of timberland in Tennessee. Bottomland hardwoods (elm-ash-cottonwood and oak-gum-cypress types), largely in West Tennessee, accounted for about 8 percent of the timberland.

Between 2004 and 2009 the only significant change in composition was a gain of about 249,000 acres in the oak-hickory group. There also appears to have been a slight rebound in the area of loblolly-shortleaf pine type group following significant losses between 1999 and 2004 (Oswalt and others 2009). This change may have resulted from the disturbance to Tennessee's southern yellow pine forests caused by the SPB outbreak of 1999 to 2002. Recent anecdotal evidence suggests that many of the impacted stands appear to be shifting to hardwood dominance due, in most cases, to the existence of hardwood regeneration in the understory. However, some stands are recovering to pine types.

In 2009, the single most common forest type across Tennessee timberland was white oak-red oak-hickory (table 17) and is found within each unit in the State. The scarcest forest type found on timberland within the State was the overcup oak-water hickory type and was only found in the West unit.

Table 16—Area of timberland by forest-type group and survey unit, Tennessee, 2009

		Survey unit				
Forest-type group	Total	West	West Central	Central	Plateau	East
				acres		
White-red-jack pine	73,228	—	—	3,276	22,991	46,961
Loblolly-shortleaf pine	888,245	259,456	155,493	17,836	174,150	281,310
Other eastern softwoods	245,209	9,718	5,916	152,661	17,715	59,200
Oak-pine	955,371	159,019	102,823	208,456	157,949	327,124
Oak-hickory	9,943,085	1,209,742	1,886,368	1,949,774	2,431,608	2,465,594
Oak-gum-cypress	317,671	252,311	17,748	23,946	13,392	10,274
Elm-ash-cottonwood	710,580	400,535	61,446	177,377	13,875	57,348
Maple-beech-birch	290,029	10,775	2,958	57,106	94,443	124,747
Other hardwoods	31,820	—	8,289	6,504	5,329	11,698
Exotic hardwoods	52,466	1,536	—	24,393	11,238	15,299
Nonstocked	39,501	10,961	—	3,269	14,840	10,430
Total	13,547,205	2,314,053	2,241,041	2,624,598	2,957,531	3,409,983

— = negligible.

Table 17—Area of timberland by forest type and survey unit, Tennessee, 2009

Forest type	Total	West	West Central	Central	Plateau	East
			acres			
Eastern white pine	59,077	—	—	3,276	13,227	42,575
Eastern white pine/eastern hemlock	4,721	—	—	—	335	4,387
Eastern hemlock	9,429	—	—	—	9,429	—
Loblolly pine	575,724	214,621	147,526	12,187	112,547	88,843
Shortleaf pine	70,988	44,835	6,487	—	4,012	15,654
Virginia pine	235,883	—	1,479	—	57,591	176,813
Pitch pine	5,650	—	—	5,650	—	—
Eastern redcedar	245,209	9,718	5,916	152,661	17,715	59,200
Eastern white pine/northern red oak/white ash	62,284	—	—	—	24,821	37,463
Eastern redcedar/hardwood	318,292	23,537	21,003	194,905	14,251	64,597
Shortleaf pine/oak	95,196	29,864	16,617	—	23,377	25,339
Virginia pine/southern red oak	250,061	—	11,832	6,005	71,521	160,703
Loblolly pine/hardwood	211,128	105,619	53,370	7,546	22,049	22,545
Other pine/hardwood	18,410	—	—	—	1,932	16,478
Post oak/blackjack oak	314,404	124,473	67,998	48,378	52,581	20,974
Chestnut oak	720,376	—	100,077	28,604	173,251	418,445
White oak/red oak/hickory	3,523,833	370,424	702,931	843,919	930,995	675,564
White oak	567,266	18,075	305,958	47,596	126,211	69,427
Northern red oak	38,490	—	—	1,464	12,844	24,183
Yellow-poplar/white oak/northern red oak	663,125	53,978	140,634	87,570	196,087	184,856
Sassafras/persimmon	165,591	12,985	16,269	61,629	26,500	48,207
Sweetgum/yellow-poplar	561,788	263,883	119,697	64,293	55,766	58,149
Scarlet oak	128,216	—	13,768	25,614	45,245	43,589
Yellow-poplar	277,944	20,532	77,842	42,192	61,896	75,482
Black walnut	20,720	4,402	—	11,782	2,665	1,872
Black locust	49,867	—	—	18,545	17,926	13,396
Chestnut oak/black oak/scarlet oak	977,865	8,064	111,531	124,114	318,468	415,687
Cherry/white ash/yellow-poplar	382,339	47,560	59,924	105,590	78,804	90,460
Elm/ash/black locust	325,042	14,476	28,822	159,500	46,876	75,369
Red maple/oak	156,801	13,447	9,275	9,517	57,103	67,460
Mixed upland hardwoods	1,069,417	257,441	131,643	269,468	228,391	182,474
Swamp chestnut oak/cherrybark oak	53,994	46,549	5,916	1,529	—	—
Sweetgum/nuttall oak/willow oak	112,766	80,576	5,916	22,417	3,857	—
Overcup oak/water hickory	4,609	4,609	—	—	—	—
Baldcypress/water tupelo	87,894	82,565	—	—	5,329	—
Sweetbay/swamp tupelo/red maple	58,408	38,013	5,916	—	4,205	10,274
River birch/sycamore	77,322	58,020	1,508	1,922	4,838	11,034
Cottonwood	10,811	8,962	—	447	1,402	—
Willow	59,045	53,707	2,127	—	3,211	—
Sycamore/pecan/American elm	120,057	67,275	29,558	18,800	4,424	—
Sugarberry/hackberry/elm/green ash	361,828	141,175	26,774	154,579	—	39,300
Silver maple/American elm	10,366	7,710	—	1,629	—	1,027
Red maple/lowland	58,862	51,396	1,479	—	—	5,986
Cottonwood/willow	12,290	12,290	—	—	—	—
Sugar maple/beech/yellow birch	165,809	4,289	2,958	34,271	40,085	84,206
Black cherry	7,391	—	—	—	—	7,391
Hard maple/basswood	116,829	6,486	—	22,835	54,358	33,150
Other hardwoods	31,820	—	8,289	6,504	5,329	11,698
Paulownia	5,992	—	—	—	1,605	4,387
Other exotic hardwoods	46,474	1,536	—	24,393	9,633	10,912
Nonstocked	39,501	10,961	—	3,269	14,840	10,430
Total	13,547,205	2,314,053	2,241,042	2,624,598	2,957,530	3,409,983

— = negligible.

Totals may not sum to due to rounding.

Standing Volume

Standing volume of all-live trees (≥5 inches d.b.h.) on timberland exceeded 27 billion cubic feet in 2009 (table 18). There were an estimated 25 and 26 billion cubic feet of volume on Tennessee timberlands in 1999 and 2004, respectively. The increase in timberland volume over the period between 1999 and 2009 equates to an additional 276 million cubic feet of material per year. Greater than 21 billion cubic feet (77 percent) of all-live standing tree volume was classified as belonging to the oak-hickory forest-type group. Oak-hickory standing tree volume declined from East to West, while forest-type groups such as oak-gum-cypress declined from West to East illustrating the physiographic differences within the State. About 29 percent of all-live standing tree volume in 2009 was located in the East unit.

Table 18—Standing volume of live trees on timberland by forest-type group and survey unit, Tennessee, 2009

Forest-type group	Total	Survey unit				
		West	West Central	Central	Plateau	East
		million cubic feet				
White-red-jack pine	300.6	—	—	11.3	82.5	206.8
Loblolly-shortleaf pine	1,329.8	483.5	197.8	57.5	151.0	440.1
Other eastern softwoods	265.1	6.0	20.1	164.6	23.2	51.2
Oak-pine	1,549.6	283.3	147.8	230.4	260.6	627.5
Oak-hickory	21,271.7	2,216.3	3,648.8	4,088.8	5,182.4	6,135.5
Oak-gum-cypress	921.4	786.8	35.1	59.0	20.7	19.8
Elm-ash-cottonwood	1,316.7	797.4	118.3	321.6	18.8	60.5
Maple-beech-birch	747.5	24.3	1.9	106.0	236.4	378.9
Other hardwoods	46.2	—	4.8	1.7	0.3	39.4
Exotic hardwoods	36.5	—	—	24.8	5.2	6.5
Nonstocked	3.5	0.9	—	0.6	1.2	0.8
Total	27,788.2	4,598.5	4,174.5	5,066.2	5,982.1	7,966.9

— = negligible.

Totals may not sum due to rounding.

All-live standing tree volume on timber-land has increased since 1980 in all five FIA units (fig. 45) as peak volume has slowly shifted to larger diameter classes (fig. 46). While the East and Central units have experienced continued increase in all-live tree volume since the beginning of the annual inventory in 1999, the West Central and Plateau units have exhibited little change over the 10-year period between 1999 and 2009. Additional forested lands in the West unit have resulted in gains in standing tree volume since 2004.

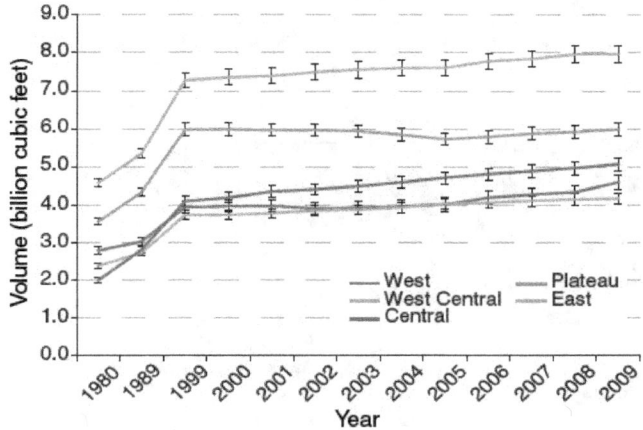

Figure 45—All-live volume of trees ≥5.0 inches d.b.h. on timberland, Tennessee, 1980–2009. Error bars represent one standard error.

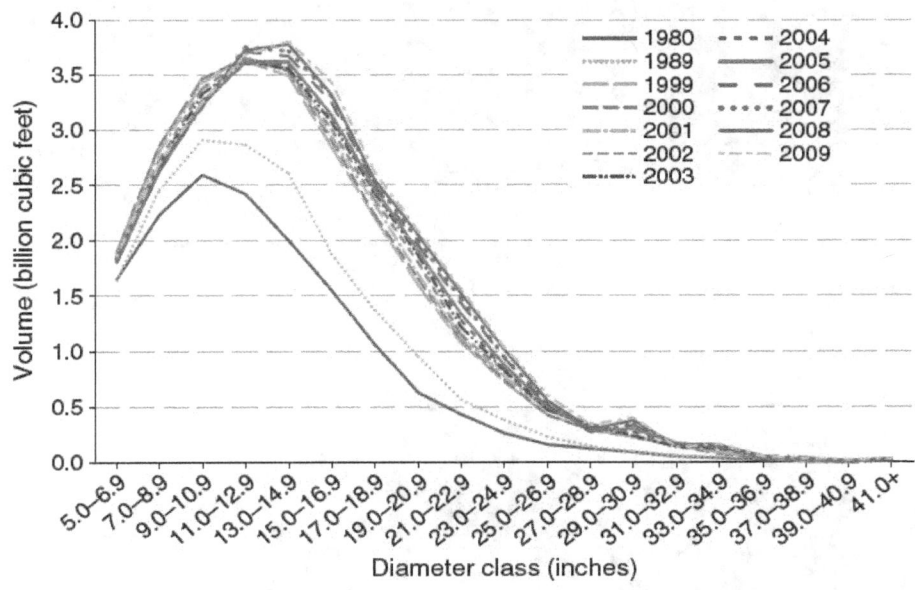

Figure 46—Volume of all-live trees on timberland by diameter class, Tennessee, 1980–2009.

In 2009 the greatest concentrations of live standing tree volume were in the East unit and in the northern regions of the remainder of the State (fig. 47). County-level standing tree volume density ranged from near 1,200 to >3,500 cubic feet per acre of timberland. Relative to all-live standing tree volume, concentrations of hardwood volume were greatest in the northern counties (fig. 48), while softwood volume concentrations were highest in southern counties (fig. 49). The largest block of counties with large percentages of standing tree volume on timberland in hardwood species was located in the northern regions of the West and West Central units. The largest block of counties with large percentages of standing tree volume on timberland in softwood species was located in southeastern Tennessee, near Chattanooga. The highest concentrations of sawtimber volume were located in southeastern part of the East unit and the northern part of the Plateau unit (fig. 50).

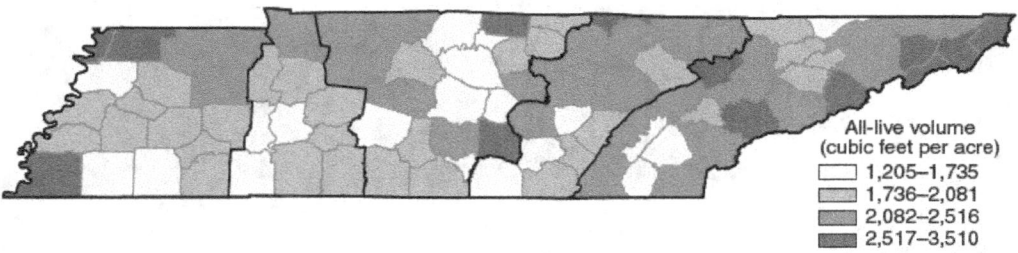

Figure 47—All-live volume on timberland, Tennessee, 2009.

Figure 48—Percent of live volume on timberland that is from hardwood species, Tennessee, 2009.

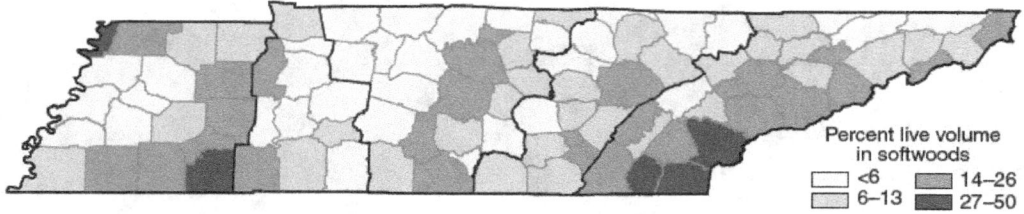

Figure 49—Percent of live volume on timberland that is from softwood species, Tennessee, 2009.

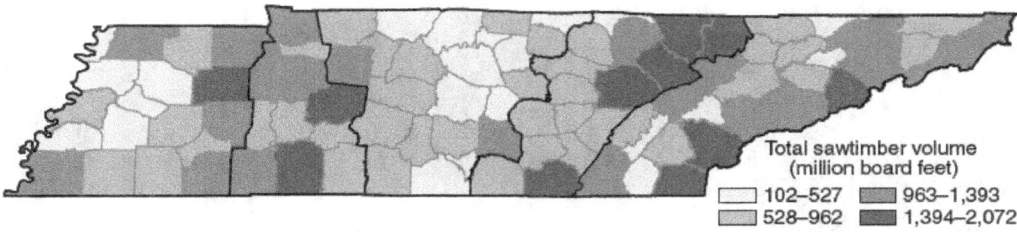

Figure 50—Total sawtimber volume on timberland, Tennessee, 2009.

Tree Quality

Tree grade is a classification that indicates the suitability of individual sawtimber size trees to yield factory grade lumber or construction strength timbers. Factory grade lumber is used in furniture, flooring, pallets, and other products. Unlike log grade, tree grade applies to the whole tree and is generally evaluated before the tree is felled. FIA adapted the hardwood tree grading system devised by Hanks (1976). The FIA system is based on the amount and distribution of surface defects, the amount of rotten wood, and the location of the utilizable log or logs within the tree.

The proportion of hardwood sawtimber volume found in grade 1 trees has declined from an estimated 22 to 7 percent over the period between 1999 and 2009 (fig. 51). Grade 3 material has accounted for about 35 percent of all hardwood sawtimber volume from 1999 to 2009, while grade 2 material, similar to grade 1 material, has declined. These estimates support the general notion based on anecdotal evidence that forests in Tennessee are experiencing a decline in sawtimber quality, particularly hardwood sawtimber quality.

Softwood sawtimber tree grade trends have differed from hardwood only and all sawtimber volume over the same time period (1999 to 2009). The sawtimber volume found within grade 1 trees has increased from 18 to 24 percent from 1999 to 2009 (fig. 52). Furthermore, sawtimber volume found in grade 3 trees has declined from 59 percent (7.2 billion board feet) of all

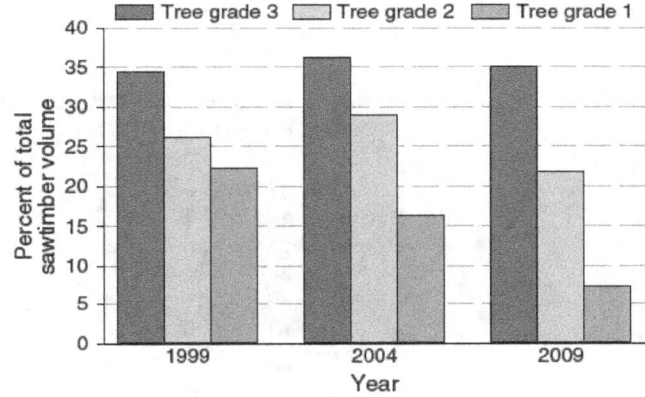

Figure 51—Percent of total sawtimber volume on timberland by tree grades 1, 2, and 3 for hardwood species, Tennessee, 1999–2009.

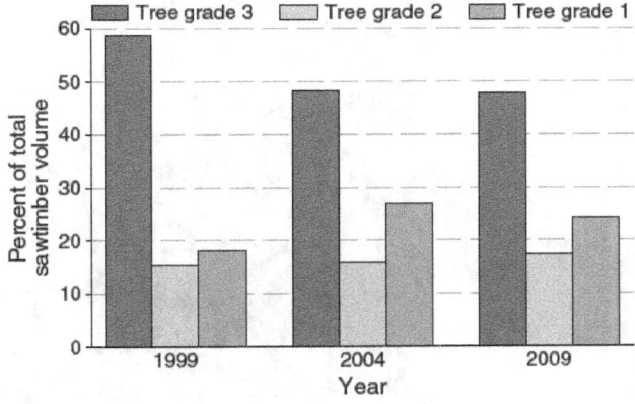

Figure 52—Percent of total sawtimber volume on timberland by tree grades 1, 2, and 3 for softwood species, Tennessee, 1999–2009.

softwood volume in 1999 to 48 percent (5.3 billion board feet) in 2009. (Note: users are cautioned when comparing estimates derived from the annual inventory design [1999 to present] to estimates derived from the periodic inventory design [pre-1999 in Tennessee]. Numerous changes in the inventory can often result in a high noise to signal ratio and confound temporal trends. Additionally, turnover in field staff can have a profound impact on the temporal trends of highly subjective variables such as tree grade [Zarnoch and Turner 2005]).

Growth

Average annual net growth (gross growth [cubic feet] minus mortality [cubic feet]) of all-live trees on timberland in Tennessee was an estimated 833 million cubic feet per year in 2009 (fig. 53). The majority of that growth was accounted for by growth on hardwood species (87 percent or 728 million cubic feet). While average annual growth for hardwood species has declined since 2002, growth for softwood species has increased since a low in 2005. The increasing softwood growth response may be due to declining mortality following

the elevated softwood mortality caused by the SPB outbreak between 1999 and 2002 (Oswalt and others 2009). In fact, in 2005, shortly after the estimated peak of the SPB outbreak, it was estimated that 99 percent of all net tree growth in Tennessee was the result of growth on hardwood tree species.

Average annual net growth differed among the five FIA units in Tennessee (fig. 53). In the West unit, average annual net growth increased for both hardwood and softwood species over the period between 1999 and 2009 and since the 1980 periodic inventory as well. Temporal trends in the West Central and Central units mimic that of the statewide trends. However, average net annual growth trends of the Plateau and East units exhibit the clear signal of the SPB outbreak that was relatively isolated to the eastern portion of the State. Estimates of average net annual growth for softwood species were positive in 2009 for the Plateau and East units for the first time since the periodic inventories prior to the most recent outbreak. At the same time, average net annual growth for hardwood species experienced larger declines for both the Plateau and East units.

Benton Mountain. (photo by Rob Howard)

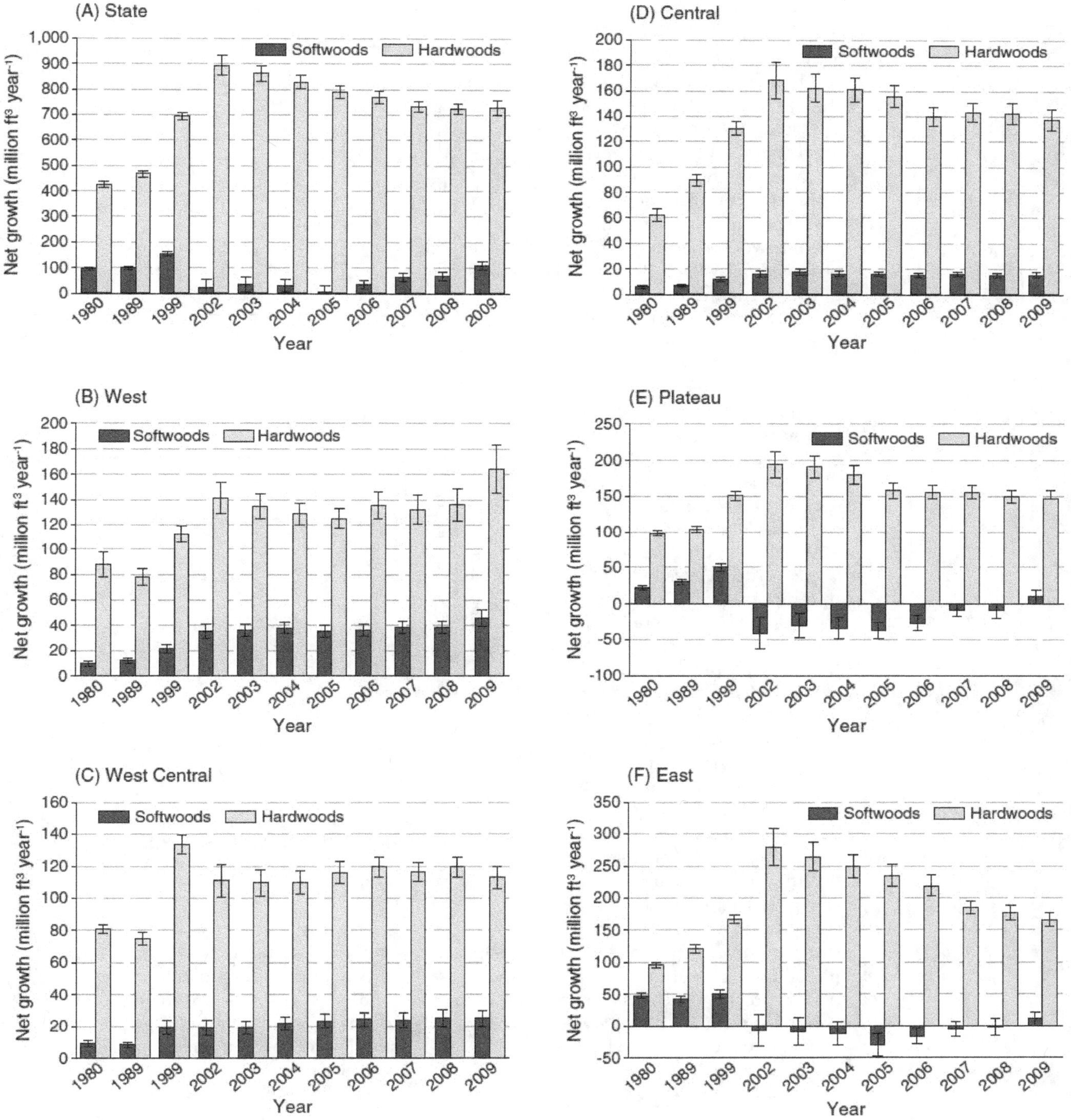

(A) State

(D) Central

(B) West

(E) Plateau

(C) West Central

(F) East

Figure 53—Average annual net growth of live trees on timberland by major species group statewide and for each survey unit, Tennessee, 1980–2009 (A) State, (B) West, (C) West Central, (D) Central, (E) Plateau, (F) East. Error bars represent one standard error.

The explanation for the decline in average annual net growth of softwood species can be mostly attributed to the SPB outbreak between 1999 and 2002 (see Oswalt and others 2009). However, not as easily explainable is the apparent decline in average annual net growth for hardwood species observed between 1999 and 2009. To further investigate this slowing in hardwood growth, average annual net growth as a proportion of total standing growing-stock inventory (cubic foot volume) and number of growing-stock trees was calculated for all species, hardwood only species and softwood only species. The impact of the SPB outbreak and the subsequent recovery is evident in temporal trends of both metrics (fig. 54). There is a significant decline in both per tree growth and growth as a percent of standing inventory following the outbreak (1999 to 2002) along with a recovery period evident in the FIA data between 2005 and 2009. During the softwood growth decline and recovery, there appears to have been a steady decline in both hardwood per tree growth and hardwood tree growth as a percent of standing inventory. However, that decline has slowed following the 2007 inventory period. At this time it is unclear why hardwood growth may have slowed during the period between 2002 and 2008.

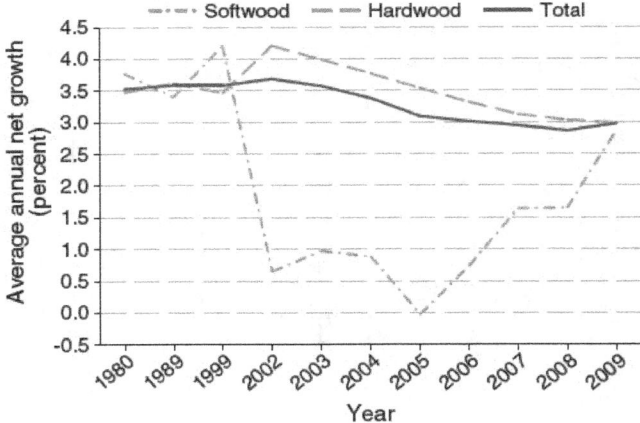

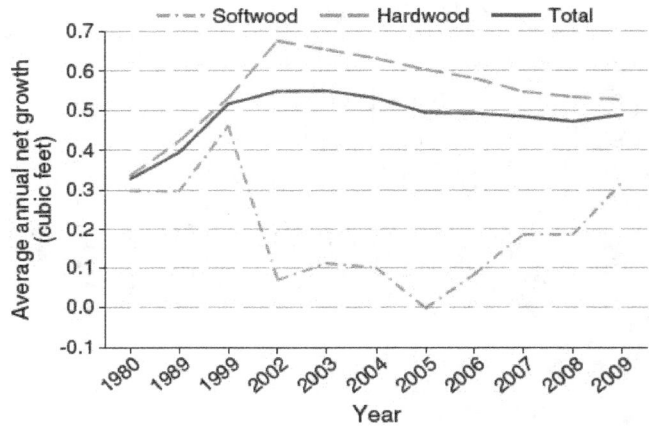

Figure 54—Average annual net growth as a percent of standing volume and average annual net growth per tree of growing stock on timberland, Tennessee, 1980–2009 (A) Percent of standing volume, (B) Growth per tree.

Forest-Management Types

Active and passive management of Tennessee timberlands helps create a diversity of products and social and ecological values that are important to citizens of and visitors to Tennessee, as well as wildlife. It is important to characterize our forests in a way that helps people understand all of the benefits the forests can provide. By characterizing the timberland in Tennessee by management type, whether actively managed or not, a clearer picture can be provided of the types of forests that are working for Tennessee.

Timberland is classified into one of six forest-management types according to stocking and stand origin. The forest-management types are pine plantation, natural pine, oak-pine, upland hardwood, lowland hardwood, and nonstocked. Across the State, the upland hardwood management type dominated timberland in Tennessee in 2009. In fact, 76 percent (10.3 million acres) of all timberland was classified as upland hardwood (table 19). Lowland hardwood (1.0 million acres) and the oak-pine (955,000 acres) management type were the second and third largest management types in Tennessee in 2009. The pine plantation management type exceeded the natural pine management type in coverage across the State by an estimated 46,000 acres. Overall, the area of pine plantations in Tennessee has increased since about 2005 (fig. 55) and seems to have stabilized recently. As compared to 2000 estimates, the increases in pine plantation coverage were concentrated in the West and West Central FIA units.

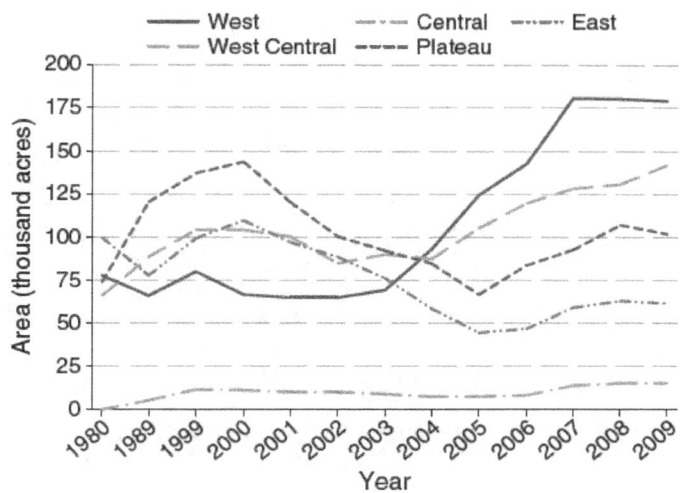

Figure 55—Area of timberland in the pine plantation management type for each survey unit, Tennessee, 1980–2009.

Table 19—Area of timberland by forest-management type and survey unit, Tennessee, 2009

| Forest-management type | Total | Survey unit | | | | |
		West	West Central	Central	Plateau	East
		acres				
Pine plantation	498,796	179,262	141,610	15,043	101,672	61,209
Natural pine	453,247	80,194	13,882	6,069	86,040	267,062
Oak-pine	955,371	159,019	102,823	208,456	157,949	327,124
Lowland hardwood	1,028,251	652,846	79,194	201,323	27,267	67,621
Upland hardwood	10,317,402	1,222,053	1,897,615	2,037,778	2,542,619	2,617,337
Nonstocked	39,500	10,961	0	3,269	14,840	10,430
Total	13,292,567	2,304,335	2,235,124	2,471,938	2,930,387	3,350,783

Totals may not sum due to rounding.

Forest Stand Treatments

Tree cutting occurred on an estimated 230,000 acres of timberland annually from 2005 to 2009 in Tennessee (table 20). Partial harvests accounted for 65 percent of the total annual area cut. Final harvests accounted for 28 percent. Seed-tree/shelterwood harvests, commercial thinning, salvage cutting, and timber stand improvement cutting accounted for a small proportion of annual area cut based on FIA observations.

Annual cutting (area) was primarily within hardwood or mixed hardwood-pine forest types, accounting for 90 percent of the total (table 20). Some type of cutting occurred on an estimated 177,000 acres of the oak-hickory forest-type group which represented the highest annual cutting rate observed in the State. Within the softwood forest types, cutting in the loblolly-shortleaf pine forest-type group accounted for 97 percent of the total. Natural regeneration was more prevalent in the hardwood forest types, while artificial regeneration (planting) was observed more often in the softwood forest types (table 20).

Among the FIA units, the average annual area experiencing cutting was highest for

Total 20—Area of timberland treated annually by forest-type group and treatment class, Tennessee, 2009

Forest-type group	Total cutting	Final harvest	Partial harvest	Seed tree/ shelter- wood harvest	Com- mercial thinning	Timber stand improve- ment	Salvage cutting	Site prepa- ration	Artificial regen- eration	Natural regen- eration	Other silvicul- tural
					thousand acres						
Softwood types											
White-red-jack pine	0.0	0.0	0.0	0.0	0.0	0.0	0.0	0.0	0.0	0.0	0.0
Loblolly-shortleaf pine	23.2	10.1	3.9	0.0	9.2	0.0	0.0	7.0	15.9	2.4	3.8
Other eastern softwoods	0.6	0.0	0.6	0.0	0.0	0.0	0.0	0.0	0.0	0.0	0.0
Total softwoods	23.8	10.1	4.5	0.0	9.2	0.0	0.0	7.0	15.9	2.4	3.8
Hardwood types											
Oak-pine	12.7	7.0	4.5	0.1	1.1	0.0	0.0	4.7	8.0	1.7	1.0
Oak-hickory	177.0	44.6	129.9	1.4	0.0	1.2	0.0	10.6	9.0	43.7	8.4
Oak-gum-cypress	3.8	0.0	2.8	0.0	0.0	0.0	1.0	0.0	0.0	1.0	1.2
Elm-ash-cottonwood	5.6	2.2	2.4	1.0	0.0	0.0	0.0	0.9	0.0	1.5	0.9
Maple-beech-birch	4.9	0.0	4.9	0.0	0.0	0.0	0.0	0.0	0.0	2.8	0.0
Other hardwoods	0.0	0.0	0.0	0.0	0.0	0.0	0.0	0.0	0.0	0.0	0.0
Exotic hardwood	1.6	0.6	1.0	0.0	0.0	0.0	0.0	0.3	0.0	0.9	0.0
Total hardwoods	205.7	54.4	145.5	2.4	1.1	1.2	1.0	16.5	17.0	51.6	11.5
Nonstocked	0.0	0.0	0.0	0.0	0.0	0.0	0.0	0.0	0.0	0.0	0.0
All groups	229.5	64.5	150.0	2.4	10.4	1.2	1.0	23.5	32.9	54.0	15.2

Totals may not sum due to rounding.

0.0 = no sample for the cell or a value of >0.0 but <0.05.

the Plateau unit, accounting for 26 percent of the statewide annual average area cut (table 21), and the West unit, accounting for 24 percent of the statewide annual average. Average annual area cut was lowest in the East unit and accounted for about 11 percent of the statewide total. Cutting intensity based on the live volume harvested from timberland was highest for the Plateau, West, and West Central units (fig. 56) and followed the pattern illustrated by average annual area treated (table 21). Even so, average annual removal of growing-stock material in Tennessee accounts for a very small proportion of the total standing volume and has been

declining recently across the State for all forest types (fig. 57), softwoods only (fig. 58), and hardwoods only (fig. 59).

Stand regeneration preferences appear to follow a geographic pattern. Artificial regeneration is much more common in the western regions of the State and decreases moving eastward. Natural regeneration appears to be the regeneration method used more often in the East and decreases as you move westward. This is possibly an artifact of the growth in plantation forestry in the western units in Tennessee and the dominance of hardwood forests in the East.

Table 21—Area of timberland treated annually by survey unit and treatment class, Tennessee, 2009

Survey unit	Total cutting	Treatment class									
		Cutting									
		Final harvest	Partial harvest	Seed tree/ shelter- wood harvest	Com- mercial thinning	Timber stand improve- ment	Salvage cutting	Site prepa- ration	Artificial regen- eration	Natural regen- eration	Other silvi- cultural
		thousand acres									
West	55.1	15.9	32.1	1.0	5.2	0.0	1.0	5.5	12.9	9.5	3.8
West Central	48.5	20.4	24.5	1.4	2.2	0.0	0.0	5.3	11.1	7.0	0.0
Central	42.1	2.1	38.9	0.0	0.0	1.2	0.0	0.0	0.0	6.6	0.0
Plateau	59.3	21.4	36.3	0.1	1.6	0.0	0.0	7.5	4.9	14.9	1.7
East	24.4	4.7	18.3	0.0	1.4	0.0	0.0	5.2	4.1	16.0	9.7

0.0 = no sample for the cell or a value of >0.0 but <0.05.

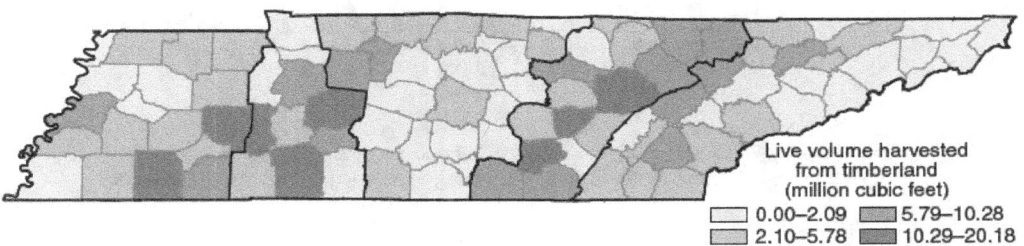

Figure 56—Average annual harvests (utilized live removals and volume killed by harvest activity) on timberland, Tennessee, 2009.

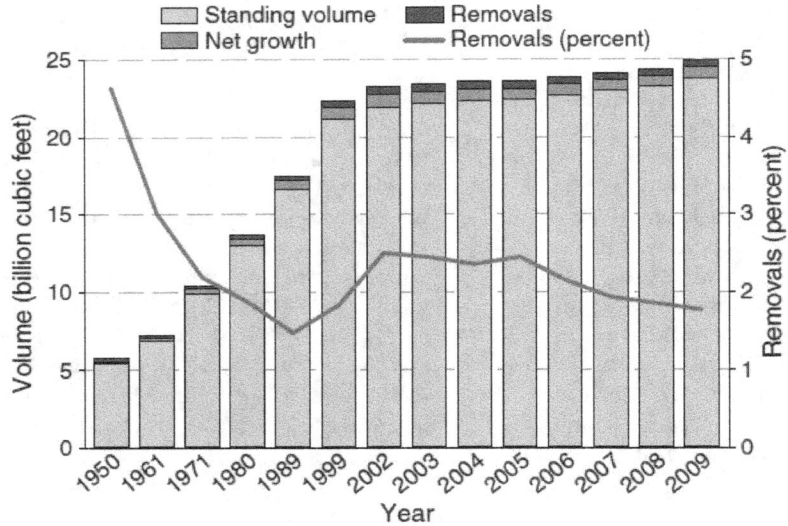

Figure 57—Standing volume, net growth, removals, and removals as a percent of standing volume of all growing stock on timberland, Tennessee, 1950–2009.

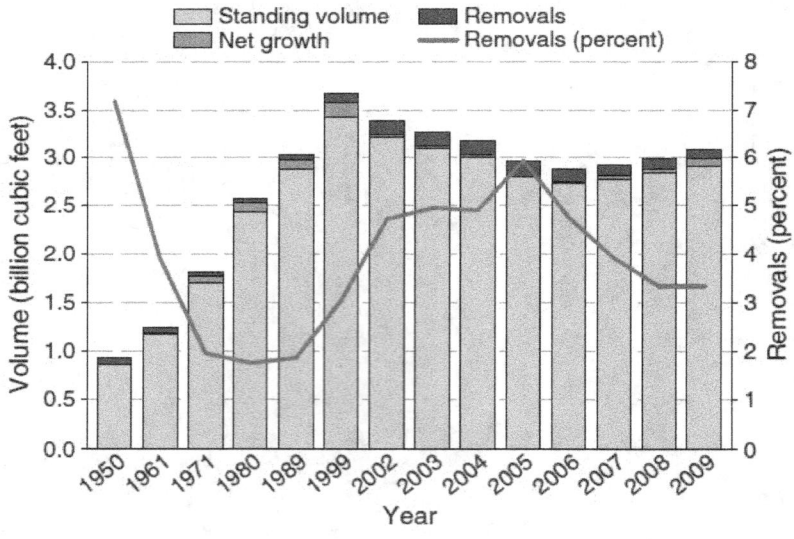

Figure 58—Standing volume, net growth, removals, and removals as a percent of standing volume of softwood growing stock on timberland, Tennessee, 1950–2009.

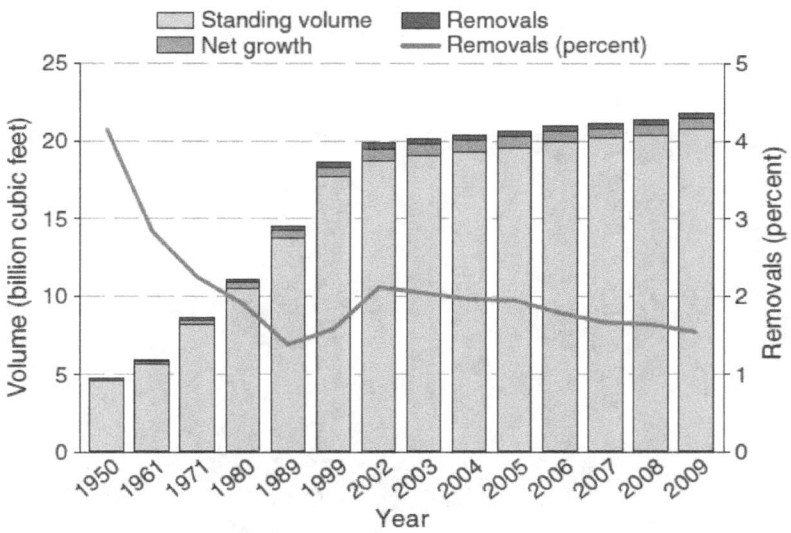

Figure 59—Standing volume, net growth, removals, and removals as a percent of standing volume of hardwood growing stock on timberland, Tennessee, 1950–2009.

Meads Quarry outside of Knoxville, Tennessee.

Roan Mountain, within the Blue Ridge Mountains, at the border between Tennessee and North Carolina. (Wikimedia.org)

Socioeconomic Benefits of Tennessee Forests

Timber Removals and Utilization

Average annual timber removals from timberland include the merchantable and nonmerchantable volume of trees harvested for products and whole trees or portions of trees cut and left behind as logging residue. Average annual removals volume also includes trees removed due to land clearing for agriculture or urban development and timberland set aside by statute prohibiting tree harvesting. The latter removals are considered land use change removals. Total removals include harvested products, logging residues, and land use removals and are reported by broad species group at the regional, State, FIA survey unit, or county level for ownership, forest type, diameter class, stand origin, and other variables.

Most FIA removal tables report only the merchantable portion or volume from a 1-foot stump to the 4-inch top in cubic feet for trees ≥5 inches d.b.h. For the sawtimber portion of sawtimber-size trees, removal volume is reported in board feet (International ¼-inch log rule), as well. Removal estimates are generated for the sawtimber portion of growing-stock trees, all other growing-stock trees ≥5 inches d.b.h., and all-live trees ≥5 inches d.b.h., which include rough and rotten cull trees. It is best to think of these categories for removals as subsets; sawtimber removals are a subset of growing-stock removals, growing-stock removals are a subset of all-live tree removals, and all of these are a subset of total aboveground tree removals which include the volume of the stumps, tops, and limbs to 1 inch in diameter. Volume of removal trees <5 inches d.b.h. have been considered noncommercial and have not been reported on a routine basis.

Reporting removals in this fashion served FIA and its users well for many decades when dealing with the traditional timber products such as saw logs, veneer logs, poles, and other solid-wood forest products. However, the traditional fiber products industries (pulpwood, composite panel, and mulch) along with the emerging bioenergy industry have and will dramatically increase the utilization of rough and cull trees, tops and limbs, a portion of trees <5 inches d.b.h., and in some cases, understory vegetation.

The majority of timber bought and sold commercially has been scaled by weight at the destination mills for many years. The forestry community has become familiar with weight as a unit of measure for timber products and has requested FIA to include weight as a reporting unit for removals. The cubic foot volumes have been converted to green tons throughout this section using 69.09 pounds of wood and bark per cubic foot of solid wood for softwoods and 77.09 pounds of wood and bark per cubic foot of solid wood for hardwoods. It is important to keep in mind that this is fresh green weight of wood and bark per cubic foot immediately after harvest.

Socioeconomic Benefits of Tennessee Forests

This section focuses on total average annual removals for all-live tree volume for trees ≥5 inches d.b.h. expressed in cubic feet and green tons. It also includes an estimate of removals for stumps, tops, and limbs and is expressed as average annual harvest removals from nonmerchantable

sources. In addition, an estimate of removals for trees <5 inches d.b.h. is discussed under the section for logging residue and is not included in total annual removals. Figure 60 shows the total annual removals by the subcategories previously discussed.

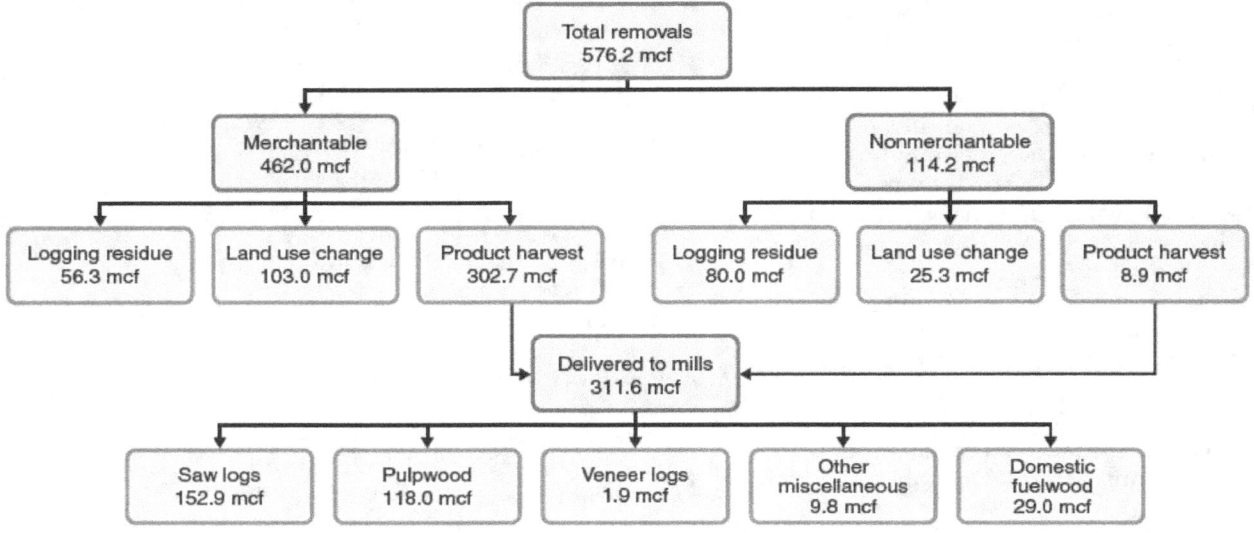

Figure 60—Total removals by merchantability and category, Tennessee, 2009.

Foothills of the Appalachian Mountains.

62

Between 2005 and 2009, total removals from all sources in Tennessee, for both softwoods and hardwoods totaled 576.2 million cubic feet, or 21.7 million green tons (table 22 and table 23). Hardwoods accounted for 78 percent of total removals, or 450.8 million cubic feet (17.4 million green tons). Volume of removals attributed to the merchantable portion of all-live tree removals accounted for 462.0 million cubic feet (17.4 million green tons), while nonmerchantable sources accounted for 114.2 million cubic feet (4.3 million green tons).

Table 22—Volume of timber removals by removals class, species group, and source, Tennessee, 2005–09

Removals class and species group	All sources	Source	
		Merchantable	Non-merchantable
		thousand cubic feet	
Timber products			
Softwood	66,340	62,769	3,571
Hardwood	245,218	239,902	5,316
Total	311,558	302,671	8,887
Logging residues			
Softwood	24,244	10,977	13,267
Hardwood	112,122	45,396	66,726
Total	136,366	56,373	79,993
Land use removals			
Softwood	34,875	28,392	6,483
Hardwood	93,417	74,584	18,833
Total	128,292	102,976	25,316
Total removals			
Softwood	125,459	102,138	23,321
Hardwood	450,757	359,882	90,875
Total	576,216	462,020	114,196

Totals may not sum due to rounding.

Table 23—Weight of timber removals by removals class, species group, and source, Tennessee, 2005–09

Removals class and species group	All sources	Source	
		Merchantable	Non-merchantable
		green tons	
Timber products			
Softwood	2,291,878	2,168,508	123,370
Hardwood	9,451,491	9,246,595	204,896
Total	11,743,369	11,415,103	328,266
Logging residues			
Softwood	837,572	379,227	458,345
Hardwood	4,321,545	1,749,708	2,571,837
Total	5,159,117	2,128,935	3,030,182
Land use removals			
Softwood	1,204,844	980,871	223,973
Hardwood	3,600,592	2,874,707	725,885
Total	4,805,436	3,855,578	949,858
Total removals			
Softwood	4,334,294	3,528,606	805,688
Hardwood	17,373,628	13,871,010	3,502,618
Total	21,707,922	17,399,616	4,308,306

Totals may not sum due to rounding.

The following sections present an average annual estimate for the merchantable and nonmerchantable portions of annual timber product output (TPO) (timber harvested and delivered to mills), land use removals, and an estimate of logging residue in Tennessee for the period 2005–09.

Timber products—A diverse forest products industry in Tennessee is made-up of a variety of mills, ranging from small- to medium-sized softwood and hardwood sawmills, pole and post mills, to the very large pulpmills. In 2009, there were about 267 sawmills, pulpwood mills, and other primary wood-processing plants distributed across the State (fig. 61). Numerous mills across the State were lost between 2004 and 2009 (fig. 62). This section presents estimates of average annual timber product harvest volume for the period 2005–09.

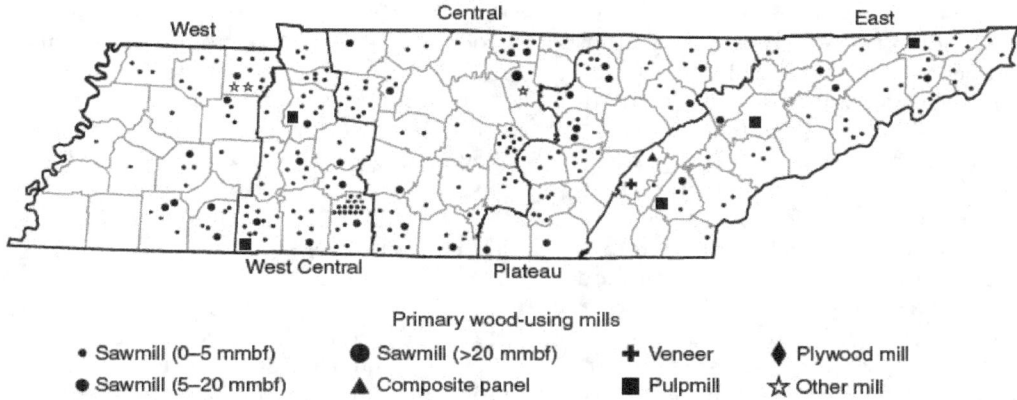

Primary wood-using mills

- Sawmill (0–5 mmbf)
- Sawmill (5–20 mmbf)
- Sawmill (>20 mmbf)
- ▲ Composite panel
- ✚ Veneer
- ■ Pulpmill
- ◆ Plywood mill
- ☆ Other mill

Figure 61—Primary wood-using mills by survey unit, Tennessee, 2009.

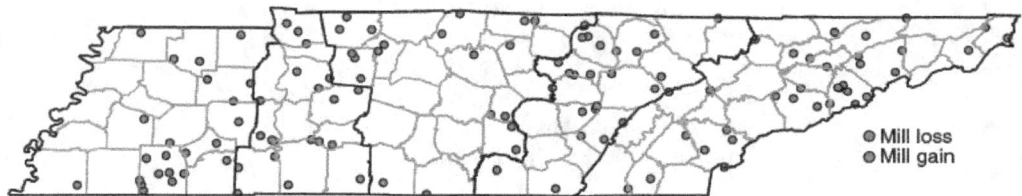

- Mill loss
- Mill gain

Figure 62—Mill loss and mill gain, Tennessee, 2004–09. (Dots have been randomly located within a given county. Dots do not represent actual mill location.)

Estimates of TPO and plant residues were obtained from canvasses (questionnaires) sent to all major primary wood-using mills in the State. The canvasses are used to determine the types and amount of round-wood or timber (i.e., saw logs, pulpwood, plywood and veneer, poles, etc.) received by each mill, the county of origin, the species used, and how the mills disposed of the bark and wood residues produced. The canvasses are conducted every 2 years by personnel from the SRS and the Tennessee Department of Agriculture, Division of Forestry. These data are used to augment the FIA annual inventory of all-live timber removals by providing the proportions

that are used for timber products. Individual TPO studies, or industry surveys, are necessary to track trends and capture changes in product output levels.

Industry surveys conducted in 2005, 2007, and preliminary findings for 2009 were used to determine average annual output for timber products and plant byproducts for the latest FIA cycle (Bentley and Schnabel 2007; Mathison and Schnabel 2009; Bentley and others 2011). Therefore, the average volumes reported in this section for individual products will not match specific year values reported in TPO publications or online query tools.

Volume harvested and delivered for products (including residential fuelwood) from all sources totaled 311.6 million cubic feet (11.7 million green tons), or 54 percent, of total removals. The merchantable portion of all-live removals accounted for 302.7 million cubic feet (11.4 million green tons), or 97 percent of timber product harvest volume. Nonmerchantable sources from all-live removals accounted for 8.9 million cubic feet (328,300 green tons), or 3 percent of product output levels (tables 22 and 23). Average annual volume harvested for hardwood products totaled 245.2 million cubic feet (9.4 million green tons) and accounted for 79 percent of the total product volume. The average annual volume harvested for softwood products saw a 48-percent decline from that reported in the previous survey period, totaling 66.3 million cubic feet (2.3 million green tons) between 2005 and 2009.

Figure 63 shows trends in average annual harvest volume by product type for the survey periods from 1961 through 2009.

Harvest volume for every major industrial product type was down from the previous survey period. As stated earlier, most of these declines by individual products were driven by the dramatic drop in softwood product output. Most products showed positive gains in hardwood output with the exception of volume harvested for hardwood saw logs.

Table 24 depicts the average annual output of timber products by survey years or the survey period, species group, hardwood proportion for each category, and the proportion of that category to total products. Volume harvested for saw-log products, used mainly for dimension lumber, was the leading product in Tennessee averaging 152.9 million cubic feet (5.8 million green tons) and accounted for 49 percent of total product output. This volume was down 16 percent from the 182.9 million cubic feet reported for the previous survey period (table 24). The total number of sawmills has

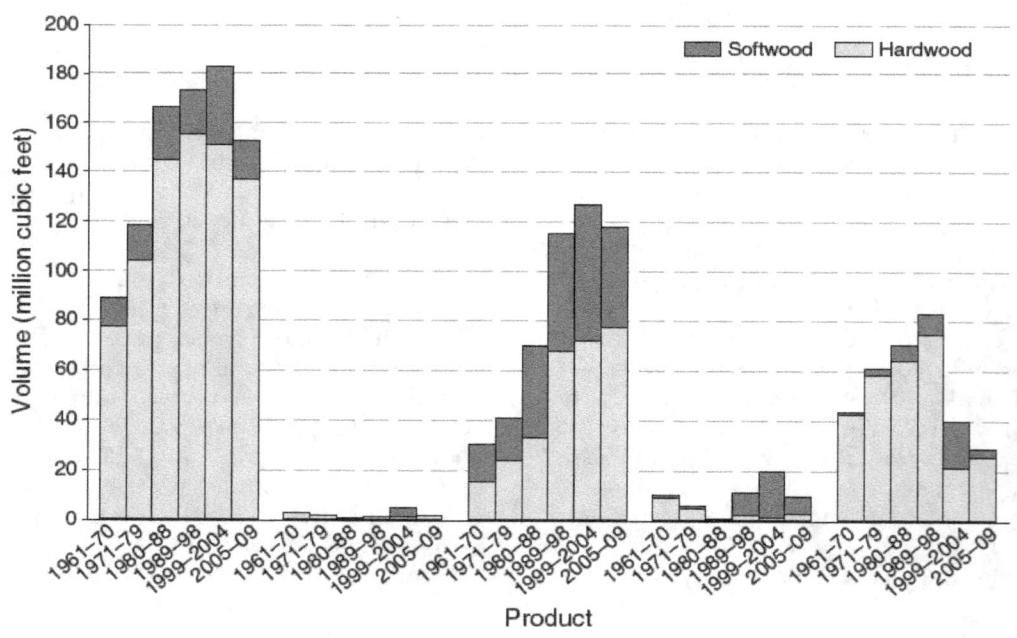

Figure 63—Average annual harvest volume of timber products by product type and species group, Tennessee, 1961–2009.

Table 24—Average annual volume of timber products by product type, survey years, and species group, Tennessee, 1961–2009

Product type and survey years	Species group			Hardwood percentage	Proportion of total	Change		
	Softwood	Hardwood	Total					
	- - - - - - *thousand cubic feet* - - - - - -			- - - - - - - - - - - - - - - - - - *percent* - - - - - - - - - - - - - - - - - -				
Saw logs								
1961–70	11,386	77,486	88,872	0.87	0.50			
1971–79	14,215	104,286	118,501	0.88	0.52			
1980–88	21,786	144,721	166,507	0.87	0.54			
1989–98	17,725	155,823	173,548	0.90	0.45			
1999–2004	31,598	151,338	182,936	0.83	0.49			
2005–09	15,847	137,016	152,863	0.90	0.49	-0.50	-0.09	-0.16
Veneer logs								
1961–70	30	2,716	2,746	0.99	0.02			
1971–79	—	1,894	1,894	1.00	0.01			
1980–88	—	737	737	1.00	0.00			
1989–98	66	1,446	1,512	0.96	0.00			
1999–2004	3,614	1,445	5,059	0.29	0.01			
2005–09	80	1,842	1,922	0.96	0.01	-0.98	0.27	-0.62
Pulpwood								
1961–70	14,734	15,821	30,555	0.52	0.17			
1971–79	16,704	24,055	40,759	0.59	0.18			
1980–88	36,888	33,163	70,051	0.47	0.23			
1989–98	47,826	67,604	115,430	0.59	0.30			
1999–2004	55,133	72,030	127,163	0.57	0.34			
2005–09	40,316	77,656	117,972	0.66	0.38	-0.27	0.08	-0.07
Other industrial								
1961–70	1,090	9,395	10,485	0.90	0.06			
1971–79	841	5,163	6,004	0.86	0.03			
1980–88	46	815	861	0.95	0.00			
1989–98	8,974	2,708	11,682	0.23	0.03			
1999–2004	19,028	1,109	20,137	0.06	0.05			
2005–09	6,666	3,104	9,770	0.32	0.03	-0.65	1.80	-0.51
Residential fuelwood								
1961–70	1,041	42,631	43,672	0.98	0.25			
1971–79	2,613	58,495	61,108	0.96	0.27			
1980–88	6,582	64,168	70,750	0.91	0.23			
1989–98	8,608	74,747	83,355	0.90	0.22			
1999–2004	18,473	21,592	40,065	0.54	0.11			
2005–09	3,431	25,600	29,031	0.88	0.09	-0.81	0.19	-0.28
All products								
1961–70	28,281	148,049	176,330	0.84				
1971–79	34,373	193,893	228,266	0.85				
1980–88	65,302	243,604	308,906	0.79				
1989–98	83,199	302,328	385,527	0.78				
1999–2004	127,846	247,514	375,360	0.66				
2005–09	66,340	245,218	311,558	0.79		-0.48	-0.01	-0.17

— = negligible.

varied between 345 in 2005 to the current number of 257 in 2009. At 137.0 million cubic feet (5.3 million green tons) hardwoods accounted for 90 percent of saw-log harvest volume (tables 25 and 26).

Because of the five pulpmills operating in Tennessee over the time period, pulpwood is the second leading wood product produced during the latest survey period. Pulpwood output as a proportion of total product output has increased from 23 percent during the 1980–88 survey period, to 34 percent during the 1999–2004 survey period. Pulpwood output during the latest remeasurement period accounted for 38 percent of total product output for the State. Average annual harvest for pulpwood (softwood and hardwood combined) was down 7 percent from that reported in the previous survey period but still totaled 118.0 million cubic feet (4.4 million green tons). Hardwood pulpwood production was up 8 percent from the previous survey

period and totaled 77.7 million cubic feet (3.0 million green tons) and accounted for 66 percent of total pulpwood harvest volume. Softwood pulpwood production was down 27 percent to 40.3 million cubic feet (1.4 million green tons).

Volume harvested for veneer products totaled 1.9 million cubic feet (73,800 green tons). Volume harvested for veneer was down 62 percent from the previous survey period and accounted for only 1 percent of total product output for the State.

Volume harvested for other miscellaneous products such as poles, posts, composite panels, and mulch totaled 9.8 million cubic feet (349,900 green tons), or about 3 percent of the State's total product output. In contrast to the other industrial products, softwoods accounted for 68 percent of the volume harvested for other miscellaneous products and totaled 6.7 million cubic feet (230,300 green tons).

Table 25—Average annual timber removals from all sources on timberland by removal type and species group, Tennessee, 2005–09

		Species group	
Removal type	All species	Softwood	Hardwood
		thousand cubic feet	
Timber products			
Saw logs	152,863	15,847	137,016
Veneer logs and bolts	1,922	80	1,842
Pulpwood	117,972	40,316	77,656
Composite panels	0	0	0
Other miscellaneous	9,770	6,666	3,104
Residential fuelwood	29,031	3,431	25,600
All products	311,558	66,340	245,218
Logging residues	136,366	24,244	112,122
Land use removals	128,292	34,875	93,417
Total removals	576,216	125,459	450,757

Totals may not sum due to rounding.

Table 26—Average annual timber removals from all sources on timberland by removal type and species group, Tennessee, 2005–09

Removal type	All species	Species group Softwood	Species group Hardwood
		green tons	
Timber products			
Saw logs	5,828,512	547,474	5,281,038
Veneer logs and bolts	73,761	2,764	70,997
Pulpwood	4,385,927	1,392,815	2,993,112
Composite panels	0	0	0
Other miscellaneous	349,931	230,293	119,638
Residential fuelwood	1,105,238	118,532	986,706
All products	11,743,369	2,291,878	9,451,491
Logging residues	5,159,117	837,572	4,321,545
Land use removals	4,805,436	1,204,844	3,600,592
Total removals	21,707,922	4,334,294	17,373,628

Totals may not sum due to rounding.

Volume used for residential fuelwood totaled 29.0 million cubic feet (1.1 million green tons) and accounted for 9 percent of total product output. At 25.6 million cubic feet (986,700 green tons), hardwoods accounted for 88 percent of the residential fuelwood harvest.

Mill residue—Mill or plant residues are defined as wood material generated in the production of timber products from roundwood at primary manufacturing plants. This material falls into three main categories:

1. coarse residues, or material such as slabs, edgings, trim, veneer cores and ends, which is suitable for chipping,

2. fine residues, or material such as sawdust, shavings, and veneer residue, which is not suitable for chipping, and

3. bark, which is used mainly for industrial fuel.

For many years, most mill residue produced in Tennessee has been utilized either for primary products such as pulp, secondary products such as mulch and animal bedding, or as fuel at wood product mills.

Table 27 depicts the average annual disposal or utilization of mill residue. Data on mill residue production and disposal generated from the averaged forest industry surveys over the time period indicated 110.4 million cubic feet of wood and bark residue was generated from primary processors. Sawmills generated the majority of the mill residue produced. Bark accounted for 33.4 million cubic feet (30 percent), coarse residues accounted for 48.2 million cubic feet (44 percent), and sawdust and shavings accounted for 28.8 million cubic feet (26 percent) of mill residue produced.

Table 27—Disposal of average annual volume of residue at primary wood-using plants by product, species group, and type of residue, Tennessee, 2005–09

Product and species group	All types	Type of residue			
		Bark	Coarse	Sawdust	Shavings
		thousand cubic feet			
Fiber products					
Softwood	925	0	925	0	0
Hardwood	30,945	0	30,945	0	0
Total	31,870	0	31,870	0	0
Particleboard					
Softwood	78	0	59	19	0
Hardwood	2,390	0	1,915	468	7
Total	2,468	0	1,974	487	7
Charcoal/ chemical wood					
Softwood	47	0	38	9	0
Hardwood	2,798	181	1,026	1,591	0
Total	2,845	181	1,064	1,600	0
Sawn products					
Softwood	0	0	0	0	0
Hardwood	3	0	3	0	0
Total	3	0	3	0	0
Industrial fuelwood					
Softwood	11,461	10,762	167	528	4
Hardwood	36,360	11,661	5,500	18,901	298
Total	47,821	22,423	5,667	19,429	302
Miscellaneous					
Softwood	1,065	355	281	365	64
Hardwood	18,100	9,200	3,720	4,961	219
Total	19,165	9,555	4,001	5,326	283
Not used					
Softwood	240	34	152	53	1
Hardwood	5,966	1,167	3,479	1,302	19
Total	6,206	1,201	3,631	1,355	20
All products					
Softwood	13,817	11,152	1,623	974	68
Hardwood	96,562	22,209	46,587	27,223	543
Total	110,378	33,360	48,210	28,197	611

Totals may not sum due to rounding.

More than 47.8 million cubic feet, or 43 percent, of mill residue produced was used for industrial fuel either at pulpmills for boiler fuel or at sawmills for dry kiln operations. Bark and sawdust, at 22.4 and 19.4 million cubic feet, respectively, accounted for 88 percent of mill residue utilized for industrial fuel. More than two-thirds of bark residue produced was utilized for fuel, with the remainder of the utilized bark going for mulch or miscellaneous products. Industrial fuel and fiber products were by far the largest uses of mill residue produced in Tennessee. Sixty-six percent of the coarse residue produced, 31.9 million cubic feet, was utilized for pulp or fiber products. Bark and wood residue not utilized totaled 6.2 million cubic feet, or nearly 6 percent of all residues produced.

Land use removals—Land use removals (land clearing or set aside forest land), or removal volume attributed to land use change, accounted for 22 percent of total removals with 128.3 million cubic feet (4.8 million green tons) (table 22). The merchantable portion of live trees accounted for 103.0 million cubic feet (3.9 million green tons), while non-merchantable sources accounted for 25.3 million cubic feet (949,900 green tons). The hardwood species group accounted for 73 percent of the land use change removals.

Logging residue—The merchantable portions of trees cut and left onsite are underutilized removals by FIA merchantability standards, while the nonmerchantable portions of trees (part of the 1-foot stump or volume in tops <4 inches) used for products are considered overutilized removals by FIA merchantability standards. Under- and over-utilization factors used to determine average annual logging residue estimates in this section were derived from preliminary estimates from the 2009 Tennessee harvest and utilization study.[1]

Logging residue has been considered a possible source for bioenergy and other timber products during recent years. It is important to keep in mind that logging residue, traditionally, has not had a marketable value. Retrieval of logging residue is a matter of economics and markets. If markets are available and a willingness to pay a reasonable price exists, then more total tree volume (including what has been left as logging residues) is utilized.

Most loggers are able to merchandise the main bole of the tree or the merchantable portion of the tree (from a 1-foot stump to a 4-inch diameter top). The current conventional logging system in Tennessee is a feller buncher, working with one or two rubber-tired grapple skidders, a delimbing gate or pull-through delimber at the deck, a knuckleboom loader, and the appropriate number of tractor trailers to haul the volume harvested. The improved mechanization and equipment capabilities have dramatically increased productivity and utilization across the South. These systems are typically capable of producing on average about 10 loads per day of tree-length wood.

Woody material typically left on a logging site includes:

1. whole trees, ≥5 inches d.b.h., or portions of the merchantable boles that have been broken and left during the felling operation (merchantable),

2. small trees, <5 inches d.b.h., damaged or killed during harvesting operations (nonmerchantable), and

3. residual stump portions, tops, and limbs or forks not utilized because of insufficient size or quality (nonmerchantable).

---

[1] Bentley, J.W. Tennessee harvest and utilization study, 2009. Manuscript in preparation. Author can be reached at U.S. Department of Agriculture Forest Service Southern Research Station. 4700 Old Kingston Pike, Knoxville, TN 37919.

The wood material left on the site is known as either merchantable or nonmerchantable logging residues. FIA calculates the merchantable portion of logging residue in a two-stage process. First, for those plots that were classified as timberland during the previous inventory and stayed in timberland for the current inventory cycle, the volume of whole trees cut and not utilized are identified by FIA field crews during the remeasurement phase of the inventory. A removal volume is derived for trees that are classified in this category.

Second, underutilization factors derived from felled-tree utilization studies are applied to the volume classified as utilized by field crews for the remainder of the merchantable portion of logging residue. For instance, felled-tree utilization studies conducted for Tennessee showed that only 5.37 percent of the merchantable softwood bole was not utilized for products, while 7.46 percent of the merchantable hardwood bole was not utilized.

It is important to remember that total removal volume is comprised of volume from the merchantable and nonmerchantable portions of removal trees. Overutilization factors from the utilization studies were used to determine how much of the nonmerchantable portion of removals was used for timber products. The nonmerchantable volume is calculated for the land use change removal estimate and added to the merchantable volume for a total land use change removal volume. With the nonmerchantable portion of timber products and land use change values calculated and subtracted from the total nonmerchantable removal volume, the remainder is the volume of nonmerchantable logging residues.

The annual logging residue volume in Tennessee from 2005 to 2009 averaged 136.4 million cubic feet per year, or 5.2 million green tons. This volume accounted for 24 percent of total timber removals. More than 112.1 million cubic feet (4.3 million green tons), or 82 percent, of the logging residues generated came from hardwoods, while nearly 24.2 million cubic feet (837,600 green tons) came from softwoods. Logging residue from the merchantable portion of all-live removals totaled 56.4 million cubic feet per year (2.1 million green tons), or 41 percent of total logging residue. While total logging residue accounted for 24 percent of total removals, the merchantable portion of logging residue for both softwood and hardwood combined accounted for about 10 percent of total live removals. For softwoods, the merchantable portion of logging residue accounted for 9 percent of the total softwood all-live tree removals which totaled 125.5 million cubic feet. The merchantable portion of hardwood logging residue accounted for 10 percent of all-live hardwood removals which amounted to 450.8 million cubic feet. Nonmerchantable sources (such as the residual stump, forks, tops, and limbs) accounted for 80.0 million cubic feet (3.0 million green tons), or 59 percent of total logging residue. Trees <5 inches d.b.h. contributed about 860,700 green tons of possible logging residue (table 28).

Also from 2005 to 2009, the area of timber harvested annually in Tennessee amounted to nearly 229,500 acres. Of this area, 64,500 acres (28 percent) underwent a final harvest, while 150,000 acres (65 percent) had a partial harvest, and 10,400 acres (5 percent) had commercial thinning. The remaining 4,600 acres, or 2 percent, had a shelterwood or some other silvicultural treatment (table 20). The removals volume attributed to timber products and logging residues are directly related to these treated acres. Based on these estimates, >73.6 tons per acre in the merchantable and nonmerchantable portion of trees

Table 28—Average annual weight of logging residue by size class and recovery potential, Tennessee, 2005–09

Logging residue in harvested trees by size class	Total		Nonrecoverable		Total available		Potentially recoverable at 60% recovery rate[a]		
			Discounted stump volume	Discounted <5" volume	Base total volume	Total	Discounted >5" volume	Total volume	Total
	green tons	tons/ acre	- - - - - - - - - green tons - - - - - - - - -			tons/ acre	- - - - green tons - - - -		tons/ acre
Merchantable volume ≥5"	2,129,935	9.3	0	0	2,128,935	9.3	797,618	1,331,317	5.8
Nonmerchantable volume ≥5"	3,030,182	13.2	652,891	0	2,377,291	10.3	1,084,631	1,292.,660	5.6
Total	5,159,117	22.5	652,891	0	4,506,226	19.6	1,882,249	2,623,977	11.4
Nonmerchantable volume <5"	860,672	3.7	0	688,538	172,134	0.8	0	172,134	0.8
All classes	6,019,789	26.2	652,891	688,538	4,678,360	20.4	1,882,249	2,796,111	12.2

Totals may not sum due to rounding.
[a] This value is calculated from the base total volume of 4,678,360 tons.

≥5 inches d.b.h. were removed annually from Tennessee timberland. Of this, nearly 51.2 tons per acre were utilized for products, while 19.6 tons per acre were left as logging residue after discounting the residual stump volume (table 28). Adding in 3.7 tons per acre for trees <5 inches d.b.h., the total logging residue amounts to 23.3 tons per acre. This volume is the equivalent of a tree-length trailer load of wood for every acre treated in Tennessee.

Potential recoverable logging residue—
Conventional logging operations are designed to haul tree length wood that fit between the stanchions of the trailer. Another possible way to handle the non-merchantable portion of removals trees—rough trees with crooked boles, tops, and limbs—is to chip this material onsite and transport the material in chip vans. Some

Tennessee loggers have begun to add whole-tree chippers and chip vans to their inventory of equipment. Current markets for chipped wood captured from logging residue are limited to facilities with wood-fired boiler systems or production of mulch. Where bioenergy or mulch markets are available, chipping this material onsite is a cost efficient way of handling and transporting rough and rotten trees, the non-merchantable portions of cut trees, as well as small trees <5 inches d.b.h.

Identifying a realistic recovery rate of logging residue in Tennessee can be challenging. Current literature and personal communications with loggers and others in the forestry field suggests that the conventional logging operations described above could capture 60 percent of what is currently being left behind as logging

residue. This recovery rate excludes residual stump volume, and would seem to be a realistic goal for possible extraction of formerly unutilized material (Perlack and others 2005).

For this assessment, the nonmerchantable portion of logging residue has been reduced by 57 percent to account for residual stump (652,900 green tons) and tops and limb volume (1.1 million green tons) that are not immediately recoverable to 1.3 million green tons (table 28). This amount, combined with the merchantable logging residue of 1.3 million green tons, leaves a total of 2.6 million green tons available from trees ≥5 inches d.b.h., or 11.4 tons per acre. Residual volume following harvest operations for trees <5 inches d.b.h. accounts for about 860,700 green tons. This report assumes only 20 percent could realistically be extracted, or 172,100 green tons.[2] This volume adds another 0.8 ton per acre. Combined, the average annual recovery of logging residue at a 60-percent recovery rate from all sources represented a potential 12.2 tons per acre added to the product stream.

Summary—Traditional markets for paper and construction materials remain dominant in the wood products industry. However, timber removals and utilization continue to change as increased demand for wood as a source for energy create new market opportunities.

FIA and TPO data indicate substantial sources of fiber that are currently underutilized and could be used for bioenergy or other timber products if effectively captured. New facilities that utilize wood for energy may provide opportunities to capture logging residue and minimize the increase to current harvest levels. This will require further study.

New markets, such as bioenergy facilities that plan to use logging residues as a primary source for fuel, must carefully assess average annual volume available in a procurement area, and consider incentives to attract loggers to invest in operations that harvest wood residues at minimum cost.

With proper assessment, investment, and operation, industries utilizing logging residues could possibly offer opportunities for a renewable energy source while creating "green" jobs. Loggers would realize additional markets for fiber and additional sources of income from each logging site. Landowners may also receive additional income with increased utilization from harvested acres and lower site preparation costs for establishing new forests.

Forest Industry in Tennessee

In 2007 the State of Tennessee ranked as the South's top producer of hardwood saw logs (Johnson and others 2009). Forest products and the forest industry also play a significant role in Tennessee's economy. In 2005, the wood products and paper manufacturing subsectors[3] combined represented 7.6 percent of the State's gross domestic product from the manufacturing sector (U.S. Department of Commerce Bureau of Economic Analysis 2011). This contribution increased slightly throughout the 2005–08 period,[4] reaching 8.7 percent in 2008 (U.S. Department of Commerce Bureau of Economic Analysis 2011).

---

[2] Personal communication. 2008. H.M. (Mac) Lupold, Lupold Consulting, Inc., 228 Chestnut Ferry Rd., Camden, SC 29020.

---

[3] Wood products and paper manufacturing correspond to the North American Industry Classification System (NAICS) manufacturing subsectors 321 and 322 respectively. A full description of the industries included in these subsectors can be found at http://www.census.gov/cgi-bin/sssd/naics/naicsrch.

[4] 2009 gross domestic product data disaggregated to the subsectors levels is not yet available at the Bureau of Economic Analysis' Web site http://www.bea.gov/regional/gsp/.

In terms of employment, these two sub-sectors supplied 28,770 jobs in Tennessee during 2009 (U.S. Department of Commerce Bureau of Economic Analysis 2011), nearly 9 percent of all manufacturing jobs in the State. However, this represents a 25-percent decline from the 2005 levels at 38,431 jobs. A large portion of those job losses came from the wood products manufacturing sector (fig. 64).

Economic impact analysis—The forest sector's importance to the State's economy was further analyzed using the IMpact Analysis for PLANning (IMPLAN) economic modeling tools. IMPLAN was developed by the Forest Service in the late 1970s and is currently owned by the Minnesota IMPLAN Group, Incorporated. Through IMPLAN's built-in economic multipliers one can assess an industry's direct economic impact on the study area, as well as the industry's indirect and induced

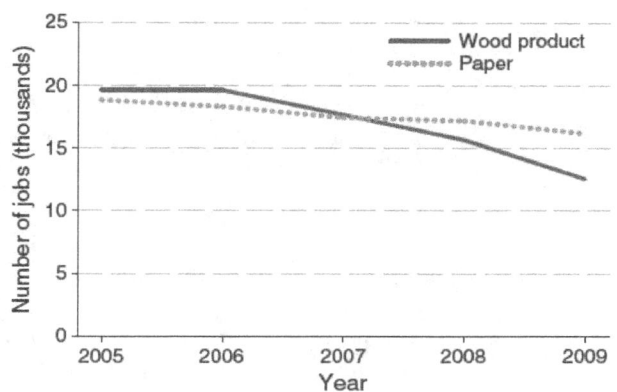

Figure 64—Employment in wood product and paper manufacturing, Tennessee, 2005–09 (Source: U.S. Bureau of Economic Analysis).

impact. According to Minnesota IMPLAN Group's (2011) term's definition, the direct effects indicate the initial changes applied to the industry by the analyst. Indirect

Forest products ready to be delivered from the mill. (photo by L. David Dwinell)

effects refer to the impact associated with the industry purchasing goods and services from other local industries. Induced effects involve the impacts resulting from the changes in household expenditures caused by the change in production from the direct effects.

For each of these impact effects IMPLAN generates estimates for employment, labor income, output, and total value added. Output represents the industry's total value of production. An industry's value added is the difference between the total output and the costs of intermediate inputs. In other words, value added is the industry's gross contribution to the overall economy of an area.

The following economic impact assessments were developed using IMPLAN Version 3.0 (Minnesota IMPLAN Group, Inc. 2009) and associated datasets for 2007 and 2009. All estimated dollar values are shown in 2009 dollars.

Forest sector in Tennessee—Tennessee's forest sector impact analysis (table 29) was generated using adjusted industrial sales. The sectors were grouped into three categories: inputs, primary products, and secondary products. A complete list of the sectors included under each category is found in appendix A.

Comparison of the economic impacts from 2007 and 2009 reveals that the forest sector experienced a downturn across all categories, reflecting the general slowdown of the economy during this period. The change in employment total impact was proportionally larger within the secondary industry, going from 64,920 employees to 49,815 employees (a 23-percent decrease). The change in the total impact of value added was more pronounced within the inputs sector (a 45-percent decrease). Primary industries, on the other hand, showed a marginal increase (3 percent) in the total effect of total value added.

Table 29—Economic impact of the forest sector by major category and impact type, Tennessee, 2007 and 2009

Major category and impact type	Economic impact					
	Employment		Total value added		Total output	
	2007	2009	2007	2009	2007	2009
	- number of jobs -		- - - - - - - millions of dollars - - - - - - -			
Inputs						
Direct	3,410	2,825	$588	$241	$1,065	$533
Total	7,559	7,292	899	498	1,612	988
Primary products						
Direct	10,717	8,857	1,397	1,823	5,713	5,520
Total	41,260	39,006	3,969	4,082	10,582	9,887
Secondary products						
Direct	29,516	22,446	1,851	1,639	7,009	5,449
Total	64,920	49,815	4,605	3,779	12,282	9,387
All categories						
Direct	43,643	34,128	3,836	3,703	13,787	11,502
Total	113,739	96,113	9,473	8,359	24,477	20,263

Source: IMPLAN version 3.0.

Primary wood-using mills—The FIA TPO bi-annual mill survey gathers a range of information from the primary wood-using plants (sawmills, veneer mills, pulpmills, and composite panel plants) in the State. Among the information collected is the number of employees at each mill. This information was used with IMPLAN data for 2009 to estimate the economic effect of the primary wood-using mills in Tennessee (table 30). The analysis shows that the 4,786 direct jobs created by the primary wood-using mills in 2009 resulted in direct labor income of 286 million dollars, and a total direct value added of 481 million dollars to the State's economy. Additionally, the total impact of primary mills is estimated at 15,734 jobs. This total includes direct, indirect, and induced effects. Likewise, the total labor income is estimated at 769 million dollars, and the total value added to the State's economy is estimated at 1.247 billion dollars.

The economic effect of primary plants, broken down by FIA survey unit (table E.2 contains a list of the counties included in each survey unit), shows the East unit as the highest in both number of jobs and total value added (table 31).[5] This unit is also the most significant contributor in terms of total impact (sum of the direct, indirect, and induced effects). The impact analysis shows the primary wood-using industry in the East unit contributing 468 million dollars of total value added to the State's economy in 2009. This is close to 46 percent of the total value added from all of the primary plants in Tennessee. Likewise, the impact on total employment is 42 percent of that estimated for the State. It is important to note, however, that this analysis assumes that 100 percent of the impact from each survey unit occurred within that unit.

---

[5] Table 31 shows only the impact within each survey unit, without considering the impact that activity on one unit might have on the remaining units. For this reason, the total from all units in table 31 does not match the total for the State shown in table 30. The State analysis (table 30) shows the total impact to the State, which considers impacts within and across units.

Table 30—Economic impact of primary wood-using plants by product type and impact type, Tennessee, 2009

Product type and impact type	Economic impact			
	Employment	Labor income	Total value added	Total output
	number of jobs	*- - - - - - millions of dollars - - - - - -*		
Sawtimber and veneer				
Direct	2,900	$96	$123	$603
Total	7,229	283	419	1,176
Pulpwood and panel				
Direct	1,886	191	358	1,397
Total	8,505	486	828	2,336
Total products				
Direct	4,786	286	481	2,000
Total	15,734	769	1,247	3,512

Source: IMPLAN version 3.0 and timber product output 2009 data.

Table 31—Economic impact of primary wood-using plants by survey unit and impact type, Tennessee, 2009

Survey unit and impact type	Economic impact		
	Employment	Total value added	Total output
	number of jobs	*- - millions of dollars - -*	
East			
Direct	1,530	$163	$849
Total	5,792	468	1,459
Central			
Direct	662	32	142
Total	1,898	121	312
Plateau			
Direct	642	25	132
Total	1,537	73	231
West			
Direct	537	23	113
Total	1,453	90	238
West Central			
Direct	1,415	166	684
Total	3,195	271	912

Source: IMPLAN version 3.0.

Employment changes in the 2005–09 period— The TPO data on employment between 2005 and 2009 reveal a considerable decline in employment from the primary industry (fig. 65). This workforce reduction is in agreement with the general downturn in the forest sector mentioned earlier. Overall, from 2005 to 2009 the reported number of employees declined by 30 percent, a loss of 2,039 jobs. Of this total, 82 percent occurred within sawmills and veneer plants.

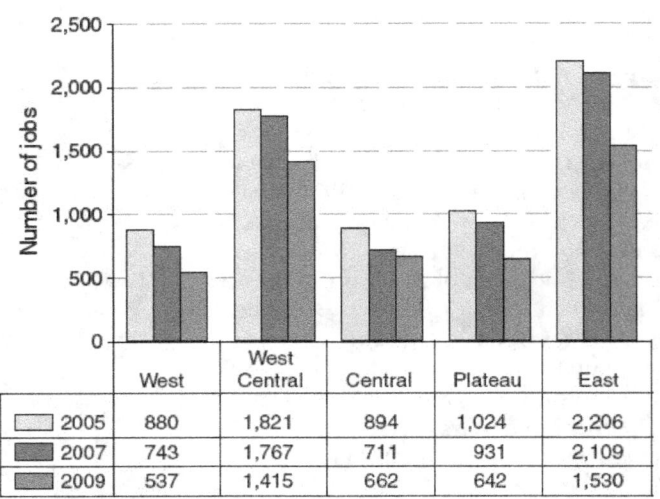

	West	West Central	Central	Plateau	East
2005	880	1,821	894	1,024	2,206
2007	743	1,767	711	931	2,109
2009	537	1,415	662	642	1,530

Figure 66—Primary wood-using mills employment by survey unit, Tennessee, 2005–09.

Although more jobs were lost in the East and the West-Central survey units (fig. 65), one has to consider that those two units are where the majority of the jobs in the primary wood-using industry in Tennessee are concentrated (fig. 66). Comparing the employment change within each survey unit revealed the West and the Plateau units experienced the largest share of job losses, with 39- and 37-percent declines, respectively. The East unit followed with 31 percent. This reduction in workforce resulted from a combination of reduced production and inactive or closed mills.

The economic effect of these job losses was evaluated using IMPLAN (table 32). Overall, the total effect from this workforce reduction impacted 5,143 jobs with an associated 336 million dollars in total value added to the States' economy.

As previously mentioned, sawmill and veneer mills experienced the largest decrease in employment during the 2005-09 period. Accordingly, the combined economic impact displayed by these two industries exceeds the impact estimated from pulpmills and composite panel plants combined. However, most of the economic impact from pulpmills and composite panel plants clusters in one area of the State. This is a direct result of mill location (the majority of the pulp and panel industry is located in the East survey area). This analysis further highlights the importance of that industry cluster to that region of the State.

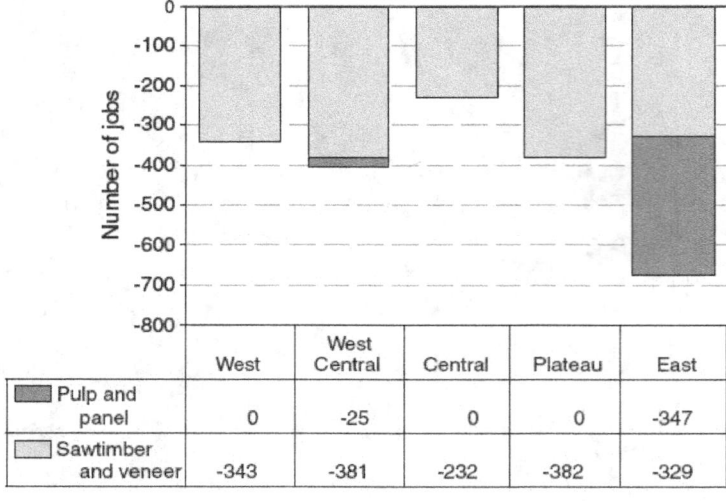

	West	West Central	Central	Plateau	East
Pulp and panel	0	-25	0	0	-347
Sawtimber and veneer	-343	-381	-232	-382	-329

Figure 65—Total employment change by survey unit and product type, Tennessee, 2005–09.

Table 32—Economic effects of job changes in the primary wood-using industry by survey unit and impact type, Tennessee, 2005–09

Survey unit and impact type	Employment	Total value added	Total output
	number of jobs lost	*- - millions of dollars - -*	
Sawmills and veneer mills			
East			
Direct	329	$14	$67
Total	732	41	120
Central			
Direct	232	11	50
Total	665	43	109
Plateau			
Direct	382	15	78
Total	915	43	138
West			
Direct	343	15	72
Total	928	58	152
West Central			
Direct	381	14	77
Total	644	29	108
Pulpmills and composite panels			
East			
Direct	347	55	190
Total	1,189	115	311
West Central			
Direct	25	5	18
Total	69	7	24
State total			
Direct	2,039	129	552
Total	5,143	336	962

Source: IMPLAN version 3.0 and timber product output employment data for 2005, 2007, and 2009.

Forest Biomass and Carbon

Forest Biomass

As the use of forest resources for human consumption broadens and the interest in additional means of quantifying our forests increases, the importance in defining forests in terms of biomass and carbon has become more common. Biomass is generally defined as the biological material from living or recently living organisms. For the most part, forest biomass commonly defines the mass of the plant material within a forest. Recent interest in forest biomass for the production of biofuels and forest carbon as a major store has heightened the need for monitoring and reporting estimates of total forest biomass and carbon stocks within forests of the United States.

In 2009, there was an estimated 770 million dry short tons of aboveground biomass in live trees and saplings within the forests of Tennessee (table 33). About 78 percent (603 million dry tons) of all-live tree and sapling biomass in Tennessee was found within oak-hickory forest types. The oak-pine forest-type group contained considerably less biomass (42 million dry tons), but represented the forest-type group with the second highest store of aboveground live tree and sapling biomass, and was followed by the loblolly-shortleaf pine forest-type group with an estimated 33 million dry tons.

The East unit contained the largest store of aboveground live tree and sapling biomass with 228 million dry tons (table 33). Total aboveground biomass

Table 33—All-live tree and sapling aboveground biomass on forest land by forest-type group and survey unit, Tennessee, 2009

Forest-type group	Total	Survey unit				
		West	West Central	Central	Plateau	East
		oven-dry short tons				
White-red-jack pine	6,207,254	—	—	202,342	1,564,403	4,440,509
Loblolly-shortleaf pine	32,707,471	11,018,037	4,932,420	1,339,859	4,233,499	11,183,657
Other eastern softwoods	6,660,841	154,536	478,158	4,293,269	560,915	1,173,963
Oak-pine	41,655,940	7,084,959	3,962,591	6,411,601	6,807,679	17,389,110
Oak-hickory	602,818,708	60,171,155	106,408,939	111,450,931	147,450,635	177,337,049
Oak-gum-cypress	22,917,217	19,543,564	876,081	1,475,980	509,258	512,334
Elm-ash-cottonwood	31,900,559	19,045,336	2,759,505	8,125,378	449,937	1,520,402
Maple-beech-birch	22,041,853	684,971	51,564	2,813,214	5,888,650	12,603,454
Other hardwoods	1,674,541	—	196,570	44,874	6,028	1,427,069
Exotic hardwoods	1,009,073	2,422	—	680,082	148,489	178,081
Nonstocked	107,460	23,108	—	14,144	50,066	20,142
Total	769,700,914	117,728,087	119,665,827	136,851,674	167,669,557	227,785,769

— = negligible.

Totals may not sum due to rounding.

in live trees and saplings increased from a low of 118 million dry tons in the West unit to a high of 228 million dry tons in the East unit. High aboveground biomass was observed in the Plateau and East units because each unit contained large multicounty blocks with high levels of total aboveground biomass (fig. 67), and most counties within the units contained high per acre aboveground biomass values (fig. 68). The highest total and per acre aboveground biomass was located in counties in the East unit, containing the Great Smoky Mountains National Park.

Forest Carbon

Forest carbon sequestration has been promoted to help mitigate the potential impacts of global climate change. Forest carbon is estimated for both aboveground and belowground stocks as well as carbon stored in the soil, understory vegetation, and forest floor litter. Soil and forest litter are important long-term stores of carbon that accumulate from the decomposition of woody biomass, foliage, and decaying leaf litter. Tree roots along with decaying litter material from the forest floor are sources of organic carbon that accumulate in the mineral soil.

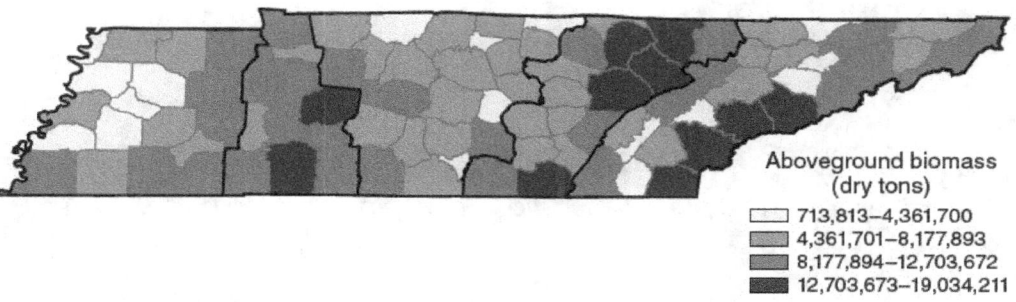

Figure 67—Aboveground biomass on forest land, Tennessee, 2009.

Figure 68—Aboveground biomass on forest land, Tennessee, 2009.

Tennessee forests stored a total of 833 million oven-dry short tons (756 metric tons) of carbon in 2009 (table 34). The largest forest carbon stocks were in aboveground live trees and saplings, and carbon in the soils. Total forest carbon was highest in the East unit and lowest in the West Central and West units. Concentrations of forest carbon appeared in the counties within the Appalachians of the East unit, in the northeast counties of the Plateau unit and in some southern counties within the West Central unit (fig. 69).

Table 34—Forest carbon found in components of the forest by survey unit, Tennessee, 2009

Component	Total	Survey unit				
		West	West Central	Central	Plateau	East
		oven-dry short tons				
Standing dead tree	17,186,922	2,816,442	2,637,786	3,273,861	3,679,444	4,779,389
Aboveground understory	16,482,561	2,605,490	2,771,576	3,080,524	3,697,777	4,327,194
Belowground understory	1,831,395	289,499	307,953	342,280	410,864	480,799
Down dead	37,149,912	5,932,554	5,760,040	6,512,773	8,076,219	10,868,326
Forest floor litter	47,008,164	7,240,407	7,370,713	8,907,826	10,253,529	13,235,689
Soil organic	252,591,018	44,770,043	40,049,493	47,590,309	53,963,804	66,217,369
Aboveground live trees and saplings	384,850,459	58,864,044	59,832,914	68,425,837	83,834,779	113,892,885
Belowground live trees and saplings	76,128,708	11,714,303	11,783,526	13,469,307	16,525,386	22,636,186
All components	833,229,139	134,232,782	130,514,001	151,602,717	180,441,802	236,437,837

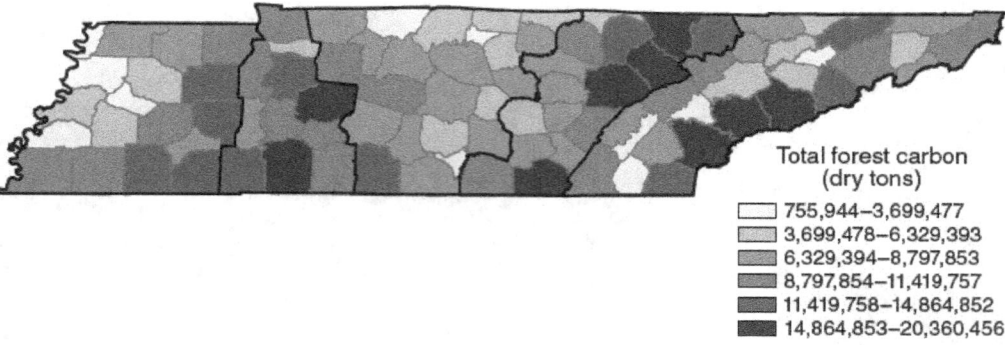

Total forest carbon (dry tons)

- 755,944–3,699,477
- 3,699,478–6,329,393
- 6,329,394–8,797,853
- 8,797,854–11,419,757
- 11,419,758–14,864,852
- 14,864,853–20,360,456

Figure 69—Total forest carbon (aboveground, belowground, live, and dead) on forest land, Tennessee, 2009.

Similar patterns of concentration existed when observing each component separately: aboveground carbon in live trees and saplings (fig. 70), aboveground carbon stored in understory forest plants (fig. 71), belowground carbon stored in understory plants (fig. 72), aboveground carbon stored in standing dead trees (fig. 73), aboveground carbon stored in down dead material (fig. 74), aboveground carbon stored in forest floor litter (fig. 75), and soil organic carbon (fig. 76).

Aboveground tree
and sapling
carbon (dry tons)

425,810–1,917,211
1,917,212–3,544,881
3,544,881–4,889,171
4,889,172–6,590,267
6,590,268–8,845,951
8,845,952–11,403,854

Figure 70—Aboveground and belowground carbon stored in trees (≥5 inches d.b.h.) and saplings (≥1 and <5 inches d.b.h.) on forest land, Tennessee, 2009.

Aboveground understory
carbon (dry tons)

12,701–67,140
67,141–119,703
119,704–173,215
173,216–234,463
234,464–310,906
310,907–437,384

Figure 71—Aboveground carbon stored in understory forest plants on forest land, Tennessee, 2009.

Figure 72—Belowground carbon stored in understory forest plants on forest land, Tennessee, 2009.

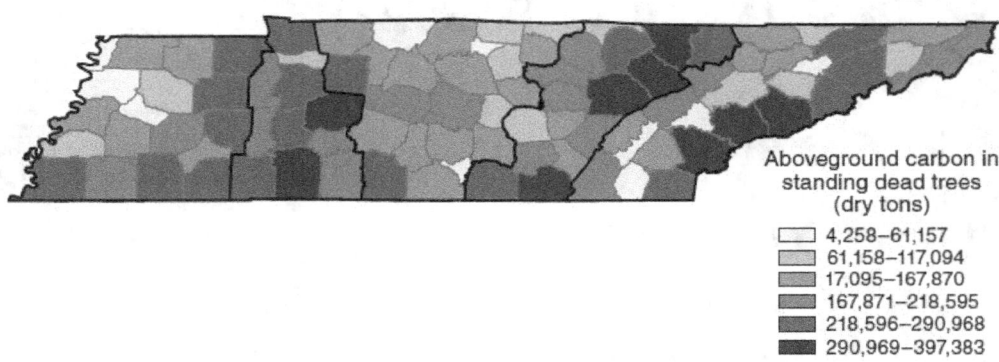

Figure 73—Aboveground carbon stored in standing dead trees (≥5 inches d.b.h.) on forest land, Tennessee, 2009.

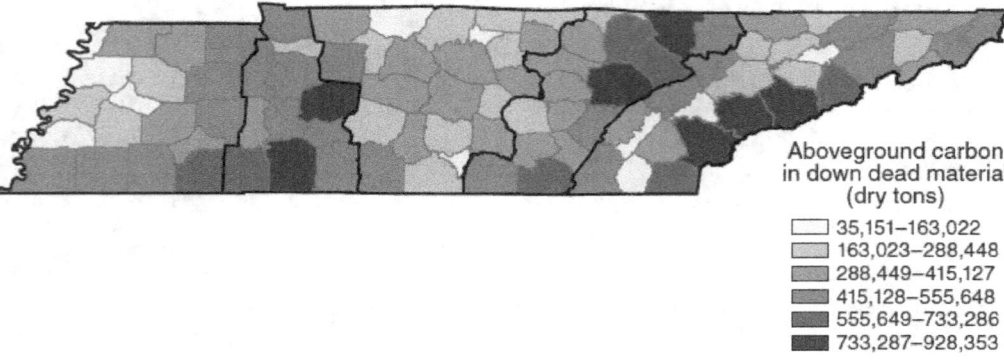

Figure 74—Aboveground carbon stored in down dead material (≥3-inch diameter pieces) on forest land, Tennessee, 2009.

Aboveground litter
carbon(dry tons)

- 45,050–209,821
- 209,822–328,897
- 328,898–454,731
- 454,732–548,153
- 548,154–710,819
- 710,820–1,198,498

Figure 75—Aboveground carbon stored in the litter layer of the forest floor (includes fine down deadwood) on forest land, Tennessee, 2009.

Soil carbon
(dry tons)

- 218,506–1,340,523
- 1,340,524–2,065,119
- 2,065,120–2,671,808
- 2,671,809–3,425,532
- 3,425,533–4,350,902
- 4,350,903–6,240,181

Figure 76—Carbon stored in organic soil on forest land, Tennessee, 2009.

Red trillium (*Trillium erectum*) flower, Newfound Gap, Great Smoky Mountains National Park, Tennessee. (photo by William M. Ciesla, Bugwood.org)

View from Pinnacle
Overlook in Cumberland
Gap National Historic
Park. (Wikimedia.org)

Indicators of Forest Health

Forest health has become a topic of great interest to the scientific and lay communities alike. The USDA Forest Service monitors forest health by measuring a combination of indicators. Forest health indicators measured by the USDA Forest Service, FIA program include invasive plants, crown structure, down woody material (DWM), soil characteristics, vegetation structure and diversity, lichen communities, and ozone damage. Through analysis of each of these variables at statewide, regional, and national levels, scientists are able to identify potential problems and pinpoint areas of concern for intensified research programs. Additionally, trends may be detected and changes tracked over time. The forest health variables presented here for Tennessee reflect monitoring conducted by two programs that were merged in 2000: forest health monitoring (FHM) and FIA. In Tennessee, forest health data collection includes variables related to invasive plants, crown structure, DWM, soil chemistry, and ozone damage.

Information about forest health is obtained in a variety of ways. First, FIA provides information in each State on rates of tree growth and death, harvesting, and changes in forest types and tree species. FIA and State agencies conduct regular ground and aerial surveys of forest damage and the causal agents, both in permanent plots and in other forest areas. In addition, universities, private industry, environmental groups, and other Forest Service scientists cooperate with FIA on a variety of forest research projects.

The FHM program is a joint Federal/State program focused on understanding forest health. This national program was developed in 1990 and is under the administration of the USDA Forest Service and partners with State foresters, other Federal and State agencies, and universities. The program goal is to monitor, assess, and report on the status, changes, and long-term trends in the health of our Nation's forests. The program involves a network of permanent plots and other off-plot areas that are regularly visited to monitor tree vigor, crown condition, and signs of damage. On a subset of the plots, plants are monitored for damage caused by ozone. Structure of the plant communities and presence of lichens (pollution-sensitive life forms that are a combination of algae and fungi) also are evaluated on a subset of the plots. The forest health information presented in this report comes primarily from FIA.

What is a Healthy Forest

From the spruce-fir forests of the Great Smoky Mountains National Park in east Tennessee to the bottomland hardwood forests within the Mississippi river floodplain of west Tennessee, the State's forests are complex ecosystems and are vital to its overall well-being. Wildlife depends on the forests for habitat, and we depend on them for food, fiber, recreation, water quality, and economic stability. A variety of factors affect the health of these forests.

Regardless of how the forests of Tennessee are viewed, their health is vital. But what is a healthy forest, and how is it defined? There are many possible definitions depending on how one views forest health. While it may be difficult to explicitly define a "healthy forest," a number of indicators can be synthesized to form the information into a larger picture of the health of the forests in the State. No single measurement or variable can summarize forest health. Instead, a wide set of indicators must be considered, and these indicators serve as a reflection of existing conditions. Monitoring of these indicators over time allows identification of trends in forest conditions and evaluates the effectiveness of actions. For example, increased tree mortality can indicate a pest or disease issue, while high levels of observed ozone damage may mean

a problem with ozone pollution, or increasing observations of nonnative invasive species may warn of future ecological or economic problems. Numerous forest health indicators must be viewed holistically in order to gain an appreciation for the overall health of our forests and the numerous threats they may be facing. We can use this information to help improve the condition of the State's forests over time.

An array of trees, herbaceous plants, animals, and microorganisms, as well as natural processes such as disturbances (e.g., fire) help maintain a healthy forest ecosystem. Careful management and harvesting also play a vital role in sustaining the health of forested ecosystems. Some forces that have a negative impact on forest health are pests, diseases, and exotic invasive species (e.g., the hemlock woolly

adelgid [*Adelges tsugae*] and the gypsy moth [*Lymantria dispar*]). In the past, large-scale overharvesting had a major impact on forest health, especially as the Nation was developing and relying heavily on forest resources. Large-scale overharvesting was not an issue in Tennessee in 2009, but some forests were declining as a result of natural maturity.

Forest Disturbance

Tennessee forests are heavily influenced by a number of disturbance events. An estimated 890,000 acres exhibited signs of some type of disturbance during the 2009 inventory. That estimate is the equivalent of about 178,000 acres disturbed annually for the period between 2004 and 2009. Thus, at current rates, an area equivalent to the entire forest land area in Tennessee

Beaver impoundments, such as this one in west Tennessee, can become very large and kill numerous trees.

is disturbed about every 79 years. Disturbances are important in defining, shaping, and changing the forests within the State. There are areas within the State, such as deep coves in the Great Smoky Mountains National Park or Dick's Cove on the escarpment of the Cumberland Plateau in southeast Tennessee, which can persist without external disturbances for longer periods of time. However, maturing forests without external disturbances are influenced by internal changes, particularly as trees age, senesce, and begin to breakup and fall over. Nevertheless, many areas in Tennessee, such as the table lands of the Middle Cumberland Plateau, are affected by multiple disturbances over short periods.

Animals (e.g., wild boar) and insects, as primary disturbance agents, accounted for the largest acreage of disturbed forest land in 2009 (fig. 77). Animal disturbances accounted for an estimated 243,000 acres of disturbed forest land (27 percent of all disturbed forest land) while insect disturbances accounted for an estimated 204,000 acres (23 percent of all disturbed forest land). In 2004 (the last survey report, see Oswalt and others 2009) insect disturbances easily ranked highest among disturbance agents in Tennessee due to the SPB epidemic that occurred between 1999 and 2002. While the actual event was documented to have occurred between 1999 and 2002 with peak activity in 2001, FIA disturbance data show a peak in estimated insect-disturbed acreage in 2005 (fig. 78). There is clearly a timelag in the ability of FIA data utilizing the temporally indifferent estimators (Bechtold and Patterson 2005) to detect large disturbance events.

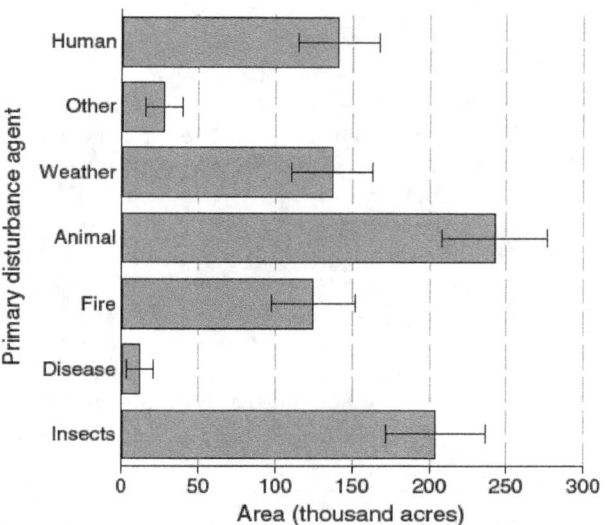

Figure 77—Area of forest land impacted by primary disturbance agents, Tennessee, 2009. Error bars represent one standard error.

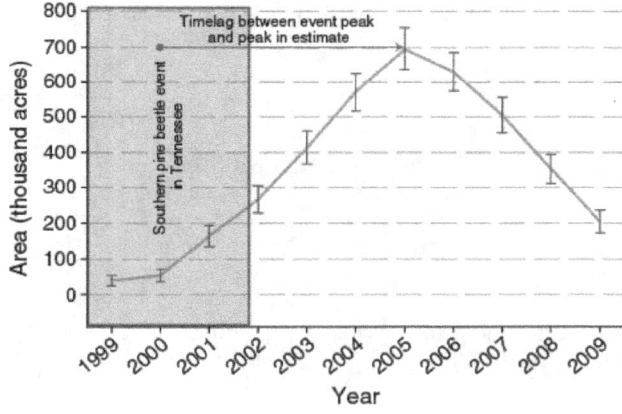

Figure 78—Area of forest land impacted by insect disturbance, Tennessee, 1999–2009. Error bars represent one standard error.

Invasive Plants

Invasive plants were detected on 1,932 plots across the State, or 71 percent of all forested plots measured (fig. 79). The maximum number of species detected on an individual plot was nine, which occurred on <1 percent of forested plots (table 35). Invasive plant presence seems to be lowest along the State's eastern border where the Cherokee National Forest and Great Smoky Mountains National Park comprise much of the land ownership, and along the Cumberland Plateau. Land management

decisions (e.g., deliberately controlling invasive plants in the national park and on the national forest) and large tracts of less-fragmented forests are likely primary reasons those forests are less impacted. Disturbance (harvests, tornadoes, etc.) and proximity to agricultural land may account for the larger proportion of impacted plots in the West-Central region of the State.

Japanese honeysuckle (*Lonicera japonica*) was the most frequently detected non-native species in Tennessee (table 36). The ubiquitous invasive vine was found on 56 percent of all forested plots surveyed, and 79 percent of all plots containing an invasive species. On average, Japanese honeysuckle foliage covered 25 percent of the subplots on which it was found. Nepalese browntop (*Microstegium vimineum*), a species whose introduction to the United States can be traced to east Tennessee, was the second most frequently detected species. It was noted on 24 percent of measured plots, with an average cover of about 24 percent on subplots where it was detected. The above mentioned species along with privet shrubs (*Ligustrum sinense/L. vulgare*), nonnative roses (*Rosa* spp.), shrubby and Chinese lespedeza (*Lespedeza bicolor/L. cuneata*), tree-of-heaven (*Ailanthus altissima*), bush honeysuckles (*Lonicera* spp.), Mimosa (*Albizia julibrissin*), and royal paulownia (*Paulownia tomentosa*) comprise the top 10 most frequently detected invasive plants surveyed for on forested plots in Tennessee (table 36).

Invasive trees were noted throughout the State (fig. 80). Tree-of-heaven was the most frequently detected invasive tree in every physiographic region in the State except east Tennessee, where mimosa was observed with equal

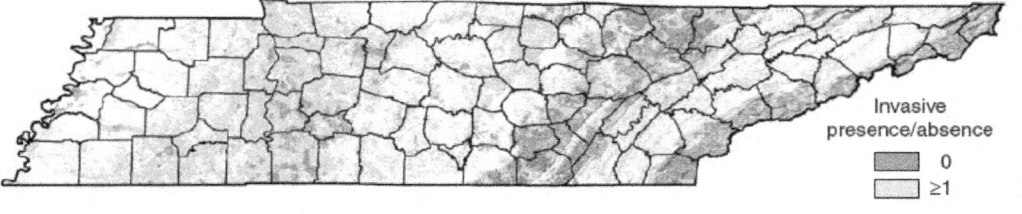

Invasive presence/absence

⬛	0
⬜	≥1

Figure 79—Presence/absence of invasive species on forest land, Tennessee, 2009.

Table 35—Invasive species on forest land, number of species detections, and the number and percent of plots, Tennessee, 2009

Count of unique species	Plots[a]	
	number	percent
1	624	23
2	561	21
3	407	15
4	240	9
5	64	2
6	25	1
7	8	<1
8	1	<1
9	2	<1
Total	1,932	71

[a] Amount of plots surveyed = 2,713.

Table 36—Invasive species detected on forest land with frequency of plot detections and mean percent subplot cover by common and scientific name, Tennessee, 2009

Common name	Scientific name	Plot detections[a]	Subplot cover[b]
		number	mean percent
Japanese honeysuckle	*Lonicera japonica*	1,530	25
Nepalese browntop	*Microstegium vimineum*	649	24
Chinese/European privet	*Ligustrum sinense/L. vulgare*	616	11
Nonnative roses	*Rosa* spp.	517	9
Shrubby lespedeza	*Lespedeza bicolor*	249	6
Tree-of-heaven	*Ailanthus altissima*	241	16
Chinese lespedeza	*Lespedeza cuneata*	191	13
Bush honeysuckles	*Lonicera* spp.	102	18
Silktree, mimosa	*Albizia julibrissin*	81	6
Princesstree, royal paulownia	*Paulownia tomentosa*	59	14
Tall fescue	*Lolium arundinaceum*	37	36
Nonnative climbing yams/air yam/Chinese yam	*Dioscorea bulbifera/D. oppositifolia*	37	5
English ivy	*Hedera helix*	34	5
Japanese/glossy privet	*Ligustrum japonicum/L. lucidum*	26	23
Kudzu	*Pueraria Montana* var. *lobata*	19	38
Nonnative bamboos	*Phyllostachys* spp., *bambus* spp.	16	31
Nonnative vincas, periwinkles	*Vinca minor/V. major*	15	31
Chinese/Japanese wisteria	*Wisteria sinensis/W. floribunda*	13	16
Sacred bamboo	*Nandina domestica*	12	10
Winter creeper	*Euonymus fortunei*	11	19
Autumn olive	*Elaeagnus umbellata*	11	13
Garlic mustard	*Alliaria petiolata*	5	19
Winged burning bush	*Euonymus alata*	3	0
Tropical soda apple	*Solanum viarum*	2	0
Russian olive	*Elaeagnus angustifolia*	2	18
Silverthorn, thorny olive	*E. pungens*	1	0

[a] Plot refers to the forested portion of all subplots measured. If a species was detected on more than one subplot, it is only counted once here.

[b] Percent cover in this column is the average cover on an individual subplot, not the whole plot.

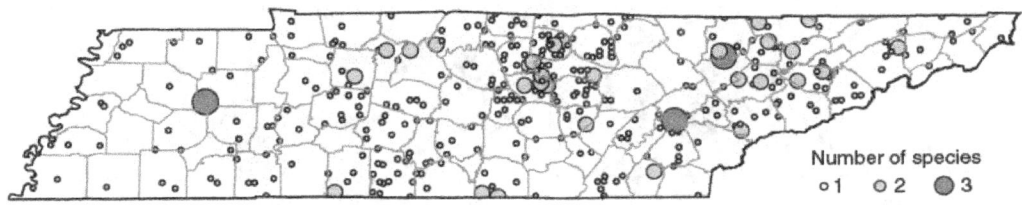

Figure 80—Number of invasive trees on plots, Tennessee, 2009.

frequency. Tree-of-heaven detections were highest in the Central unit, where it was noted on 21 percent of plots. Invasive shrubs and vines are the most frequently recorded invasive plants in Tennessee forests (figs. 81 and 82), with many plots containing two or more species. Japanese honeysuckle is the most commonly detected vine and was recorded on 81, 73, 53, 50, and 30 percent of plots in the West, Central, West Central, East, and Plateau units, respectively. No other invasive vine was detected on >4 percent of plots in any region. Chinese/European privet (*Ligustrum sinense/L. vulgare*) and non-native roses were the two most frequently detected shrubs on Tennessee forest land. Chinese/European privet occupies 26, 18, 34, 11, and 24 percent of plots in the West, West Central, Central, Plateau, and East Tennessee units, respectively, while nonnative roses occupied a fairly high proportion of plots in Central Tennessee (30 percent) and <20 percent in all other regions.

Japanese stiltgrass (*Microstegium vimineum*) was the most frequently detected invasive grass in Tennessee (fig. 83) and it was detected on 31, 27, 30, 15, and 19 percent of plots in West, West Central, Central, Plateau, and East Tennessee units, respectively. Invasive herbs were most common in West Central and West Tennessee (fig. 84), and consisted primarily of Shrubby and Chinese lespedezas.

Invasive species are common on forested plots across the State of Tennessee. The prevalence of invasive plants on Tennessee forest land illustrates the need for public education regarding the ecological and economic costs of invasive plants, and the need for concentrated control and management efforts for invasive plants.

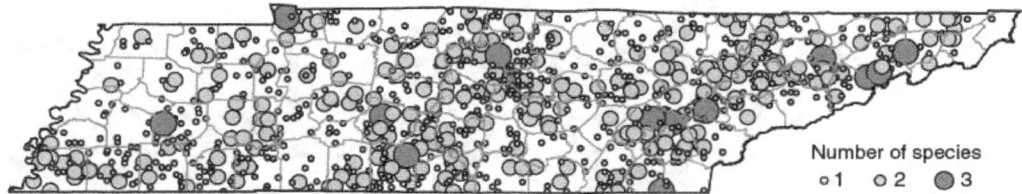

Figure 81—Number of invasive shrubs on plots, Tennessee, 2009.

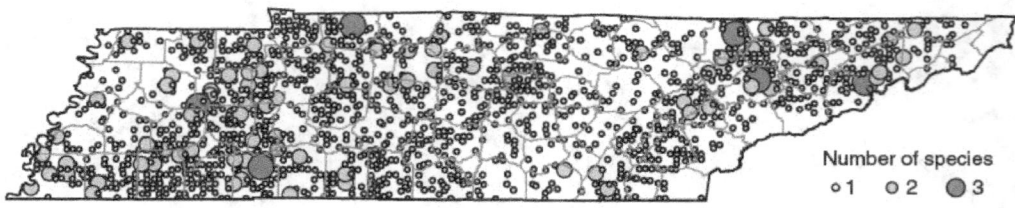

Figure 82—Number of invasive vines on plots, Tennessee, 2009.

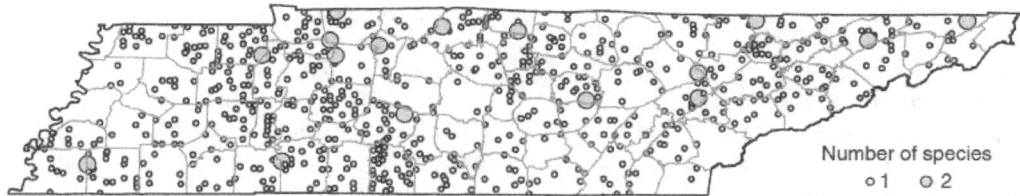

Figure 83—Number of invasive grasses on plots, Tennessee, 2009.

Number of species
o 1   o 2

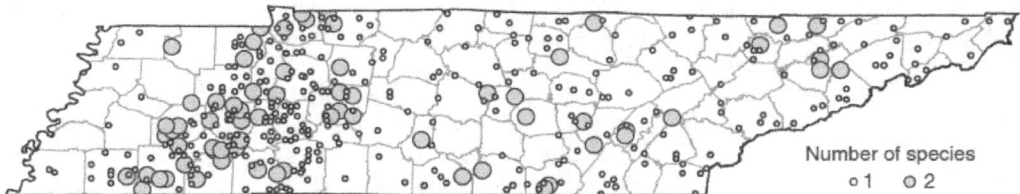

Figure 84—Number of invasive herbs on plots, Tennessee, 2009.

Number of species
o 1   o 2

A butterfly rests on a thistle in a forest opening.

93

Deadwood

Deadwood is extremely important to forest ecosystems because it performs a number of key ecological functions. For example, it serves as nurse logs for the growth of plants and moss, is critical to nutrient cycling and as an element of wildlife habitat, and is a major component of forest fuel loads (Waddell 2002, Bate and others 2004). A multitude of organisms rely on DWM to provide structural and/or thermal protection, foraging sites, or travel corridors (Bate and others 2004). For example, Mannan and others (1996) describe 13 small mammal species that depend on coarse woody material for all three of their life-history requirements: food, shelter, and reproduction. However, too much deadwood in the forest can result in excess fuel loads, sustaining damaging wildfires over large areas. Therefore, forest managers must strike a balance between maintaining enough deadwood to sustain wildlife, insect, and plant communities, while avoiding unacceptably high fuel accumulations.

A major contributing factor to deadwood pools is standing dead trees. In 2009 there were an estimated 156 million standing dead trees within Tennessee's forests. Thirty-nine percent were in the East unit (fig. 85). The high level of standing dead trees in the East unit is likely due to the SPB epidemic that occurred mostly in eastern Tennessee forests between 1999 and 2002 (see Forest Disturbance section for additional information). The peak in estimated standing dead wood occurred in 2005 and was evident in the East and Plateau FIA units (fig. 86). The remaining units appeared to be impacted very little.

The forest-type groups with the greatest number of estimated standing dead trees were the oak-hickory, oak-pine, and elm-ash-cottonwood pine groups (fig. 87). However, as a percentage of total standing population, the other hardwood, exotic hardwood, and maple-beech-birch appeared to have the greatest standing dead population.

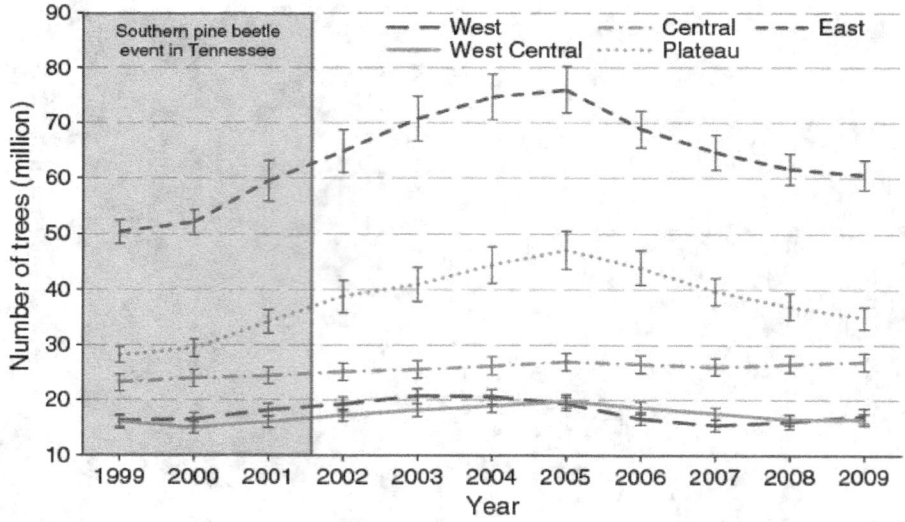

Figure 85—Number of standing dead trees ≥ 5 inches d.b.h. on forest land for each survey unit, Tennessee, 1999–2009. Error bars represent one standard error.

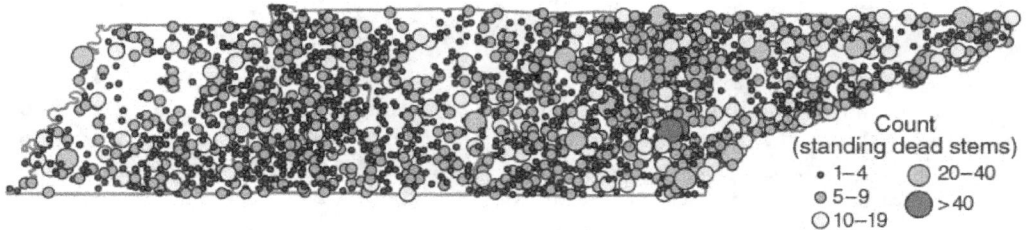

Figure 86—Distribution of standing dead stems sampled, Tennessee, 2009.

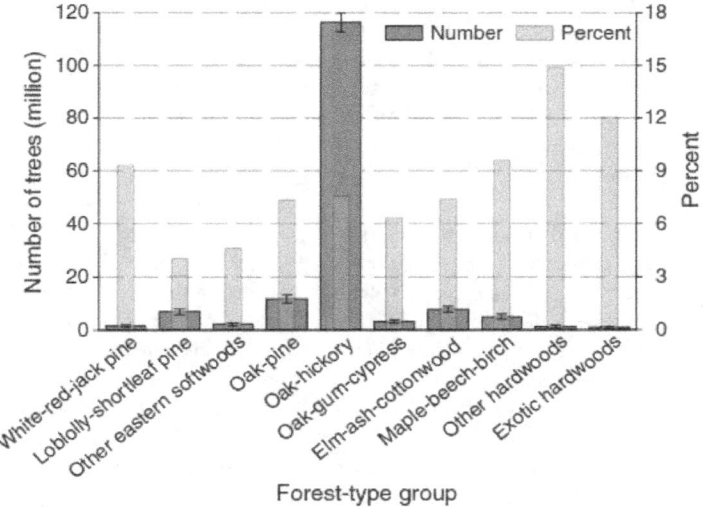

Figure 87—Number of standing dead trees ≥ 5 inches d.b.h. and number of standing dead trees as a percent of number of all standing trees on forest land by forest-type group, Tennessee, 2009. Error bars represent one standard error.

Deadwood along the side of a forest road in east Tennessee. (photo by Rachel Weeks)

Tree Crowns

FIA includes visual assessments of individual tree crown condition on the phase 3 subset of its inventory plots to aid in the monitoring of changes and trends in forest health. Tree crown condition can be used to track forest health because a tree undergoing stress reacts by slowing growth and shedding parts of its crown (Millers and others 1989). The shedding of foliage and fine twigs not only changes the tree's appearance, but also alters its rate of photosynthesis and carbohydrate production. Thus, poor crown conditions can be a signal of declining growth rates and degraded forest health.

FIA reports on three tree crown condition variables, crown density, crown dieback, and foliage transparency, and one sapling crown condition variable, sapling crown vigor. Each of the three tree crown variables are visually assessed by a two-person field crew and recorded in increments of 5 percent from 0 to 99 for all-live trees. Sapling crown vigor is recorded in one of three categories for all-live saplings. All crown assessments are made in the summer during leaf-on season.

All four crown condition indicators were summarized by FIA species group for the years 2005–09. In addition, trees and saplings measured in years 2005–09 were paired with their first measurement in 2000–04 to determine whether crown conditions improved, declined, or remained stable during the 5-year remeasurement period.

Crown dieback is a symptom of recent stress demonstrated by the death of fine twigs and branches in the upper and outer portions of the crown. Crown dieback may result from a disruption in water and nutrient transport from the roots to the crown, direct injury to the crown, or even normal physiological processes such as heavy seed production. Overall, 84.4 percent of the trees assessed exhibited <5-percent crown dieback. Mean dieback was 0.9 percent for softwoods and 2.7 percent for hardwoods and ranged as high as 8.3 percent for the tupelo and blackgum species group (table 37). The mean and standard error for tupelo and blackgum are unusually high. Closer inspection of this species group revealed that 85.9 percent of the tupelo and blackgum trees had crown dieback

Damage from the Hemlock woolly adelgid may be similar to this Balsam woolly adelgid damage near Clingman's Dome, Tennessee. (Photo by Ronald F. Billings, Bugwood.org)

Table 37—Mean crown dieback and other statistics[a] for live trees (≥5 inches d.b.h.) on forest land by species group, Tennessee, 2009

Species group	Plots[b]	Trees	Mean	SE[c]	Minimun	Median	90th percentile	Maximum
	--- number ---		----------------------- percent -----------------------					
Softwoods								
Loblolly and shortleaf pines	25	122	0.3	0.2	0	0	0	5
Other yellow pines	20	118	0.6	0.2	0	0	0	10
Eastern white and red pines	10	49	1.4	0.7	0	0	5	20
Eastern hemlock	8	28	0.7	0.6	0	0	0	15
Other eastern softwoods	31	169	1.6	0.8	0	0	0	95
Total	67	486	0.9	0.3	0	0	0	95
Hardwoods								
Select white oaks	85	303	2.3	0.6	0	0	5	99
Select red oaks	35	57	1.2	0.5	0	0	5	25
Other white oaks	47	235	1.9	0.5	0	0	5	45
Other red oaks	70	194	3.4	0.8	0	0	5	95
Hickory	79	299	1.3	0.5	0	0	0	99
Yellow birch	1	1	0.0	—	0	0	0	0
Hard maple	40	119	0.1	0.1	0	0	0	5
Soft maple	67	277	3.2	1.2	0	0	5	99
Beech	19	37	0.7	0.5	0	0	0	15
Sweetgum	37	146	2.6	1.6	0	0	0	99
Tupelo and blackgum	42	71	8.3	5.6	0	0	20	99
Ash	53	140	2.9	1.1	0	0	8	90
Cottonwood and aspen	1	1	0.0	—	0	0	0	0
Basswood	4	4	3.8	—	0	3	10	10
Yellow-poplar	77	306	1.6	0.6	0	0	5	99
Black walnut	17	23	0.4	0.3	0	0	0	5
Other eastern soft hardwoods	97	340	4.1	0.8	0	0	10	99
Other eastern hard hardwoods	45	91	3.2	1.3	0	0	5	99
Eastern noncommercial hardwoods	67	201	4.1	1.3	0	0	5	99
Total	159	2,845	2.7	0.4	0	0	5	99
Species total	162	3,331	2.4	0.3	0	0	5	99

Data collected from 2005 to 2009; d.b.h. = diameter at breast height; SE = standard error.

— = negligible; 0.0 = no sample for the cell or a value of >0.0 but <0.05.

[a] The mean, SE, and median calculations consider the clustering of trees on plots.

[b] Total number of plots on which trees were measured. Plot totals are not cumulative because multiple species may occur on any given plot.

[c] Standard errors are not presented for species groups with the number of trees <20.

of ≤5 percent and most plot means were <6 percent (fig. 88), which does not suggest a problem statewide. Indeed, this is the case as the trees with crown dieback of ≥15 percent were concentrated on the five plots which had mean dieback >5 percent (fig. 88).

Crown density is a measure of the amount of foliage present on the tree and is recorded as the percentage of light blocked through the projected crown outline by live and dead branches, foliage, and reproductive structures. Within individual species, higher crown densities typically represent healthier trees. Most crown densities ranged from 30.0 to 55.0 percent (fig. 89).

Mean crown density was 39.2 percent for softwoods, 44.5 percent for hardwoods, and among the species groups with ≥20 sampled trees, ranged from 37.6 percent for loblolly and shortleaf pines to 49.6 percent for beech (table 38).

Foliage transparency is an indicator of the amount of foliage present on the tree and is measured as the percent of skylight visible through the live, normally foliated portion of the crown. As with crown density, mean foliage transparency tends to be species-specific; however, there is typically less variation among the foliage transparency means than there is among the crown density means. In general, lower foliage

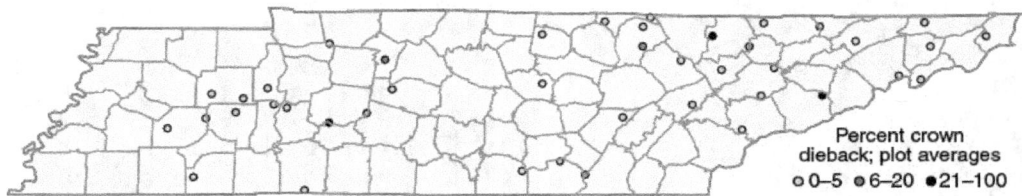

Figure 88—Mean crown dieback by plot for tupelo and blackgum, Tennessee, 2009. (Plot locations are approximate).

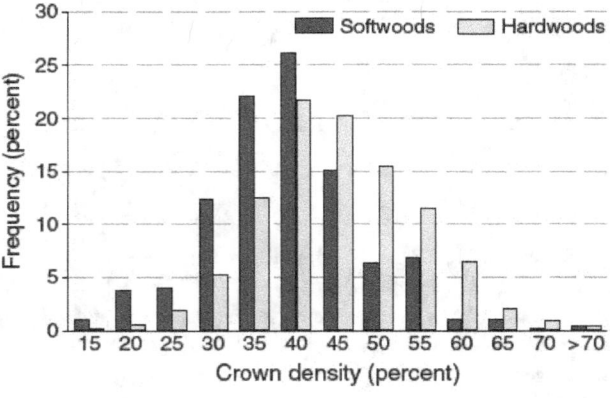

Figure 89—Crown density frequency distribution, Tennessee, 2009.

Table 38—Mean crown density and other statistics[a] for live trees (≥5 inches d.b.h.) on forest land by species group, Tennessee, 2009

Species group	Plots[b]	Trees	Mean	SE[c]	Minimum	Median	Maximum
	- - - number - - -		- - - - - - - - - - - - - - - - - percent - - - - - - - - - - - - - - - - -				
Softwoods							
Loblolly and shortleaf pines	25	122	37.6	1.4	25	35	65
Other yellow pines	20	118	39.5	1.8	20	40	65
Eastern white and red pines	10	49	39.6	1.9	20	40	60
Eastern hemlock	8	28	43.0	3.4	30	40	80
Other eastern softwoods	31	169	39.3	2.1	15	40	70
Total	67	486	39.2	1.0	15	40	80
Hardwoods							
Select white oaks	85	303	44.3	1.0	0	45	75
Select red oaks	35	57	47.5	1.6	25	50	70
Other white oaks	47	235	43.3	0.9	10	40	95
Other red oaks	70	194	44.9	1.3	5	45	80
Hickory	79	299	47.5	1.2	0	45	80
Yellow birch	1	1	45.0	—	45	45	45
Hard maple	40	119	47.5	1.6	25	45	70
Soft maple	67	277	43.4	0.9	0	45	70
Beech	19	37	49.6	1.7	35	50	75
Sweetgum	37	146	46.2	1.1	10	45	70
Tupelo and blackgum	42	71	42.7	2.4	0	45	70
Ash	53	140	43.9	1.0	20	45	65
Cottonwood and aspen	1	1	35.0	—	35	35	35
Basswood	4	4	45.0	—	35	43	60
Yellow-poplar	77	306	46.5	1.4	0	45	75
Black walnut	17	23	44.3	2.0	25	45	65
Other eastern soft hardwoods	97	340	41.9	0.8	0	40	80
Other eastern hard hardwoods	45	91	41.5	1.4	0	40	70
Eastern noncommercial hardwoods	67	201	42.4	1.3	0	45	65
Total	159	2,845	44.5	0.5	0	45	95
Species total	162	3,331	43.8	0.5	0	45	95

Data collected from 2005 to 2009; d.b.h. = diameter at breast height; SE = standard error.

— = negligible.

[a] The mean, SE, and median calculations consider the clustering of trees on plots.

[b] Total number of plots on which trees were measured. Plot totals are not cumulative because multiple species may occur on any given plot.

[c] Standard errors are not presented for species groups with the number of trees <20.

transparency ratings indicate healthier trees. Ninety percent of all trees had foliage transparency values of ≤25 percent (fig. 90). Mean foliage transparency was 20.6 percent for all trees combined and among the species groups with at least 20 sampled trees ranged from a low of 18.7 percent for the hard maples to a high of 26.6 percent for the other yellow pines (table 39).

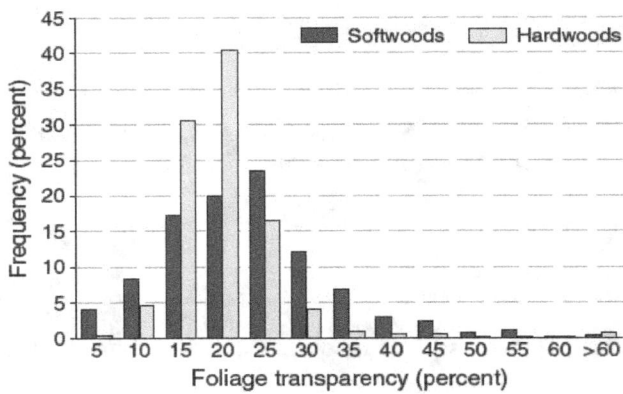

Figure 90—Foliage transparency frequency distribution, Tennessee, 2009.

A Great blue heron sits proudly atop an eastern redcedar while viewing its domain.

Table 39—Mean foliage transparency and other statistics[a] **for live trees (≥5 inches d.b.h.) on forest land by species group, Tennessee, 2009**

Species group	Plots[b]	Trees	Mean	SE[c]	Minimim	Median	Maximum
	- - - number - - -		- - - - - - - - - - - - - - - - - - percent - - - - - - - - - - - - - - - -				
Softwoods							
Loblolly and shortleaf pines	25	122	20.0	1.4	5	20	40
Other yellow pines	20	118	26.6	1.9	5	25	65
Eastern white and red pines	10	49	22.4	2.9	10	25	35
Eastern hemlock	8	28	22.1	2.4	5	25	35
Other eastern softwoods	31	169	23.4	4.5	0	20	60
Total	67	486	23.1	1.8	0	25	65
Hardwoods							
Select white oaks	85	303	18.9	0.6	0	20	99
Select red oaks	35	57	19.2	1.0	5	20	40
Other white oaks	47	235	21.0	0.6	10	20	45
Other red oaks	70	194	20.6	1.2	5	20	80
Hickory	79	299	19.0	0.7	5	20	99
Yellow birch	1	1	15.0	—	15	15	15
Hard maple	40	119	18.7	0.6	10	20	40
Soft maple	67	277	20.8	0.6	0	20	99
Beech	19	37	19.2	1.8	10	20	60
Sweetgum	37	146	19.4	0.9	5	20	99
Tupelo and blackgum	42	71	22.5	3.2	10	20	99
Ash	53	140	18.9	0.8	5	20	45
Cottonwood and aspen	1	1	10.0	—	10	10	10
Basswood	4	4	15.0	—	10	15	20
Yellow-poplar	77	306	19.6	0.6	10	20	99
Black walnut	17	23	21.7	1.4	15	20	30
Other eastern soft hardwoods	97	340	22.0	0.7	0	20	99
Other eastern hard hardwoods	45	91	22.5	1.1	5	20	99
Eastern noncommercial hardwoods	67	201	20.8	1.1	0	20	99
Total	159	2,845	20.2	0.3	0	20	99
Species total	162	3,331	20.6	0.4	0	20	99

Data collected from 2005 to 2009; d.b.h. = diameter at breast height; SE = standard error.

— = negligible.

[a] The mean, SE, and median calculations consider the clustering of trees on plots.

[b] Total number of plots on which trees were measured. Plot totals are not cumulative because multiple species may occur on any given plot.

[c] Standard errors are not presented for species groups with the number of trees <20.

Sapling crowns are not developed enough to assess the three crown condition indicators applied to larger trees. Instead, they are categorized based upon the amount and condition of foliage present into three broad vigor classes of good, fair, and poor. Overall, 71.3 percent of the sapling crowns were categorized as good (table 40). Among the species groups with at least 20 sampled saplings, the ash group had the lowest percentage of saplings in the good category and the other eastern hard hardwoods group had the highest percentage of saplings in the poor category (table 40).

Table 40—Distribution of sapling crown vigor class for all-live saplings (1.0 to <5.0 inches d.b.h.) on forest land by species group, Tennessee, 2009

Species group	Plots[a]	Trees	Good	SE[b]	Fair	SE[b]	Poor	SE[b]
	--- number ---		--------------- percent ---------------					
Softwoods								
Loblolly and shortleaf pines	5	5	80.0	—	20.0	—	0.0	—
Other yellow pines	7	17	47.1	—	47.1	—	5.9	—
Eastern white and red pines	6	24	91.7	8.6	0.0	0.0	8.3	8.6
Eastern hemlock	3	8	75.0	—	12.5	—	12.5	—
Other eastern softwoods	24	61	68.9	8.5	23.0	8.1	8.2	5.1
Total	37	115	71.3	7.4	20.9	7.2	7.8	3.3
Hardwoods								
Select white oaks	16	23	87.0	6.2	8.7	6.2	4.3	3.5
Select red oaks	4	4	50.0	—	25.0	—	25.0	—
Other white oaks	11	16	75.0	—	25.0	—	0.0	—
Other red oaks	9	12	66.7	—	25.0	—	8.3	—
Hickory	29	45	75.6	6.2	24.4	6.2	0.0	0.0
Hard maple	24	49	75.5	7.5	22.4	7.5	2.0	2.1
Soft maple	43	94	79.8	5.1	14.9	4.5	5.3	2.8
Beech	13	20	95.0	5.0	5.0	5.0	0.0	0.0
Sweetgum	15	65	84.6	7.3	13.8	6.4	1.5	1.6
Tupelo and blackgum	31	65	63.1	6.8	35.4	6.8	1.5	1.5
Ash	12	21	47.6	10.7	47.6	12.1	4.8	4.6
Basswood	2	4	50.0	—	25.0	—	25.0	—
Yellow-poplar	23	86	77.9	5.1	15.1	3.3	7.0	3.2
Other eastern soft hardwoods	57	127	68.5	5.1	29.9	4.8	1.6	1.1
Other eastern hard hardwoods	41	88	51.1	8.1	39.8	7.6	9.1	3.7
Eastern noncommercial hardwoods	46	88	69.3	4.9	29.5	4.7	1.1	1.1
Total	138	807	71.3	2.6	25.0	2.3	3.7	0.8
Species total	141	922	71.3	2.7	24.5	2.4	4.2	0.8

Data collected from 2005 to 2009; d.b.h. = diameter at breast height; SE = standard error.

— = negligible; 0.0 = no sample for the cell or a value of >0.0 but <0.05.

[a] Total number of plots on which trees were measured. Plot totals are not cumulative because multiple species may occur on any given plot.

[b] SE calculations consider the clustering of trees on plots. Standard errors are not presented for species groups with the number of trees <20.

Change over time—Among the trees that survived the 5-year remeasurement period, crown conditions remained relatively stable with only small changes in mean conditions. Mean crown density improved slightly from 41.5 to 43.8 percent whereas foliage transparency and crown dieback declined, biologically speaking, from 19.5 to 20.6 percent and 1.2 to 2.6 percent, respectively (table 41). Among the saplings that survived, 67.5 percent demonstrated no change in vigor class. An improvement in vigor class was observed for 9.1 percent of the surviving saplings, and a decline in vigor class was recorded for the remaining 23.4 percent.

Table 41—Mean crown conditions and other statistics[a] for live trees ≥5.0 inches d.b.h. by species group, Tennessee, 2004[b] compared to 2009[c]

Crown indicator and species group			Paired trees only[d]				
			2004		2009		t-test[g]
	Plots[e]	Trees	Mean	SE[f]	Mean	SE[f]	P-value[h]
	- - - number - - -		- - - - - - - - -percent - - - - - - - -				
Crown density							
Softwoods	54	351	39.6	0.9	38.4	1.2	0.3991
Hardwoods	142	2,184	41.8	0.4	44.7	0.6	<0.0001
All trees	144	2,535	41.5	0.4	43.8	0.6	<0.0001
Crown dieback							
Softwoods	54	351	1.6	0.6	1.1	0.4	0.1449
Hardwoods	142	2,184	1.1	0.1	2.8	0.4	0.0001
All trees	144	2,535	1.2	0.2	2.6	0.4	0.0005
Foliage transparency							
Softwoods	54	351	20.7	0.9	23.3	2.0	0.3134
Hardwoods	142	2,184	19.3	0.3	20.2	0.3	0.0754
All trees	144	2,535	19.5	0.3	20.6	0.4	0.0593

d.b.h. = diameter at breast height; SE = standard error.

[a] The mean and SE calculations consider the clustering of trees on plots.

[b] Data collected from 2000 to 2004.

[c] Data collected from 2005 to 2009.

[d] Includes only the trees measured during both specified time periods.

[e] Total number of plots on which trees were measured. Plot totals are not cumulative because multiple species may occur on any given plot.

[f] Standard errors are not presented for species groups with the number of trees <20.

[g] t-tests are not performed for species groups where n plots is <10.

[h] For crown density and foliage transparency, the probability of obtaining a larger t-value under the null hypothesis that the difference between the two means equals 0. For crown dieback, the probability of obtaining a larger t-value under the null hypothesis that the ratio of the two means equals 1.

As an indicator of degraded health, poor crown conditions are potential signals of impending mortality. On average, trees that died between the two assessments had poorer crown conditions, and in particular higher crown dieback (fig. 91), than the trees that survived. Likewise, saplings with poor crown vigor suffered a larger percentage of mortality than saplings with good or fair crown vigor (fig. 92).

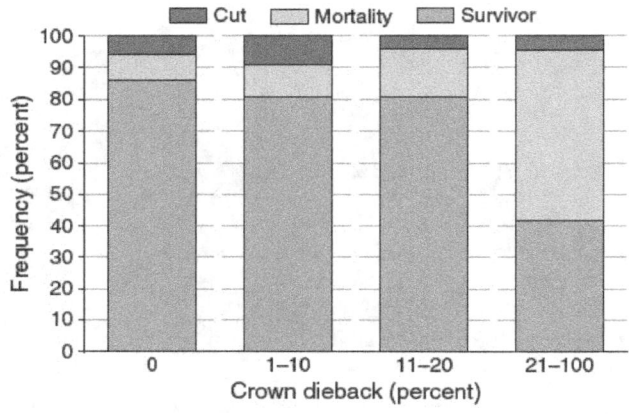

Figure 91—Crown dieback distribution by tree survivorship for remeasured trees, Tennessee, 2004–09.

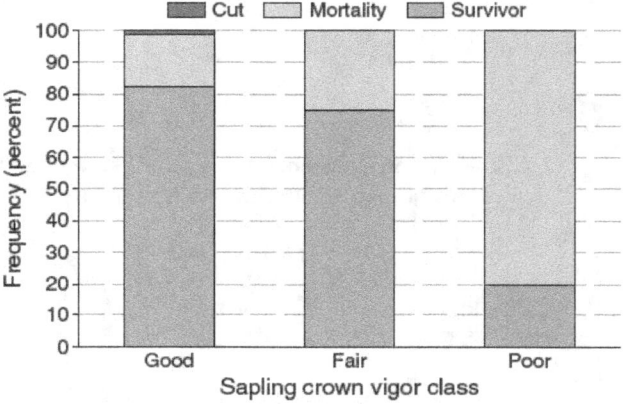

Figure 92—Sapling crown vigor class distribution by tree survivorship for remeasured trees, Tennessee, 2004–09.

Southern pine beetle (*Dendroctonus frontalis*) damage in east Tennessee. (Photo by Richard Spriggs, Bugwood.org)

Species of interest—Black walnut (*Juglans nigra*)—Black walnut was observed on 17 phase 3 plots (fig. 93). The movement of black walnut logs and lumber has been quarantined in Anderson, Blount, Knox, and Union Counties in east Tennessee, due to confirmed cases of thousand cankers disease (TCD). Mean crown conditions for black walnut on plots in these counties (fig. 93) are typical for the species and showed no decline between the current and previous inventory cycle. Since the earliest symptoms of TCD infection are yellowing foliage and branch mortality, future decline of black walnut crown conditions on these plots in particular could indicate the spread of TCD.

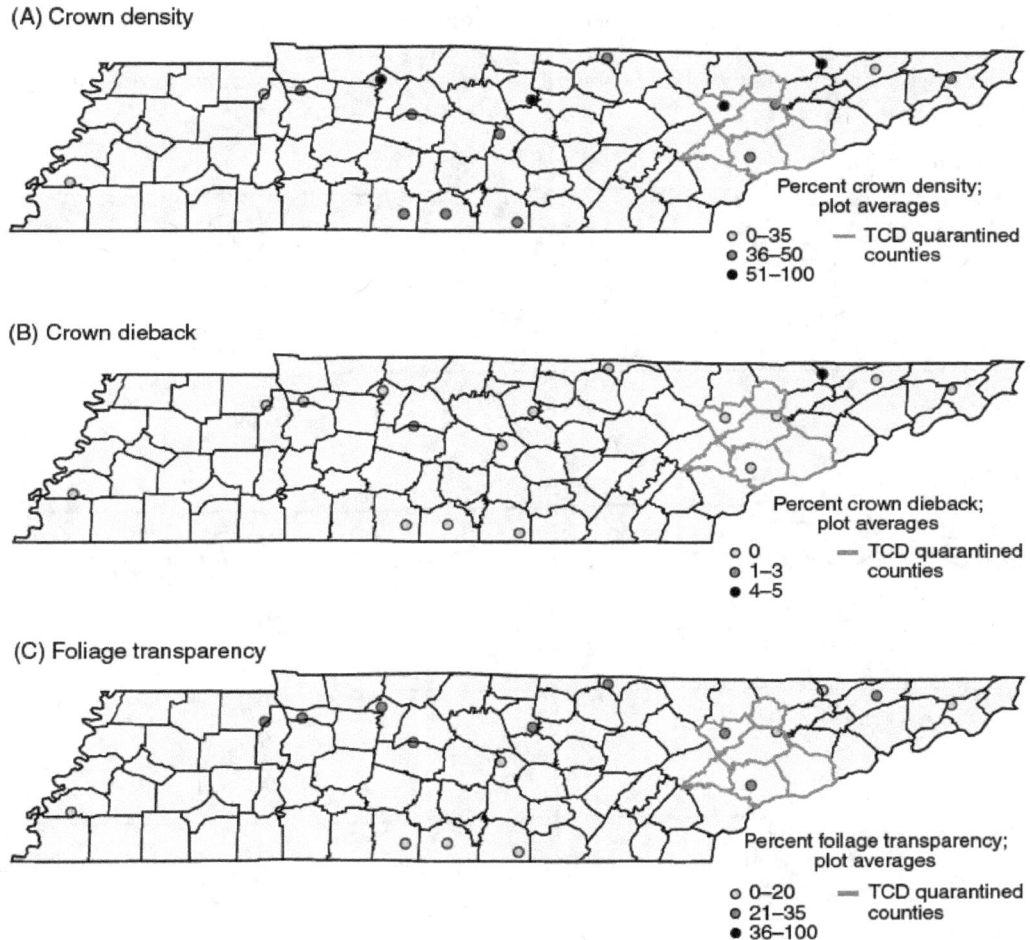

Figure 93—Mean crown conditions by plot for black walnut trees and thousand cankers disease (TCD) quarantined counties, Tennessee, 2009 (A) Crown density, (B) Crown dieback, (C) Foliage transparency. (Plot locations are approximate.)

Ash (*Fraxinus americana* and *F. penn-sylvanica*)—Due to the discovery of the emerald ash borer (EAB, *Agrilus planipennis* Fairmaire) the movement of ash has been quarantined in Knox, Grainger, and Loudon Counties (Note: Due to the fact that intensified monitoring is occurring, these estimates and counties reflect the situation at the time of development. It is understood that the area of impact by EAB will expand in the future). Ash trees were observed on 53 phase 3 plots (fig. 94) but not on any of the phase 3 plots in these quarantined counties. Mean crown conditions for ash in the counties surrounding Knox and Loudon provide no indication of impact by the EAB at this time, but should be monitored closely for declines in the future.

Eastern hemlock (*Tsuga canadensis*)—The hemlock woolly adelgid was found in east Tennessee in 2002. The Hemlock woolly adelgid feeds on the sap in the needles, and infested trees suffer from discolored and prematurely dropped needles. Eastern hemlock trees are scattered throughout Tennessee but were recorded on only eight phase 3 plots, none of which consistently demonstrated poor conditions across the three tree crown condition indicators (fig. 95).

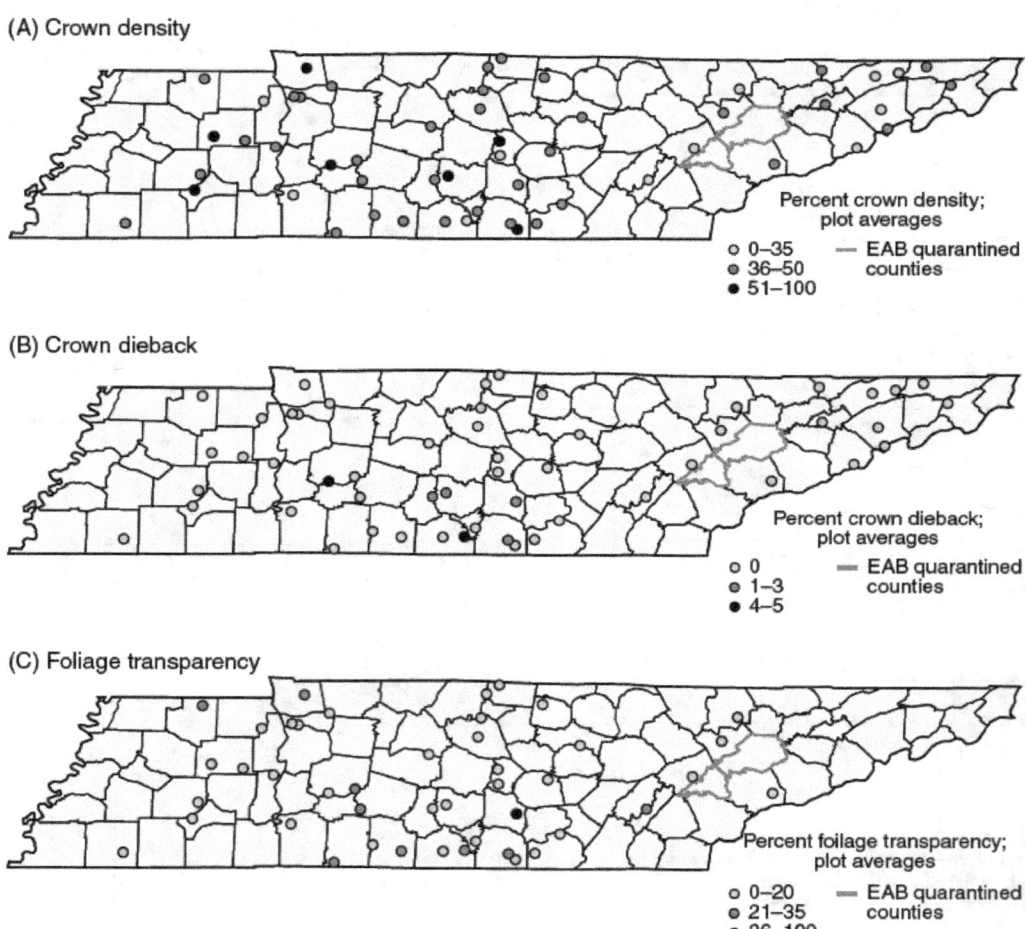

Figure 94—Mean crown conditions by plot for ash trees and emerald ash borer (EAB) quarantined counties, Tennessee, 2009 (A) Crown density, (B) Crown dieback, (C) Foliage transparency. (Plot locations are approximate.)

106

(A) Crown density

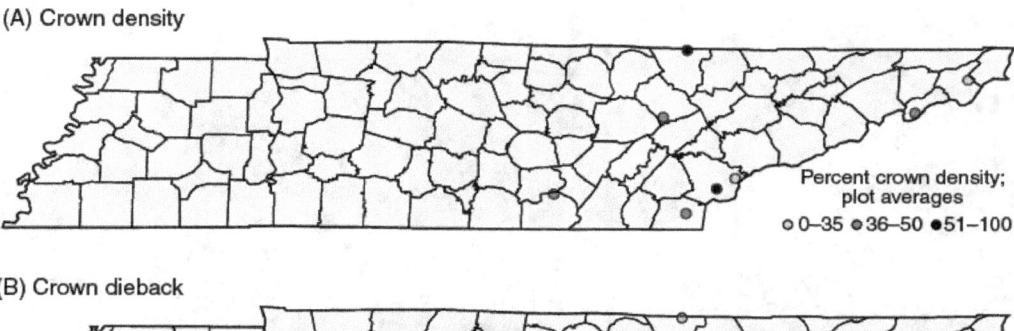

Percent crown density;
plot averages
o 0–35 ◐ 36–50 ● 51–100

(B) Crown dieback

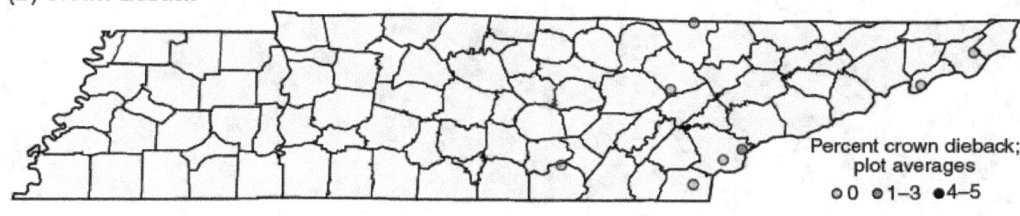

Percent crown dieback;
plot averages
o 0 ◐ 1–3 ● 4–5

(C) Foliage transparency

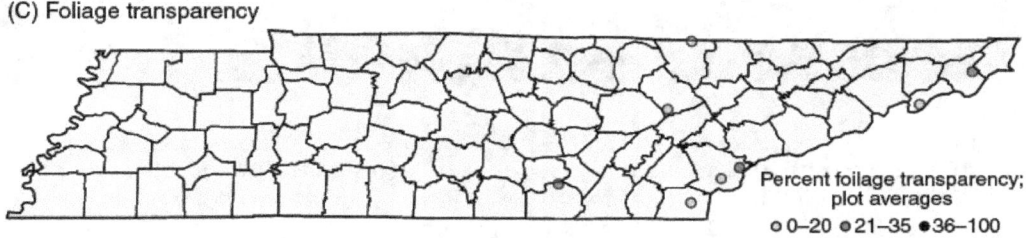

Percent foilage transparency;
plot averages
o 0–20 ◐ 21–35 ● 36–100

Figure 95—Mean crown conditions by plot for eastern hemlock trees, Tennessee, 2009 (A) Crown density, (B) Crown dieback, (C) Foliage transparency. (Plot locations are approximate.)

Emerging Threats

Recent announcements have revealed that both the EAB and TCD have been found in east Tennessee. This is in addition to the relatively recent threat of the Hemlock woolly adelgid. The EAB is a nonnative invasive beetle that has caused ash (*Fraxinus* spp.) mortality in the United States since it was first discovered in Michigan in 2002. EAB is considered a significant threat to ash trees in Tennessee. TCD is a pest complex (caused by a fungus (*Geosmithia* sp. *nov.*) and transported by the walnut twig beetle (*Pityophthorus juglandis*) that has caused walnut mortality in many western States. The recent observation of TCD in east Tennessee is the first within the native range of black walnut and poses a serious threat to the species in Tennessee and the Eastern United States.

Hemlock woolly adelgid (*Adelges tsugae*). (photo by Chris Evans, Bugwood.org)

In Tennessee, TCD poses a threat to the estimated 29 million black walnut trees (≥1-inch d.b.h.) found in the State. In addition, the estimated 224 million cubic feet of wood volume found in trees ≥5 inches d.b.h., if lost to TCD, would amount to a significant economic loss to industry professionals and Tennessee landowners interested in black walnut wood products. Black walnut is primarily found in the Central and East regions of Tennessee (fig. 96). Populations appear to be largest in the Central FIA unit (fig. 97). A quarantine that limits the transport of potentially infected wood material has been placed on several counties in the area. About 6 percent of the statewide total volume is located in the TCD quarantine counties, while an additional 9 percent is located within the buffer regulated counties.

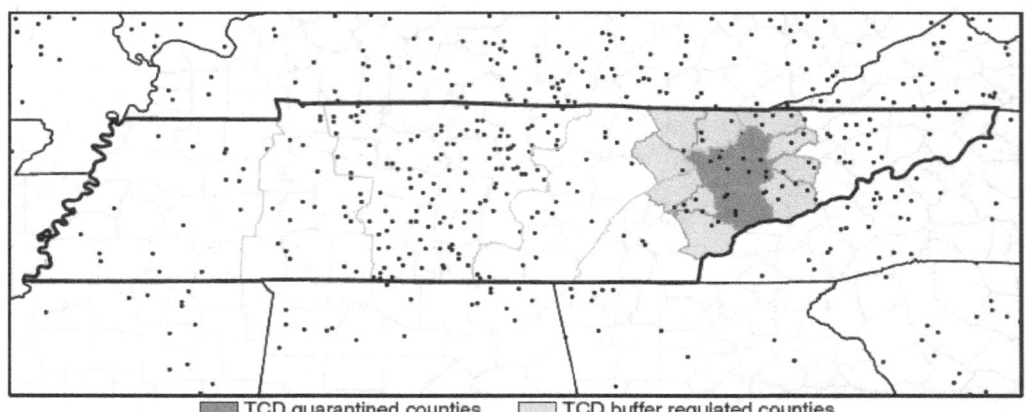

■ TCD quarantined counties   □ TCD buffer regulated counties

Figure 96—Black walnut (*Juglans nigra*) distribution and thousand cankers disease (TCD) quarantined and buffer regulated counties, Tennessee, 2009. (Plot locations are approximate.)

Figure 97—Population of walnut species on forest land by county, Tennessee, 2009.

Ash trees are found throughout the State (fig. 98). EAB could potentially have a much larger impact because the ash resource is much larger in Tennessee than the walnut resource. In 2009, ash species accounted for a total of 926 million cubic feet of standing wood volume in over 61 million trees $\geq$5 inches d.b.h. Currently, <1 percent of ash volume is located within the EAB quarantined counties with the largest populations in the West and Central FIA units (fig. 99).

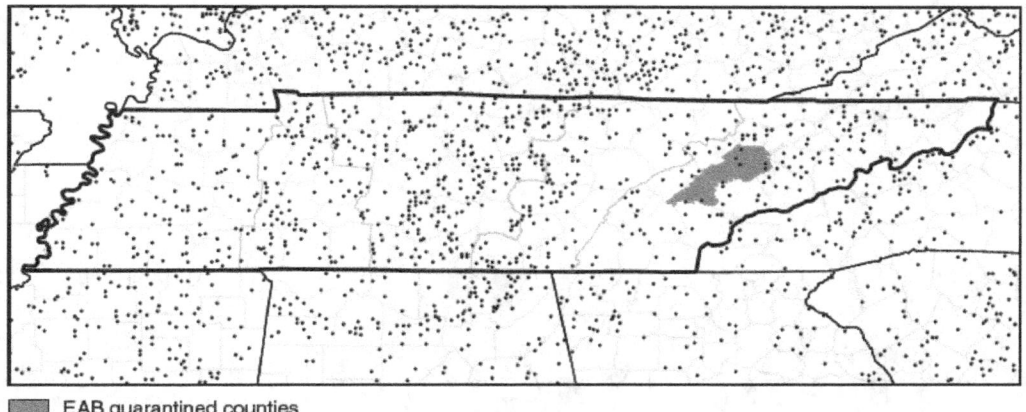

▨ EAB quarantined counties

Figure 98—Ash (*Fraxinus* spp.) distribution and emerald ash borer (EAB) quarantined counties, Tennessee, 2009. (Plot locations are approximate.)

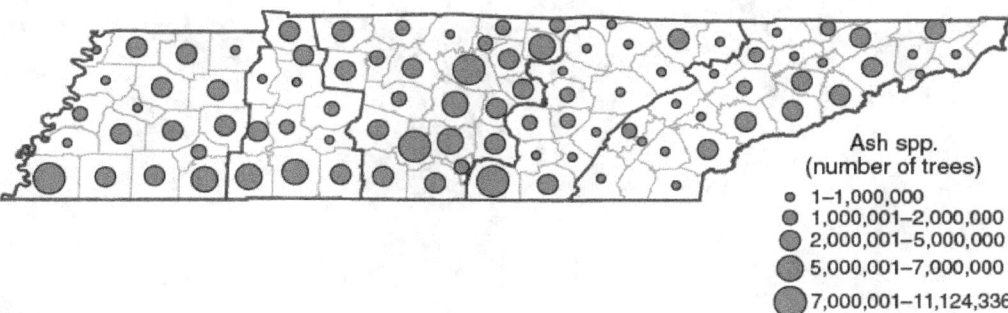

Figure 99—Population of ash species on forest land by county, Tennessee, 2009.

The hemlock woolly adelgid, while present in Western North America since 1924, was first reported in the Eastern United States in 1951 near Richmond, Virginia. In the absence of natural control elements, this introduced insect pest attacks on both eastern (Canadian) and Carolina hemlock, which are often damaged and killed within a few years of becoming infested. The hemlock woolly adelgid is now established from northeastern Georgia to southeastern Maine, and as far west as eastern Kentucky and Tennessee. Species of hemlock are found only in the East and Plateau FIA units (fig. 100), and therefore this threat is limited to the eastern regions of the State's forests.

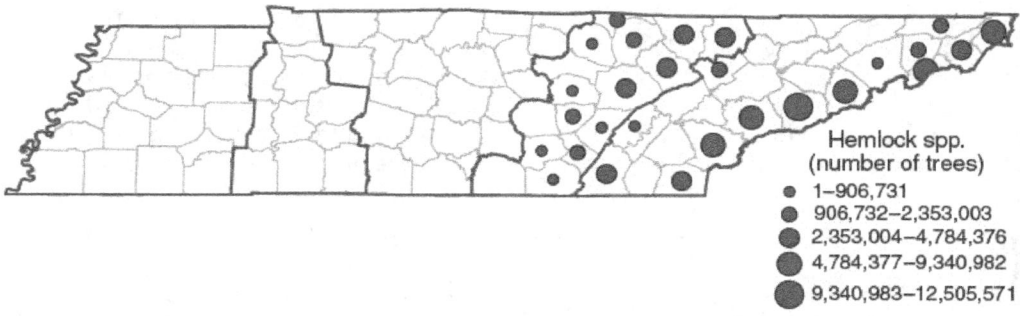

Hemlock spp.
(number of trees)

- 1–906,731
- 906,732–2,353,003
- 2,353,004–4,784,376
- 4,784,377–9,340,982
- 9,340,983–12,505,571

Figure 100—Population of hemlock species on forest land by county, Tennessee, 2009.

Adult emerald ash borer (*Agrilus planipennis*). (photo by David Cappaert, Michigan State University)

American Society for Quality Control. 1994. American national standard: specifications and guidelines for quality systems for environmental data collection and environmental technology programs. ANSI/ASQC E4–1994. Milwaukee, WI: American Society for Quality Control, Energy and Environmental Quality Division, Environmental Issues Group. 32 p.

Baskin, J.M.; Baskin, C.C. 2003. The vascular flora of cedar glades of the Southeastern United States and its phytogeographical relationships. The Journal of the Torrey Botanical Society. 130(2): 101–118.

Bate, L.J.; Torgersen, T.R.; Wisdom, M.J.; Garton, E.O. 2004. Performance of sampling methods to estimate log characteristics for wildlife. Forest Ecology and Management. 199(1): 83–102.

Bechtold, W.A.; Patterson, P.L., eds. 2005. The enhanced forest inventory and analysis program—national sampling design and estimation procedures. Gen. Tech. Rep. SRS–80.Asheville, NC: U.S. Department of Agriculture Forest Service Southern Research Station. 85 p.

Beers, T.W.; Miller, C.L. 1964. Point sampling: research results, theory, and applications. Res. Bull. 786. West Lafayette, IN: Purdue University Agricultural Experiment Station. 56 p.

Bentley, J.W.; Schnabel, D. 2007. Tennessee's timber industry—an assessment of timber product output and use, 2005. Resour. Bull. SRS–126. Asheville, NC: U.S. Department of Agriculture Forest Service Southern Research Station. 31 p.

Bentley, J.W.; Johnson, T.G.; Schnabel, D. 2011. Tennessee's timber industry—an assessment of timber product output and use, 2009. Resour. Bull. SRS–173. Asheville, NC: U.S. Department of Agriculture Forest Service Southern Research Station. 28 p.

Franklin, J.F.; Cromack, K., Jr.; Denison, W. [and others]. 1981. Ecological characteristics of old-growth douglas-fir forests. Gen. Tech. Rep. PNW–118. Portland, OR: U.S. Department of Agriculture Forest Service, Pacific Northwest Research Station. 48 p.

Hanks, L.F. 1976. Hardwood tree grades for factory lumber. Res. Pap. NE–333. Broomall, PA: U.S. Department of Agriculture Forest Service Northeastern Forest Experiment Station. 81 p.

Johnson, T.G.; Bentley, J.W.; Howell, M. 2009. The South's timber industry—an assessment of timber product output and use, 2007. Resour. Bull. SRS–164. Asheville, NC: U.S. Department of Agriculture Forest Service Southern Research Station. 52 p.

Mannan, R.W.; Conner, R.N.; Marcot, B.; Peek, J.M. 1996. Managing forest lands for wildlife. In: Bookhout, T.A., ed. Research and management techniques for wildlife and habitats. Bethesda, MD: The Wildlife Society: 689–721.

Mathison, R.M.: Schnabel, D. 2009. Tennessee's timber industry—an assessment of timber product output and use, 2007. Resour. Bull. SRS–152. Asheville, NC: U.S. Department of Agriculture Forest Service Southern Research Station. 29 p.

Millers, I.; Shriner, D.; Rizzo, D. 1989. History of hardwood decline in the Eastern United States. Gen. Tech. Rep. NE–126. Radnor, PA: U.S. Department of Agriculture Forest Service Northeastern Forest Experiment Station. 75 p.

Minnesota IMPLAN Group, Inc. 2009. IMPLAN system (data and software). Hudson, WI: Minnesota IMPLAN Group, Inc. www.implan.com. [Date accessed unknown].

Minnesota IMPLAN Group, Inc. 2011. Glossary of terms. http://implan. com/V4/indes.php?option=com_ glossary&Itemid=12. [Date accessed unknown].

Oliver, C.D.; Larson, B.C. 1990. Forest stand dynamics. New York: McGraw-Hill. 467 p.

Oswalt, C.M.; Oswalt, S.N.; Johnson, T.G. [and others]. 2009. Tennessee's forests, 2004. Resour. Bull. SRS–144. Asheville, NC: U.S. Department of Agriculture Forest Service Southern Research Station. 96 p.

Oswalt, S.N.; Johnson, T.G.; Howell, M.; Bentley, J.W. 2009. Fluctuations in national forest timber harvest and removals: the southern regional perspective. Resour. Bull. SRS–148. Asheville, NC: U.S. Department of Agriculture Forest Service Southern Research Station. 30 p.

Perlack, R.D.; Wright, L.L.; Turhollow, A. [and others]. 2005. Biomass as feed-stock for a bioenergy and bioproducts industry: the technical feasibility of a billion-ton annual supply. Washington, DC: U.S. Department of Energy and U.S. Department of Agriculture Forest Service. ORNL/TM-2005/6. 673 p. http:// www1.eere.energy.gov/biomass/pdfs/ final billionton_vision_report2.pdf. [Date accessed unknown].

Reams, G.A.; Smith, W.D.; Hansen, M.H. [and others]. 2005. The forest inventory and analysis sampling frame. In: Bechtold, W.A.; Patterson, P.L., eds. The enhanced forest inventory and analysis program—national sampling design and estimation procedures. Gen. Tech. Rep. SRS–80. Asheville, NC: U.S. Department of Agriculture Forest Service Southern Research Station: 11–26.

Rosson, J.F., Jr.; Rose, A.K. 2010. Arkansas' forests, 2005. Resour. Bull. SRS–166. Asheville, NC: U.S. Department of Agriculture Forest Service Southern Research Station. 126 p.

Smith, G.C.; Smith, W.D.; Coulston, J.W. 2007. Ozone bioindicator sampling and estimation. Gen. Tech. Rep. NRS–20. Newtown Square, PA: U.S. Department of Agriculture Forest Service, Northern Research Station. 34 p.

U.S. Department of Agriculture Forest Service. 2004a. National report on sustainable forest—2003. For. Serv. Publ. FS–766. Washington, DC: U.S. Department of Agriculture Forest Service, Washington Office. 139 p.

U.S. Department of Agriculture Forest Service. 2004b. White paper, forest products marketing and utilization report. U.S. Department of Agriculture Forest Service, Region 8, State and Private Forestry Technology Marketing Unit Forest Products Laboratory, and Southern Group of State Foresters. Un-published report. On file with: Southern Research Station, Forest Inventory and Analysis, 4700 Old Kingston Pike, Knoxville, TN 37919.

U.S. Department of Commerce, Bureau of Economic Analysis. 2011. Regional economic accounts. http://www.bea. gov/regional/index.htm. [Date accessed unknown].

Waddell, K.L. 2002. Sampling coarse woody debris for multiple attributes in extensive resource inventories. Ecological Indicators. 1(3): 139–153.

Zarnoch, S.J.; Turner, J.A. 2005. Adjustments to forest inventory and analysis estimates of 2001 saw-log volumes for Kentucky. Res. Pap. SRS–38. Asheville, NC: U.S. Department of Agriculture Forest Service Southern Research Station. 4 p.

Fire pink (*Silene virginica*) is often found in forests of Tennessee. (www.forestryimages.org)

Afforestation—Area of land previously classified as nonforest that is converted to forest by planting of trees or by natural reversion to forest.

Average annual mortality—Average annual volume of trees ≥5.0 inches d.b.h. that died from natural causes during the intersurvey period.

Average annual removals—Average annual volume of trees ≥5.0 inches d.b.h. removed from the inventory by harvesting, cultural operations (such as timber-stand improvement), land clearing, or changes in land use during the intersurvey period.

Average net annual growth—Average annual net change in volume of trees ≥5.0 inches d.b.h. in the absence of cutting (gross growth minus mortality) during the intersurvey period.

Basal area—The area in square feet of the cross section at breast height of a single tree or of all the trees in a stand, usually expressed in square feet per acre.

Bioindicator species—A tree, woody shrub, or nonwoody herb species that responds to ambient levels of ozone pollution with distinctive visible foliar symptoms.

Biomass—The aboveground fresh weight of solid wood and bark in live trees ≥1.0-inch d.b.h. from the ground to the tip of the tree. All foliage is excluded. The weight of wood and bark in lateral limbs, secondary limbs, and twigs <0.5 inch in diameter at the point of occurrence on sapling-size trees is included but is excluded on poletimber and sawtimber-size trees.

Blind check—A remeasurement done by a qualified inspection crew without production crew data on hand; a full remeasurement of the plot is recommended for the purpose of obtaining a measure of data quality. If a full plot remeasurement is not possible, then it is strongly recommended that at least two full subplots be completely remeasured along with all the plot level information. The two datasets are maintained separately. Discrepancies between the two sets of data are not reconciled. Blind checks are done on production plots only. This procedure provides a quality assessment and evaluation function. The statistics band recommends a random subset of plots be chosen for remeasurement.

Bole—That portion of a tree between a 1-foot stump and a 4-inch top d.o.b. in trees ≥5.0 inches d.b.h.

Census water—Streams, sloughs, estuaries, canals, and other moving bodies of water ≥200-feet wide, and lakes, reservoirs, ponds, and other permanent bodies of water ≥4.5 acres in area.

Coarse woody debris or coarse woody material—Down pieces of wood leaning >45 degrees from vertical with a diameter of at least 3.0 inches and a length of at least 3.0 feet (decay classes 1 through 4). Decay class 5 pieces must be at least 5.0 inches in diameter, at least 5.0 inches high from the ground, and at least 3.0 feet in length.

Cold check—An inspection done either as part of the training process, or as part of the ongoing QC program. Normally the installation crew is not present at the time of inspection. The inspector has the completed data in hand at the time of inspection. The inspection can include the whole plot or a subset of the plot. Data errors are corrected. Cold checks are done on production plots only. This type of quality control measurement is a "blind" measurement in that the crews do not know when or which of their plots will be remeasured by the inspection crew and cannot therefore alter their performance because of knowledge that the plot is a QA plot.

Compacted area—Type of compaction measured as part of the soil indicator. Examples include the junction areas of skid trails, landing areas, work areas, etc.

Condition class—The combination of discrete landscape and forest attributes that identify, define, and stratify the area associated with a plot. Examples of such attributes include condition status, forest type, stand origin, stand size, owner group, reserve status, and stand density.

Crown—The part of a tree or woody plant bearing live branches or foliage.

Crown density—The amount of crown stem, branches, twigs, shoots, buds, foliage, and reproductive structures that block light penetration through the visible crown. Dead branches and dead tops are part of the crown. Live and dead branches below the live crown base are excluded. Broken or missing tops are visually reconstructed when forming this crown outline by comparing outlines of adjacent healthy trees of the same species and d.b.h./d.r.c. (root collar diameter).

Crown dieback—This is recent mortality of branches with fine twigs, which begins at the terminal portion of a branch and proceeds toward the trunk. Dieback is only considered when it occurs in the upper and outer portions of the tree. When whole branches are dead in the upper crown, without obvious signs of damage such as breaks or animal injury, assume that the branches died from the terminal portion of the branch. Dead branches in the lower portion of the live crown are assumed to have died from competition and shading. Dead branches in the lower live crown are not considered part of crown dieback, unless there is continuous dieback from the upper and outer crown down to those branches.

D.b.h. (diameter at breast height)—Tree diameter in inches (outside bark) at breast height (4.5 feet aboveground).

Decay class—Qualitative assessment of stage of decay (5 classes) of coarse woody debris based on visual assessments of color of wood, presence/absence of twigs and branches, texture of rotten portions, and structural integrity.

Diameter class—A classification of trees based on tree d.b.h. Two-inch diameter classes are commonly used by FIA, with the even inch as the approximate midpoint for a class. For example, the 6-inch class includes trees 5.0–6.9 inches d.b.h.

D.o.b. (diameter outside bark)—Stem diameter including bark.

Down woody material (DWM)—Woody pieces of trees and shrubs that have been uprooted (no longer supporting growth) or severed from their root system, not self-supporting, and are lying on the ground. Previous named down woody debris (DWD).

Duff—A soil layer dominated by organic material derived from the decomposition of plant and animal litter and deposited on either an organic or a mineral surface. This layer is distinguished from the litter layer in that the original organic material has undergone sufficient decomposition that the source of this material (e.g., individual plant parts) can no longer be identified.

Effective cation exchange capacity (ECEC)—The sum of cations that a soil can adsorb in its natural pH. Expressed in units of centimoles of positive charge per kilogram of soil.

Erosion—The wearing away of the land surface by running water, wind, ice, or other geological agents.

Fine woody debris or fine woody material—Down pieces of wood with a diameter <3.0 inches, not including foliage or bark fragments.

Foliage transparency—The amount of skylight visible through micro-holes in the live portion of the crown, i.e. where you see foliage, normal or damaged, or remnants of its recent presence. Recently defoliated branches are included in foliage transparency measurements. Macro-holes are excluded unless they are the result of recent defoliation. Dieback and dead branches are always excluded from the estimate. Foliage transparency is different from crown density because it emphasizes foliage and ignores stems, branches, fruits, and holes in the crown.

Forest floor—The entire thickness of organic material overlying the mineral soil, consisting of the litter and the duff (humus).

Forest land—Land at least 10 percent stocked by forest trees of any size, or formerly having had such tree cover, and not currently developed for nonforest use. The minimum area considered for classification is 1 acre. Forested strips must be at least 120-feet wide.

Forest management type—A classification of timberland based on forest type and stand origin.

Pine plantation—Stands that (1) have been artificially regenerated by planting or direct seeding, (2) are classed as a pine or other softwood forest type, and (3) have at least 10-percent stocking.

Natural pine—Stands that (1) have not been artificially regenerated, (2) are classed as a pine or other softwood forest type, and (3) have at least 10-percent stocking.

Oak-pine—Stands that have at least 10-percent stocking and classed as a forest type of oak-pine.

Upland hardwood—Stands that have at least 10-percent stocking and classed as an oak-hickory or maple-beech-birch forest type.

Lowland hardwood—Stands that have at least 10-percent stocking with a forest type of oak-gum-cypress, elm-ash-cottonwood, palm, or other tropical.

Nonstocked stands—Stands <10 percent stocked with live trees.

Forest type—A classification of forest land based on the species forming a plurality of live-tree stocking. Major eastern forest-type groups are:

White-red-jack pine—Forests in which eastern white pine, red pine, or jack pine, singly or in combination, constitute a plurality of the stocking. (Common associates include hemlock, birch, and maple.)

Spruce-fir—Forests in which spruce or true firs, singly or in combination, constitute a plurality of the stocking. (Common associates include maple, birch, and hemlock.)

Longleaf-slash pine—Forests in which longleaf or slash pine, singly or in combination, constitute a plurality of the stocking. (Common associates include oak, hickory, and gum.)

Loblolly-shortleaf pine—Forests in which loblolly pine, shortleaf pine, or other southern yellow pines, except longleaf or slash pine, singly or in combination, constitute a plurality of the stocking. (Common associates include oak, hickory, and gum.)

Oak-pine—Forests in which hardwoods (usually upland oaks) constitute a plurality of the stocking but in which pines account for 25 to 50 percent of the stocking. (Common associates include gum, hickory, and yellow-poplar.)

Oak-hickory—Forests in which upland oaks or hickory, singly or in combination, constitute a plurality of the stocking, except where pines account for 25 to 50 percent, in which case the stand would be classified oak-pine. (Common associates include yellow-poplar, elm, maple, and black walnut.)

Oak-gum-cypress—Bottomland forests in which tupelo, blackgum, sweetgum, oaks, or southern cypress, singly or in combination, constitute a plurality of the stocking, except where pines account for 25 to 50 percent of stocking, in which case the stand would be classified as oak-pine. (Common associates include cottonwood, willow, ash, elm, hackberry, and maple.)

Elm-ash-cottonwood—Forests in which elm, ash, or cottonwood, singly or in combination, constitute a plurality of the stocking. (Common associates include willow, sycamore, beech, and maple.)

Maple-beech-birch—Forests in which maple, beech, or yellow birch, singly or in combination, constitute a plurality of the stocking. (Common associates include hemlock, elm, basswood, and white pine.)

Nonstocked stands—Stands <10 percent stocked with live trees.

Forested tract size—The area of forest within the contiguous tract containing each FIA sample plot.

Fresh weight—Mass of tree component at time of cutting.

Fuel bed—Accumulated mass of all DWM components above the top of the duff layer. The fuel bed does not include live shrubs or herbs.

Fuel hour classes—Fuel classes defined by the approximate amount of time it takes for moisture conditions to fluctuate. Larger coarse woody material will takes longer to dry out than smaller fine woody pieces (Small = 1 hour, Medium = 10 hour, Large = 100 hour, Coarse woody material = 1,000 hour).

Gross growth—Annual increase in volume of trees ≥5.0 inches d.b.h. in the absence of cutting and mortality. (Gross growth includes survivor growth, ingrowth, growth on ingrowth, growth on removals before removal, and growth on mortality before death.)

Growing-stock trees—Living trees of commercial species classified as sawtimber, poletimber, saplings, and seedlings. Trees must contain at least one 12-foot or two 8-foot logs in the saw-log portion, currently or potentially (if too small to qualify), to be classed as growing stock. The log(s) must meet dimension and merchantability standards to qualify. Trees must also have, currently or potentially, one-third of the gross board-foot volume in sound wood.

Growing-stock volume—The cubic-foot volume of sound wood in growing-stock trees ≥5.0 inches d.b.h. from a 1-foot stump to a minimum 4.0-inch top d.o.b. of the central stem.

Hardwoods—Dicotyledonous trees, usually broadleaf and deciduous.

Soft hardwoods—Hardwood species with an average specific gravity of ≤0.50, such as gums, yellow-poplar, cottonwoods, red maple, basswoods, and willows.

Hard hardwoods—Hardwood species with an average specific gravity >0.50, such as oaks, hard maples, hickories, and beech.

Hexagonal grid (Hex)—A hexagonal grid formed from equilateral triangles for the purpose of tessellating the FIA inventory sample. Each hexagon in the base grid has an area of 5,937 acres (2,403.6 ha) and contains one inventory plot. The base grid can be subdivided into smaller hexagons to intensify the sample.

Humus—A soil layer dominated by organic material derived from the decomposition of plant and animal litter and deposited on either an organic or a mineral surface. This layer is distinguished from the litter layer in that the original organic material has undergone sufficient decomposition that the source of this material (e.g., individual plant parts) can no longer be identified.

Land area—The area of dry land and land temporarily or partly covered by water, such as marshes, swamps, and river floodplains (omitting tidal flats below mean high tide), streams, sloughs, estuaries, and canals <200-feet wide, and lakes, reservoirs, and ponds <4.5 acres in area.

Lichen—An organism generally appearing to be a single small leafy, tufted or crust-like plant that consists of a fungus and an alga or cyanobacterium living in symbiotic association.

Lichen community indicator—The set of macrolichen species collected on a FIA lichen plot using standard protocols, which serves as an indicator of ecological condition (e.g., air quality or climate) of the plot.

Lichen plot—The FIA lichen plot is a circular area, total 0.935 acre (0.4 ha), with a 120-foot (36.6 m) radius centered on subplot 1, and excluding the 4 subplots.

Litter—Undecomposed or only partially decomposed organic material that can be readily identified (e.g., plant leaves, twigs, etc.).

Live trees—All living trees. All size classes, all tree classes, and both commercial and noncommercial species are included.

Measurement quality objective (MQO)—A data user's estimate of the precision, bias, and completeness of data necessary to satisfy a prescribed application (e.g., Resource Planning Act, assessments by State foresters, forest planning, forest health analyses). Describes the acceptable tolerance for each data element. MQOs consist of two parts: a statement of the tolerance and a percentage of time when the collected data are required to be within tolerance. Measurement quality objectives can only be assigned where standard methods of sampling or field measurements exist, or where experience has established upper or lower bounds on precision or bias. Measurement quality objectives can be set for measured data elements, observed data elements, and derived data elements.

Mineral soil—A soil consisting predominantly of products derived from the weathering of rocks (e.g., sands, silts, and clays).

Net annual change—Increase or decrease in volume of live trees ≥5.0 inches d.b.h. Net annual change is equal to net annual growth minus average annual removals.

Noncommercial species—Tree species of typically small size, poor form, or inferior quality that normally do not develop into trees suitable for industrial wood products.

Nonforest land—Land that has never supported forests and land formerly forested where timber production is precluded by development for other uses.

Nonstocked stands—Stands <10 percent stocked with live trees.

Other forest land—Forest land other than timberland and productive reserved forest land. It includes available and reserved forest land which is incapable of producing annually 20 cubic feet per acre of industrial wood under natural conditions, because of adverse site conditions such as sterile soils, dry climate, poor drainage, high elevation, steepness, or rockiness.

Other removals—The growing-stock volume of trees removed from the inventory by cultural operations such as timber stand improvement, land clearing, and other changes in land use, resulting in the removal of the trees from timberland.

Ozone. O₃—A gaseous air pollutant produced primarily through sunlight-driven chemical reactions of NO_2 and hydrocarbons in the atmosphere and causing foliar injury to deciduous trees, conifers, shrubs, and herbaceous species.

Ozone bioindicator site—An open area in which ozone injury to ozone-sensitive species is evaluated. The area must meet certain site selection guidelines regarding size, condition, and plant counts to be used for ozone injury evaluations in FIA.

Ownership—The property owned by one ownership unit, including all parcels of land in the United States.

National forest land—Federal land that has been legally designated as national forests or purchase units, and other land under the administration of the Forest Service, including experimental areas and Bankhead-Jones Title III land.

Forest industry land—Land owned by companies or individuals operating primary wood-using plants.

Nonindustrial private forest land—Privately owned land excluding forest industry land.

Corporate—Owned by corporations, including incorporated farm ownerships.

Individual—All lands owned by individuals, including farm operators.

Other public—An ownership class that includes all public lands except national forests.

Miscellaneous Federal land—Federal land other than national forests.

State, county, and municipal land—Land owned by States, counties, and local public agencies or municipalities or land leased to these governmental units for ≥50 years.

Phase 1 (P1)—FIA activities related to remote-sensing, the primary purpose of which is to label plots and obtain stratum weights for population estimates.

Phase 2 (P2)—FIA activities conducted on the network of ground plots. The primary purpose is to obtain field data that enable classification and summarization of area, tree, and other attributes associated with forest land uses.

Phase 3 (P3)—FIA activities conducted on a subset of phase 2 plots. Additional attributes related to forest health are measured on phase 3 plots.

Poletimber-size trees—Softwoods 5.0 to 8.9 inches d.b.h. and hardwoods 5.0 to 10.9 inches d.b.h.

Productive-reserved forest land—Forest land sufficiently productive to qualify as timberland but withdrawn from timber utilization through statute or administrative regulation.

Quality assurance (QA)—The total integrated program for ensuring that the uncertainties inherent in FIA data are known and do not exceed acceptable magnitudes, within a stated level of confidence. Quality assurance encompasses the plans, specifications, and policies affecting the collection, processing, and reporting of data. It is the system of activities designed to provide program managers and project leaders with independent assurance that total system quality control is being effectively implemented.

Quality control (QC)—The routine application of prescribed field and laboratory procedures (e.g., random check cruising, periodic calibration, instrument maintenance, use of certified standards, etc.) in order to reduce random and systematic errors and ensure that data are generated within known and acceptable performance limits. Quality control also ensures the use of qualified personnel; reliable equipment and supplies; training of personnel; good field and laboratory practices; and strict adherence to standard operating procedures.

Reforestation—Area of land previously classified as forest that is regenerated by tree planting or natural regeneration.

Rotten trees—Live trees of commercial species not containing at least one 12-foot saw log, or two noncontiguous saw logs, each ≥8 feet, now or prospectively, primarily because of rot or missing sections, and with less than one-third of the gross board-foot tree volume in sound material.

Rough trees—Live trees of commercial species not containing at least one 12-foot saw log, or two noncontiguous saw logs, each ≥8 feet, now or prospectively, primarily because of roughness, poor form, splits, and cracks, and with less than one-third of the gross board-foot tree volume in sound material; and live trees of noncommercial species.

Sapling—Live trees 1.0 to 4.9 inches (2.5 to 12.5 cm) in diameter (d.b.h.).

Saw log—A log meeting minimum standards of diameter, length, and defect, including logs ≥8-feet long, sound and straight, with a minimum diameter inside bark for softwoods of 6 inches (8 inches for hardwoods).

Saw-log portion—The part of the bole of sawtimber trees between a 1-foot stump and the saw-log top.

Saw-log top—The point on the bole of sawtimber trees above which a conventional saw log cannot be produced. The minimum saw-log top is 7.0 inches d.o.b. for softwoods and 9.0 inches d.o.b. for hardwoods.

Sawtimber-size trees—Softwoods ≥9.0 inches d.b.h. and hardwoods ≥11.0 inches d.b.h.

Sawtimber volume—Growing-stock volume in the saw-log portion of sawtimber-size trees in board feet (International ¼-inch rule).

Seedlings—Trees <1.0-inch d.b.h. and >1-foot tall for hardwoods, >6 inches tall for softwoods, and >0.5 inch in diameter at ground level for longleaf pine.

Select red oaks—A group of several red oak species composed of cherrybark, Shumard, and northern red oaks. Other red oak species are included in the "other red oaks" group.

Select white oaks—A group of several white oak species composed of white, swamp chestnut, swamp white, chinkapin, Durand, and bur oaks. Other white oak species are included in the "other white oaks" group.

Site class—A classification of forest land in terms of potential capacity to grow crops of industrial wood based on fully stocked natural stands.

Softwoods—Coniferous trees, usually evergreen, having leaves that are needles or scalelike.

Yellow pines—Loblolly, longleaf, slash, pond, shortleaf, pitch, Virginia, sand, spruce, and Table Mountain pines.

Other softwoods—Cypress, eastern red-cedar, white-cedar, eastern white pine, eastern hemlock, spruce, and fir.

Soil bulk density—The mass of soil per unit volume. A measure of the ratio of pore space to solid materials in a given soil. Expressed in grams per cubic cm of oven dry soil.

Soil compaction—A reduction in soil pore space caused by heavy equipment or by repeated passes of light equipment that compress the soil and break down soil aggregates. Compaction disturbs the soil structure and can cause decreased tree growth, increased water runoff, and soil erosion.

Soil texture—The relative proportions of sand, silt, and clay in a soil.

Stand age—The average age of dominant and codominant trees in the stand.

Stand origin—A classification of forest stands describing their means of origin.

Planted—Planted or artificially seeded.

Natural—No evidence of artificial regeneration.

Stand-size class—A classification of forest land based on the diameter class distribution of live trees in the stand.

Sawtimber stands—Stands at least 10 percent stocked with live trees, with one-half or more of total stocking in sawtimber and poletimber trees, and with sawtimber stocking at least equal to poletimber stocking.

Poletimber stands—Stands at least 10 percent stocked with live trees, with one-half or more of total stocking in poletimber and sawtimber trees, and with poletimber stocking exceeding sawtimber stocking.

Sapling-seedling stands—Stands at least 10 percent stocked with live trees, in which saplings and seedlings account for more than one-half of total stocking.

Nonstocked stands—Stands <10 percent stocked with live trees.

Stocking—The degree of occupancy of land by trees, measured by basal area or the number of trees in a stand and spacing in the stand, compared with a minimum standard, depending on tree size, required to fully utilize the growth potential of the land.

Density of trees and basal area per acre required for full stocking:

D.b.h. class	Trees per acre for full stocking	Basal area
inches		square feet per acre
Seedlings (<1 inch)	600	—
2	560	—
4	460	—
6	340	67
8	240	84
10	155	85
12	115	90
14	90	96
16	72	101
18	60	106
20	51	111

— = not applicable.

Timberland—Forest land capable of producing 20 cubic feet of industrial wood per acre per year and not withdrawn from timber utilization.

Transect diameter—Diameter of a coarse woody piece at the point of intersection with a sampling plane.

Tree—Woody plant having one erect perennial stem or trunk ≥3 inches d.b.h., a more or less definitely formed crown of foliage, and a height of ≥13 feet (at maturity).

Tree grade—A classification of the saw-log portion of sawtimber trees based on: (1) the grade of the butt log or (2) the ability to produce at least one 12-foot or two 8-foot logs in the upper section of the saw-log portion. Tree grade is an indicator of quality; grade 1 is the best quality.

Upper-stem portion—The part of the main stem or fork of sawtimber trees above the saw-log top to a minimum top diameter of 4.0 inches outside bark or to the point where the main stem or fork breaks into limbs.

Vigor class—A visual assessment of the apparent crown vigor of saplings. The purpose is to separate excellent saplings with superior crowns from stressed individuals with poor crowns.

Volume of live trees—The cubic-foot volume of sound wood in live trees ≥5.0 inches d.b.h. from a 1-foot stump to a minimum 4.0-inch top d.o.b. of the central stem.

Volume of saw-log portion of sawtimber trees—The cubic-foot volume of sound wood in the saw-log portion of sawtimber trees. Volume is the net result after deductions for rot, sweep, and other defects that affect use for lumber.

South Fork of Citico Creek located in Citico Creek Wilderness within the Cherokee National Forest in Monroe County, Tennessee.

Data Sources and Techniques

A State-by-State inventory of the Nation's forest land began in the mid-1930s. These surveys primarily were designed and conducted to provide estimates of forest area, wood volume, tree growth, removals, and mortality. Throughout the years, numerous technical innovations and national concerns over perceived and real trends in forest resource conditions have led to many improvements (Reams and others 2005). The primary purpose for conducting forest inventories has remained unchanged, but the methods have undergone substantial change. The following is a general description of the current sample design used to collect the information and procedures used to derive the forest resource estimates provided in this report. A brief discussion of past sample designs and procedures is included to alert users to substantive changes.

The seventh survey of Tennessee's forest marked a shift in design, intensity, and timeliness of data collection. The Agricultural Research Extension and Education Reform Act of 1998 (Farm Bill) mandated

annual surveys of U.S. forests. The annual surveys feature: (1) a nationally consistent, fixed-radius, four-point plot configuration; (2) a systematic national sampling design consisting of a base grid of approximately 6,000-acre hexagons; (3) integration of the forest inventory and forest health monitoring sample designs; (4) annual measurement of a fixed proportion of permanent plots across the State; (5) reporting of data or data summaries within 6 months after yearly sampling; (6) an annual estimator based on a default 5-year moving average, with provisions for optional estimators based on techniques for updating information; and (7) a summary report every 5 years. Additional information about annual surveys is available at www.fia.fs.fed.us.

Current Sample Design

Current phase 1: forest area estimates—Following the 1999 inventory, Forest Inventory and Analysis (FIA) now bases the three phases of the current sampling method on a hex-grid design (fig. A.1) with each successive phase sampled with less intensity. There are 16 phase 2 hexes for every phase 3 hex, and 27 phase 1 hexes for

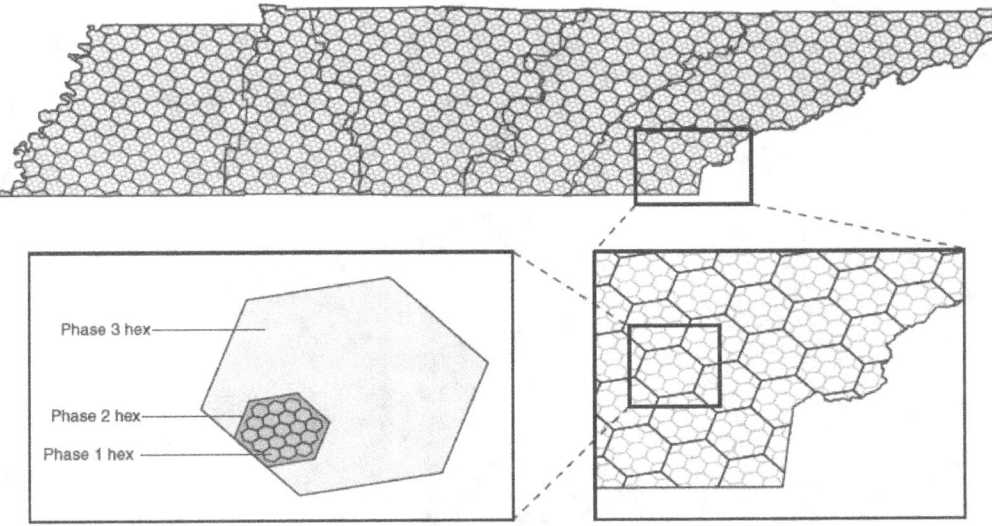

Figure A.1—The forest inventory and analysis hexagonal grid system for locating phase 1, 2, and 3 plots, Tennessee.

every phase 2 hex. Phase 1 hexes represent about 222 acres, while phase 2 and phase 3 hexes represent roughly 6,000 acres and 96,000 acres, respectively.

The current phase 1 design stratifies the land base into one of four distinct strata (1) interior forest, (2) nonforest, (3) forest edge, and (4) nonforest edge, based on pixel classification of the national land cover data. Forest edge and nonforest edge are assigned based primarily on classified pixels with considerations for the relative makeup of nearby pixel classifications. Forest edge signifies a forested pixel within a 2-pixel range of a forest/nonforest edge. Nonforest edge signifies a nonforest pixel within a 2-pixel range of a forest/nonforest edge. Forest area is then estimated by the summation of pixel counts across strata in conjunction with the mean area from the measured phase 2 plots. This method places significantly more weight on the phase 2 plots than in previous periodic inventories in Tennessee. The approach, through stratifying acreage into 'like' categories, improves the precision of the estimate or reduces the sample variance around the estimate.

Current phase 2: forest inventory—
In the 2009 inventory, the plot design employed a fixed-plot composed of four subplots spaced 120 feet apart (fig. A.2). The sample area of these four subplots was 1/6 of an acre, while the footprint of the cluster was about 1 acre. Trees ≥5.0 inches in diameter at breast height (d.b.h.) were measured on each subplot (1/24 of an acre; 24-foot radius). Trees 1.0–4.9 inches in d.b.h. and seedlings (<1.0 inch in d.b.h.) were measured on a microplot (1/300 of an acre; 6.8 foot radius) on each of the four subplots. The cluster of four fixed-area subplots sampled forest land at 2,344 ground sample locations.

A unique feature of this plot design was in the mapping of different land use and forest conditions that are encountered on the plot cluster. Since the plots were placed on the ground without bias, i.e., systematically but at a scale large enough so that placement could be considered random, there was a probability that the plot cluster might straddle more than one type of land use or forest condition. Furthermore, the four subplots were not relocated into the same land use. If a plot happened to straddle

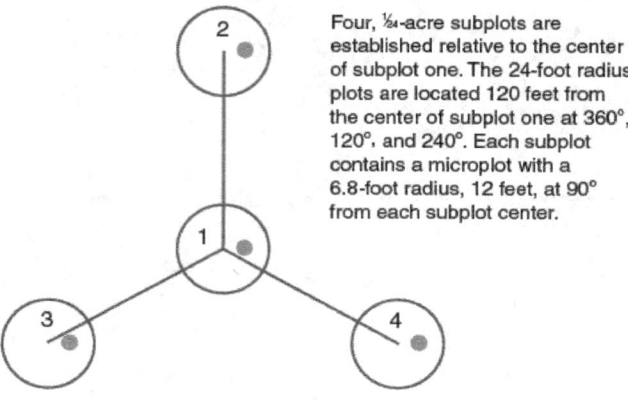

Four, ¼-acre subplots are established relative to the center of subplot one. The 24-foot radius plots are located 120 feet from the center of subplot one at 360°, 120°, and 240°. Each subplot contains a microplot with a 6.8-foot radius, 12 feet, at 90° from each subplot center.

Figure A.2—Layout of annual fixed-radius plot design. The cluster plot is a circle circumscribing the outer edge of the four subplots.

multiple land uses and forest conditions then the crew identified the differences encountered on the plot. There were two steps in the mapping process. The first step involved identifying forest and nonforest areas on the plot and establishing a boundary line on the plot if both were present. The second step involved identifying differing conditions in the forested portion of the plot based on six factors: forest type, stand size, ownership, stand density, regeneration status, and reserved status. These, too, were mapped into separate entities.

Estimates of growth, removals, and mortality were determined from the remeasurement of 2,119 permanent sample plots established in the previous inventory. Remeasurement information was used in the calculation of seven components of change: (1) survivor growth, (2) ingrowth, (3) growth on ingrowth, (4) mortality, (5) growth on mortality, (6) removals, and (7) growth on removals. Estimates of gross growth, net growth, and net change were made following Beers and Miller (1964).

Phase 3: forest health—In the 2009 inventory, forest health variables (phase 3) were collected on about 1/16th of the phase 2 sample plots. Phase 3 data are coarse

descriptions, and are meant to be used as general indicators of overall forest health over large geographic areas. This dataset was not collected in Tennessee until 2000 so there is no previous methodology to compare and contrast.

Phase 3 data collection includes variables pertaining to tree crown health, down woody material (DWM), foliar ozone injury, lichen diversity, and soil composition. Tree crown health, DWM, and soil composition measurements were collected using the same plot design used during phase 2 data collection, while lichen data were collected within a 120-foot radius circle centered on subplot 1 of each FIA phase 3 field plot.

Biomonitoring sites for ozone data collection were chosen based on specific criteria and were located independently of the FIA grid. Sites chosen were 1-acre fields or similar open areas adjacent to or surrounded by forest land, and contained a minimum of at least two identified bioindicator plant species (Smith and others 2007). Plants were evaluated for ozone injury, and voucher specimens were submitted to a regional expert for verification of ozone-induced foliar injury.

American chestnut (*Castanea dentata*) fall color. (photo by Chris Evans, Bugwood.org)

125

Annual versus Periodic

Previous surveys of Tennessee (prior to the year 2000) were done periodically; all of the plots were measured in 1 to 2 years with remeasurement about every 10 years. The current, annual inventory design was implemented to provide more up-to-date information about forest resources. The goal of the annual inventory system is to measure 20 percent (referred to as a panel or subcycle) of the total plots in the State each year so that all plots are measured within a 5-year period (one cycle). Each year's panel of plots is selected on a subgrid which is slightly offset from the previous year's plots, thus each year covers essentially the same sample area (both spatially and in intensity) as the prior year. In the sixth year, the plots that were measured in the first panel are remeasured. This marks the beginning of the next cycle of data collection.

After field measurements are completed, a cycle of data (consisting of data from five panels of plots) is available for a 5-year report. This dataset consists of data collected at different times: 20 percent of the data would be <1-year old, 20 percent >1- but <2-years old, etc.

One of the major impacts on data interpretation and analyses of switching to the annual inventory design is the length of time for data collection (5 years, versus 1 or 2 years). Data collected over a longer period of time has a higher probability of sampling a specific event, (e.g., a tornado or fire), but only on a small proportion of the sample. However, data collected over a shorter time span may miss an event entirely until the next periodic measurement takes place, at which time all of the sample plots reflect the event. This may be further complicated by the number of years passing since the event, before remeasurement occurs.

Prescribed fire ignition along plowed break. (photo by Dale Wade, Rx fire doctor, Bugwood.org)

Statistical Reliability

A relative standard of accuracy has been incorporated into the forest survey. This standard satisfies user demands, minimizes human and instrumental sources of error, and keeps costs within prescribed limits. The two primary types of error are measurement error and sampling error.

Measurement Error

There are three elements of measurement error: (1) bias, which is caused by instruments which are not properly calibrated; (2) compensating, which is caused by instruments of moderate precision; and (3) accidental, which is caused by human error in measuring and compiling. All of these are held to a minimum by a system that incorporates training, check plots, and editing and checking for consistency. Editing checks screen out logical and data entry errors for all plots. It is not possible to determine measurement error statistically, but it is possible to hold it to a minimum.

Sampling Error

Sampling error is associated with the natural and expected deviation of the sample from the true population mean. This deviation is susceptible to a mathematical evaluation of the probability of error. Table B.1 lists the 2009 estimates of land area, inventory volume, and 2005–09 components of change on timberland, along with sampling errors, expressed as percentages.

Forest Inventory and Analysis (FIA) inventories supported by the full complement of sample plots are designed to achieve reliable statistics for the region. Sampling error increases as the area or volume considered decreases in magnitude. Sampling errors and associated confidence intervals are often unacceptably high for small components of the total resource. However, there may be instances where a smaller component does not have

Table B.1—Statistical reliability estimates, Tennessee, 2009

Variable	Sample estimate	Sampling error
		percent
Area (*1,000 acres*)		
Forest land	14,003.3	0.74
Timberland	13,547.2	0.80
Reserved and other	456.1	7.93
All-live trees (*million trees*)		
Inventory (forest land)	7,971.0	1.53
Inventory (timberland)	7,758.9	1.58
All-live volume (*million cubic feet*)		
Inventory (forest land)	29,176.2	1.36
Inventory (timberland)	27,788.2	1.42

a proportionately larger sampling error. This can happen when the post-defined strata are more homogeneous than the larger strata, thereby having a smaller variance. For specific post-defined strata the sampling error is available from online retrievals using the forest inventory data online (FIDO) at http://199.128.173.26/fido/mastf/index.html, or can be calculated using the following formula. (Note: Sampling errors obtained by this method are only approximations of reliability because this process assumes constant variance across all subdivisions of totals.)

$$SE_s = SE_t \ \frac{\sqrt{X_t}}{\sqrt{X_s}}$$

where

SE_s = sampling error for subdivision of State total

SE_t = sampling error for State total

X_s = sum of values for the variable of interest (area or volume) for subdivision of State

X_t = total area or volume for State

Precautions

Users are cautioned to be aware of the highly variable accuracy and questionable reliability of small subsets of the data, e.g., volume estimates by county. When summarizing statistics from the FIA database, users should familiarize themselves with the procedures used to compute sampling error as outlined above.

Hatachie National Wildlife Refuge, Haywood County, Tennessee. (photo by Thomas R. Machnitzki, Wikimedia.org)

Inventory Quality Assurance and Quality Control

The goal of the Forest Inventory and Analysis (FIA) quality assurance (QA) program is to provide a framework that ensures that forest assessments meet given standards for completeness, accuracy, and absence of bias. This program is organized in accordance with the protocols set forth in the American National Standard for Quality of Environmental Data collection (Part B of American Society for Quality Control 1994). One of the goals of the FIA program is to include data quality documentation in all nationally available reports, including State reports and national summary reports. This report includes a summary of phase 2 variables and measurement quality objective (MQO) analyses from FIA blind check measurements. Quality assessments of the phase 3 data will be addressed in future reports. Quality control procedures include feedback to field staff to provide assessment and improvement of crew performance. Additionally, data quality is assessed and documented using performance measurements and post survey assessments. These assessments then are used to identify areas of the data collection process that need improvement or refinement in order to meet quality objectives of the program.

Quality Assurance and Quality Control Methods

FIA implements QA methods in several different ways. These methods include nationally standardized field manuals, portable data recorders (PDR), training and certification of field crews, and field audits. The PDRs help assure that specified procedures are followed. The minimum national standards for annual training of field crews are: (1) a minimum of 40 hours for new employees, and (2) a minimum of 8 hours for return employees. Field crew members are certified via an *in situ* test plot. All crews are required to have at least one certified person present on the plot at all times.

Field Audits

A hot check is an inspection normally done as part of the training process. The inspector is present with crew to document crew performance as they measure plots. The recommended intensity for hot checks is 2 percent of the plots installed.

Cold checks are done at regular intervals throughout the field season. The crew that installed the plot is not present at the time of inspection and does not know when or which plots will be remeasured. The inspector visits the completed plot, evaluates the crew's data collection, and notes corrections where necessary. The recommended intensity for cold checks is 5 percent of the plots installed.

A blind check is a complete reinstallation measurement of a previously completed plot. However, the QA crew remeasurement is done without the previously recorded data. The first measurement of the plot is referred to as the field measurement and the second measurement as the QA measurement. The field crews do not know in advance when or which of their plots will be measured by a QA crew. This type of blind measurement provides a direct, unbiased observation of measurement precision from two independent crews. Plots selected for blind checks are chosen to be a representative subsample of all plots measured and are randomly selected. Blind checks are planned to be made within 2 weeks following completion of the field measurement. The recommended intensity for blind checks is 3 percent of the plots installed.

Measurement Quality Objectives

Each variable collected by FIA is assigned a MQO with desired levels of tolerance for data analyses. The MQOs are documented in the FIA national field manual (U.S. Department of Agriculture 2004a). In some instances, the MQOs were established as a "best guess" of what experienced field crews should be able to consistently achieve. Tolerances are somewhat arbitrary and were based on the ability of crews to make repeatable measurements or observations within the assigned MQO. Evaluation of field crew performance is accomplished by calculation of the differences between the field crew and QA crew data collected on blind check plots. Results of these calculations are compared to the established MQOs.

In the analysis of blind check data, an observation is within tolerance when the difference between the field crew and QA crew observations does not exceed the assigned tolerance for that variable. For many categorical variables, the tolerance is "no error" allowed, so only observations that are identical are within the tolerance level. The tables below (tables C.1–C.3) show the percent of observations that fell within the program tolerances in Tennessee and the Southern region during 2005–09.

Table C.1—Performance of data collection on achieving measurement quality objectives for Tennessee and the Southern Region between 2005 and 2009 for plot-level variables

Plot-level variables	Tolerance	Observations	Percent within tolerance	
			Tennessee	Southern Region
		- number -	- - - - - percent - - - - -	
Distance road	No tolerance	53	81.1	76.6
Water on plot	No tolerance	41	82.9	87.9
Latitude	± 2.3 degrees	60	95.0	97.1
Longitude	± 2.3 degrees	60	91.7	91.9
Elevation	No tolerance	39	41.0	37.0
Elevation with tolerance	± 5 feet	39	41.0	49.5
Regional variables				
Distance to agriculture	No tolerance	37	70.3	73.4
Distance to urban area	No tolerance	37	86.5	69.8
Human debris	No tolerance	23	87.0	85.3
Accessibility	No tolerance	26	96.2	86.4
Number of conditions	No tolerance	26	76.9	59.1

Table C.2—Performance of data collection on achieving measurement quality objectives for Tennessee and the Southern Region between 2005 and 2009 for condition-level variables

Condition-level variables	Tolerance	Observations	Percent within tolerance	
			Tennessee	Southern Region
		- number -	- - - - - percent - - - - -	
Condition status	No tolerance	500	99.6	99.8
Reserve status	No tolerance	364	98.1	99.0
Owner group	No tolerance	472	99.8	98.0
Owner class	No tolerance	472	98.7	98.1
Owner status	No tolerance	361	98.3	97.8
Forest type (type)	No tolerance	364	89.6	85.1
Forest type (group)	No tolerance	364	95.6	91.4
Stand size	No tolerance	364	89.6	85.9
Regeneration status	No tolerance	364	96.7	96.7
Regeneration species	No tolerance	364	97.0	96.7
Tree density	No tolerance	344	99.1	99.5
Stand age	± 10 percent	364	69.8	62.2
Disturbance 1	No tolerance	37	97.3	91.1
Disturbance year 1	± 1 year	2	100.0	91.4
Disturbance 2	No tolerance	17	100.0	99.6
Disturbance 3	No tolerance	15	100.0	100.0
Treatment 1	No tolerance	37	97.3	94.8
Treatment year 1	± 1 year	6	83.3	78.2
Treatment 2	No tolerance	18	83.3	95.7
Treatment year 2	± 1 year	3	100.0	88.5
Treatment 3	No tolerance	17	88.2	98.9
Physiographic class	No tolerance	457	93.2	90.8
Land use	No tolerance	467	97.6	97.8
Tract size	No tolerance	468	99.4	98.3
Stand structure	No tolerance	472	93.4	92.3
Distance to water	± 10 feet	435	83.0	83.0
Prescribed fire	No tolerance	472	98.9	97.4
Grazing	No tolerance	472	99.2	98.2
Site class	± 1 class	54	81.5	84.8
Urban-land use	No tolerance	32	100.0	100.0
Water source	No tolerance	435	89.4	89.4

Table C.3—Performance of data collection on achieving measurement quality objectives for Tennessee and the Southern Region between 2005 and 2009 for tree-level variables

Tree-level variables	Tolerance	Observations	Percent within tolerance	
			Tennessee	Southern Region
		- number -	- - - - - percent - - - - -	
D.b.h.	± 0.1/20 inch	744	87.4	83.2
DRC	± 0.1/20 inch	8	100.0	86.2
Azimuth	± 10 degrees	803	96.4	96.6
Horizontal distance	± 0.2 /1.0 ft	800	97.6	95.3
Species	No tolerance	878	95.7	96.1
Genus	No tolerance	878	99.2	99.1
Tree status	No tolerance	878	99.1	98.9
Reconcile	No tolerance	138	97.8	96.6
Total length	± 10 percent	694	82.4	72.6
Actual length	± 10 percent	38	60.5	56.8
Compacted crown ratio	± 10 percent	747	87.2	80.5
Crown class	No tolerance	748	83.4	83.2
Decay class	± 1class	95	98.9	95.2
Standing dead	No tolerance	117	100.0	98.8
Cause of death	No tolerance	87	93.1	89.2
Mortality year	± 1 year	87	93.1	93.3
Tree class	No tolerance	67	74.6	91.3
Tree grade	No tolerance	552	99.6	75.2
Utilization class	No tolerance	548	94.5	99.0
Board-foot cull	± 10 percent	521	96.5	96.7
Cubic-foot cull	± 10 percent	662	100.0	97.1

D.b.h. = diameter at breast height; DRC = diameter at root collar.

Table D.1—Species list by common and scientific name, Tennessee, 2009

Common name	Scientific name[a] [b]	Common name	Scientific name[a] [b]
Fraser fir	*Abies fraseri*	Butternut	*Juglans cinerea*
Florida maple	*Acer barbatum*	Black walnut	*J. nigra*
Boxelder	*A. negundo*	Eastern redcedar	*Juniperus virginiana*
Striped maple	*A. pensylvanicum*	Sweetgum	*Liquidambar styraciflua*
Red maple	*A. rubrum*	Tuliptree	*Liriodendron tulipifera*
Silver maple	*A. saccharinum*	Osage orange	*Maclura pomifera*
Sugar maple	*A. saccharum*	Cucumber-tree	*Magnolia acuminata*
Yellow buckeye	*Aesculus flava*	Mountain or fraser magnolia	*M. fraseri*
Ohio buckeye	*A. glabra*	Bigleaf magnolia	*M. macrophylla*
Ailanthus	*Ailanthus* Desf.	Umbrella-magnolia	*M. tripetala*
Mimosa, silktree	*Albizia julibrissin*	Sweetbay	*M. virginiana*
Serviceberry spp.	*Amelanchier* spp.	Southern crab apple	*Malus angustifolia*
Pawpaw	*Asimina triloba*	White mulberry	*Morus alba*
Yellow birch	*Betula alleghaniensis*	Red mulberry	*M. rubra*
Sweet birch	*B. lenta*	Water tupelo	*Nyssa aquatica*
River birch	*B. nigra*	Swamp tupelo	*N. biflora*
American hornbeam, musclewood	*Carpinus caroliniana*	Blackgum	*N. sylvatica*
Mockernut hickory	*Carya alba*	Eastern hophornbeam	*Ostrya virginiana*
Water hickory	*C. aquatica*	Sourwood	*Oxydendrum arboreum*
Bitternut hickory	*C. cordiformis*	Paulownia, princesstree	*Paulownia tomentosa*
Pignut hickory	*C. glabra*	Red spruce	*Picea rubens*
Pecan	*C. illinoensis*	Shortleaf pine	*Pinus echinata*
Shellbark hickory	*C. laciniosa*	Table Mountain pine	*P. pungens*
Shagbark hickory	*C. ovata*	Pitch pine	*P. rigida*
Sand hickory	*C. pallida*	Eastern white pine	*P. strobus*
American chestnut	*Castanea dentata*	Loblolly pine	*P. taeda*
Chinese chestnut	*C. mollissima*	Virginia pine	*P. virginiana*
Southern catalpa	*Catalpa bignonioides*	Planertree	*Planera aquatica*
Sugarberry	*Celtis laevigata*	American sycamore	*Platanus occidentalis*
Hackberry	*C. occidentalis*	Eastern cottonwood	*Populus deltoides*
Eastern redbud	*Cercis canadensis*	Bigtooth aspen	*P. grandidentata*
Kentucky yellowwood	*Cladrastis kentukea*	American plum	*Prunus americana*
Flowering dogwood	*Cornus florida*	Pin cherry	*P. pensylvanica*
Cockspur hawthorn	*Crataegus crus-galli*	Black cherry	*P. serotina*
Downy hawthorn	*C. mollis*	Chokecherry	*P. virginiana*
Hawthorn spp.	*C.* spp.	White oak	*Quercus alba*
Common persimmon	*Diospyros virginiana*	Swamp white oak	*Q. bicolor*
American beech	*Fagus grandifolia*	Scarlet oak	*Q. coccinea*
White ash	*Fraxinus americana*	Southern red oak	*Q. falcata*
Green ash	*F. pennsylvanica*	Shingle oak	*Q. imbricaria*
Blue ash	*F. quadrangulata*	Laurel oak	*Q. laurifolia*
Waterlocust	*Gleditsia aquatica*	Overcup oak	*Q. lyrata*
Honeylocust	*G. triacanthos*	Bur oak	*Q. macrocarpa*
Kentucky coffeetree	*Gymnocladus dioicus*	Blackjack oak	*Q. marilandica*
Carolina silverbell	*Halesia carolina*	Swamp chestnut oak	*Q. michauxii*
Silverbell	*Halesia* Ellis ex L	Chinkapin oak	*Q. muehlenbergii*
American holly	*Ilex opaca* Alton var. *opaca*	Water oak	*Q. nigra*

continued

Table D.1—Species list by common and scientific name, Tennessee, 2009 (continued)

Common name	Scientific name[a][b]	Common name	Scientific name[a][b]
Cherrybark oak	*Q. pagoda*	Baldcypress	*Taxodium distichum*
Pin oak	*Q. palustris*	American basswood	*Tilia americana*
Willow oak	*Q. phellos*	Unknown dead hardwood	*Tree broadleaf*
Chestnut oak	*Q. prinus*	Other or unknown live tree	*Tree unknown*
Northern red oak	*Q. rubra*	Eastern hemlock	*Tsuga canadensis*
Shumard oak	*Q. shumardii*	Carolina hemlock	*T. caroliniana*
Bottomland post oak	*Q. similis*	Winged elm	*Ulmus alata*
Post oak	*Q. stellata*	American elm	*U. americana*
Texas red oak	*Q. texana*	Siberian elm	*U. pumila*
Black oak	*Q. velutina*	Slippery elm	*U. rubra*
Black locust	*Robinia pseudoacacia*	September elm	*U. serotina*
Black willow	*Salix nigra*	Rock elm	*U. thomasii*
Sassafras	*Sassafras albidum*		

[a] Little (1979).
[b] USDA Plants database.

Vibrant colored leaves such as these maple leaves provide a brilliant display each autumn.

Table E.1—Description of the forest sector industry groups

Forest sector group	NAICS 2007 code	IMPLAN sector	Description
Inputs	1131-2	15	Forestry, forest products, and timber tract production
	1133	16	Commercial logging
Primary			
Solid, primary	3211	95	Sawmills and wood preservation
Panel	321211-2	96	Veneer and plywood manufacturing
	321219	98	Reconstituted wood product manufacturing
Pulp and paper	32211	104	Pulpmills
	32212	105	Paper mills
	32213	106	Paperboard mills
Secondary			
Solid, secondary	321213-4	97	Engineered wood member and truss manufacturing
	32191	99	Wood windows and doors and millwork manufacturing
	32192	100	Wood container and pallet manufacturing
	321991	101	Manufactured home (mobile home) manufacturing
	321992	102	Prefabricated wood building manufacturing
	321999	103	All other miscellaneous wood product manufacturing
	33711	295	Wood kitchen cabinet and countertop manufacturing
	337122	297	Nonupholstered wood household furniture manufacturing
	337129	300	Wood television, radio, and sewing machine cabinet manufacturing
	337211-12	301	Office furniture and custom architectural woodwork and millwork manufacturing
Pulp and paper products	32221	107	Paperboard container manufacturing
	322221-2	108	Coated and laminated paper, packaging paper and plastics film manufacturing
	322223-6	109	All other paper bag and coated and treated paper manufacturing
	32223	110	Stationery product manufacturing
	322291	111	Sanitary paper product manufacturing
	322299	112	All other converted paper product manufacturing

NAICS = North American industry classification system; IMPLAN = IMpact analysis for PLANning.

Table E.2—Counties by survey unit, Tennessee, 2009

		Survey unit		
East	Central	Plateau	West	West Central
Anderson	Bedford	Bledsoe	Carroll	Benton
Blount	Cannon	Campbell	Chester	Decatur
Bradley	Cheatham	Cumberland	Crockett	Hardin
Carter	Clay	Fentress	Dyer	Hickman
Claiborne	Coffee	Franklin	Fayette	Houston
Cocke	Davidson	Grundy	Gibson	Humphreys
Grainger	DeKalb	Marion	Hardeman	Lawrence
Greene	Dickson	Morgan	Haywood	Lewis
Hamblen	Giles	Overton	Henderson	Perry
Hamilton	Jackson	Pickett	Henry	Stewart
Hancock	Lincoln	Putnam	Lake	Wayne
Hawkins	Macon	Scott	Lauderdale	
Jefferson	Marshall	Sequatchie	Madison	
Johnson	Maury	Van Buren	McNairy	
Knox	Montgomery	Warren	Obion	
Loudon	Moore	White	Shelby	
McMinn	Robertson		Tipton	
Meigs	Rutherford		Weakley	
Monroe	Smith			
Polk	Sumner			
Rhea	Trousdale			
Roane	Williamson			
Sevier	Wilson			
Sullivan				
Unicoi				
Union				
Washington				